At a time when the relations between morality, the social fabric and the inner world are causing distress throughout the world, Rob Weatherill provides a searching study of the growing impoverishment of life in Western society. He addresses himself to the role of ideals in psychoanalysis and brings a Kleinian perspective to bear on the schizoid nature of modern culture; the emptiness of the addict; the crisis in schools and education; feminism and the shattering of male narcissism. All who have an interest in working with others to reach a better understanding of human needs, anxiety and values will respond to this book.

ROB WEATHERILL'S background is in education, and he has for many years been in private practice as a psychoanalytic psychotherapist in Dublin. He is an executive member of both the Irish Forum for Psychoanalytic Psychotherapy, and the Irish Psychoanalytical Association. He teaches psychoanalysis on graduate and postgraduate courses in Dublin.

CULTURAL COLLAPSE

ROB WEATHERILL

'an association in which the free development of
each is the condition of the free development of all'

Free Association Books / London / 1994

Published in 1994 by
Free Association Books Ltd
26 Freegrove Road
London N7 9RQ

ISBN 1 85343 320 9

A CIP catalogue record for this book is available from the
British Library.

Typeset from author's disc by Archetype, Stow-on-the-Wold
Printed in the EC by The Cromwell Press, Broughton Gifford

CONTENTS

Acknowledgements   vii
Preface   ix

1   The common sense of psychoanalysis   1
2   Limits to growth   18
3   Culture: A mainly Kleinian perspective   46
4   Feminist outrage   90
5   Childcare and the growth of apathy   112
6   The empty self   135
7   The crisis in authority   154
A conclusion   177

Notes   187
Bibliography   196
Index   205

In memory of my parents

ACKNOWLEDGEMENTS

Parts of this book have been presented before in spoken or written form. Chapter 1 is based on the text of a lecture delivered in Trinity College, Dublin, in November 1988. This was one of a series of lectures given by various speakers to mark the centenary of Jonathan Hanaghan, the founder of psychoanalysis in Ireland. A much condensed version of Chapters 5 and 6 was given as a paper to the First World Family Therapy Congress, held in Trinity College in June 1989. Chapter 7 was derived from three papers written for *The Secondary Teacher* (the journal of the Irish Post-primary Teachers' Association), during 1988-9. These were 'Crisis in authority' (vol. 17 no. 2), 'Lifeskills' (vol. 17 no. 3), and 'The reaction against lifeskills' (vol. 18 no. 1). Part of Chapter 2 appeared as an article for the *Journal of the Irish Forum for Psychoanalytic Psychotherapy*: 'Humanistic and psychoanalytic psychotherapies compared – limits to growth' (1989, vol. 1 no. 3). And a modified version of Chapter 3, Section II was written for the same journal, under the title 'The fragmentation of culture' (1990, vol. 1 no. 4). 'The psychical realities of modern culture', an article based on this book, was written for *The British Journal of Psychotherapy* (1991, vol. 7 no. 3. pp. 268-73).

I have many friends and colleagues to thank for their many helpful comments, criticisms, discussions and arguments that helped in the preparation of this work.

I should like also to thank Collins, the publishers, for permission to quote from Thomas Gordon's book, *How to be an Effective Parent*, and Paul Tillich's *The Boundary of Our Being*. Thanks also to the McGraw-Hill Publishing Company for permission to quote from Hopson and Scally's *Lifeskills Education*. I should also like to thank Sigmund Freud Copyrights, the Institute of Psychoanalysis and the Hogarth Press for permission to quote from *The Standard Edition of the Complete Psychological Works of Sigmund Freud*, translated and edited by James Strachey. I am grateful to the Runa Press, Dublin, for permission to quote from the writings of Jonathan Hanaghan. Quotes from Anna Freud's *The Ego and the Mechanisms of Defence* are reprinted by permission of Mark Paterson and Associates for the Estate of Anna Freud.

I am most grateful, also, to the staff of Free Association Books for their interest in this work – most importantly Robert Young,

Ann Scott and Karl Figlio, whose detailed editing of this book was invaluable.

Finally, I should like to thank my patients for the things that they have felt able to share with me in the many hours we have spent together.

PREFACE

All his perversities, phoney charades, excessive and exaggerated attitudinising derived from one source and one source alone: all through his childhood Mr Luis had known *no limits*. It was total permissiveness to everyone . . . Nature had endowed him with high brain power, so that as he grew he had brought everything, almost everything under his ego-omnipotence. What he couldn't manage was to get into his own person . . . It was a sordid existence . . . He had no capacities within, with which to operate. (Khan, 1988, p. 98)

This book is for anyone with a concern about modern culture. What is the effect of that culture on the internal or psychical world? How do cultural forces, consumerism, the media, personal liberation, the break-up of the family, impact upon the cauldron of unconscious forces that makes the internal world? The central paradox explored in this book is that while we enjoy greater freedom and abundance than ever before, at least in the rich parts of the world, we can't help noticing a corresponding *inner* weakness and loss of control. This is a psychical depletion that leaves us prey to powerful and primitive unconscious forces. Carried away by the pursuit of economic growth and lifestyles freed from any constraint, we have squandered our psychical resources in much the same way as we have plundered our natural environmental resources. The awareness of our psychological impoverishment is underlined by our alarm over sex abuse, rape, hard porn, violence and so on. The noise of the emotional underworld, now unrestrained, has reached such a pitch that even the strongest advocates of the unfettered pursuit of economic well-being are having to sit up and take notice.

There is nothing new in these concerns; they have been voiced throughout the modern period. But the severance of meanings, of roots, the presence of real absence, the expropriation of desire, can lead to terrible and extreme consequences upon which psycho-analysis can and must make more comment.

The book has emerged out of my work in psychoanalysis and education over the past twenty years. My aim has been to understand aspects of modern culture in the light of some basic psychoanalytic ideas. The question for me has always been: what contribution does 'the unconscious' make to any given cultural manifestation? So much cultural discussion ignores the impact of the unconscious. Yet unconscious meanings and significations are always present and operative alongside our conscious and rational thoughts and actions. This of course applies to individuals in psychotherapy as well as to broad cultural movements and events. Avoidance of the unconscious restricts experience and potentiality and creates a situation whereby what is avoided and repressed returns in a more virulent form.

From the viewpoint of the unconscious, all conscious certainties become undetermined, superficial adjustments are rendered untenable, decisions made and loyalties struck can be subverted and overturned. Political and ideological convictions can move towards the daemonic and the moral stance be invaded by its opposite. It is to explore these disquieting and often tragic paradoxes that this book is written. But it does not represent – and this cannot be overstressed – an attempt to reduce modern cultural trends to a handful of obscure psychoanalytic interpretations. Neither is it intended to be an academic study of psychoanalytic thought on cultural experience, at one remove from the lived reality. In both the above approaches, a clash of textual interpretations is invited: psychoanalytic texts versus a feminist, a Marxist or an ecological text. A fight develops as to where one's loyalties lie. There are winners and losers in an essentially intellectual battle about theories, sometimes far removed from the search for the *meaning* of experience, which is what psycho-analysis is about.

Instead, this book proceeds from *direct* experience of a culture and an attempt to think about that experience – to grasp some fragment of it and articulate it in broadly psychoanalytic terms. It represents to an extent a collaborative effort, in that it has arisen out of discussions and arguments with friends, some of whom are psychoanalytically informed and orientated, while others indeed would be hostile to psychoanalysis.

I am of the opinion that the psychoanalytic space is a good space, if one can think in terms of 'cultural spaces'. This space is provided by the psychoanalytic therapist, who has had a good training, but who has also developed his or her own psychoanalytic idiom; while all the time realising that when one tries to define what one does (as I do in Chapter 1) one is always wrong, or at the very least limited. Psychoanalysis is always about something else, something other. It is precisely this fact, taken thoughtfully, that makes it a good space. In other words, if the analyst doesn't think in holistic terms, if this pressure can be resisted, then this has a great liberating effect on the therapeutic process. But the goodness of the space is far from being immediately apparent. Often, under the impact of transference, it does not feel good to either analysand or analyst.

Let us take the example of Paul,[1] who comes to psychoanalytic therapy because of bouts of depression. He is able to 'function' (his word) in his work, but recently does so without any zest or enthusiasm. He is in one of the helping professions. He is from a very large family, where he got very little attention by today's standards. His father even used to forget his name. To compensate for not being known, Paul works very hard at helping everyone, but gets exhausted. During therapy Paul finds out very painfully that he has never had anything of his own, not even his name.

Now my point is, where else could Paul experience that? Where else can people thaw out by really just being listened to? There aren't many good places like this left any more. In other places there is often forcing or ideology. This is why analysis can be so good, because it allows freedom – in particular, freedom to hate and be bitter over extended periods of time. Because of this listening, it has something to say about the human condition and contemporary culture, even though, as I shall have to admit, it is often said in the wrong way.

Paul could of course take anti-depressants, or he could take up aerobics, or some kind of behavioural-cognitive therapy that would help him to think in better ways. These might cure his depression, indeed, but where would they leave him? Still unspoken to.

Anna's presenting problem was anxiety states that made her see her life and her work as a series of disasters. She was therefore forced to control everything to an impossible degree. Her doctor had given her medication that had been a help, but she wanted to try 'talking it out', as she put it. At first, she was quite unable to speak and communicate meaning. In time, her therapist was able to put words on these raw affective states, when they appeared vividly in the sessions, so that Anna was better able to separate her conscious mind and thought from her unconscious. Less flooded by intense affects, she became better able to speak.

There are many different psychoanalytic models: Freud, Klein, Bion, Lacan, the object relations school, and so on. These models have explanatory value for individuals and perhaps for a whole culture, but the crucial fact about all models is that they are only representational. They always miss the point. And for psychoanalysts, what is always most interesting is what is in the margin. So the models can only be applied with a light touch, and with a certain element of play. This is not always the case here. And indeed some of the issues raised are so important that something much tougher is called for.

This book ranges from the banal to the subtle. It covers many old ideas, but also a few new ones. But Bion is always helpful: 'True thought requires neither formulation nor thinker. The lie is a thought to which a formulation and a thinker are essential.'

Chapter 1 outlines the process of a psychoanalytic treatment and takes account of some of the criticisms commonly levelled at psychoanalysis as a theory and a method. Psychoanalysis has come of age since the immediate post-war years, when it was seen by some as a cure-all. However, the true value of psychoanalysis as a treatment for mental illness and as a theory of culture is a long way from being generally understood.

Chapter 2 attempts to situate psychoanalysis within the broader religious framework of Western thought. Many of the new psychotherapies, it is argued, have become substitute personal religions in their own right. But psychoanalysis is different because it cannot offer any kind of personal salvation, and therefore it is not a religion. However, there remains the enigmatic and evocative *presence* of the analyst, which offers a unique opportunity to the analysand for the elaboration of a personal idiom.

Chapter 3 looks psychoanalytically at the frenetic nature of modern and postmodern culture and traces the progressive loss of coherence, of stable realities and of solidarity. Increasingly competitive and paranoid personally, culturally and internationally, we feel forced to retreat into ourselves, into a smaller and smaller world of family and self.

Chapter 4 focuses on the women's movement and raises some questions about the decline of patriarchy and the unconscious of both men and women. With aggression no longer turned against herself the new assertive woman feels justified in her attack on male power, which has far-reaching consequences for both sexes, for the family and for children.

The last three chapters broadly deal with the changing position of children in relation to parents and authority generally. **Chapter 5** traces the emergence of the modern child, now to be positioned at the centre of the modern family, out of the old medieval social matrix. The consequences of the progressive demoralisation of parents by the conflicting fashions of the medical and psychiatric establishments are explored. The results, discussed in **Chapter 6**, involve children being left exposed to the potential gratification of every need, which has had disastrous consequences in terms of the depleting of the self. And finally, **Chapter 7** looks at how schools have had to change radically in an attempt to contain the breakdown in communal life. Education and youth generally have become a battleground for conflicting ideologies of the Left and Right which threaten the needs of the adolescent for a private space in which to mature.

A recurrent theme in this book is the notion of how what Freud called *die Seele* has become occluded. *Die Seele* is most appropriately translated as 'soul' or 'psyche', rather than 'mind', which has become too closely associated with, and is perhaps the agent of, this occlusion. What has become lost is our sense of, and a necessary respect for, the unconscious, for otherness, for mystery, for death. Trapped by an alienation in the mind, in the ego, in a minimalist mentality, we have increasingly been forced into a contraction of the self, preoccupied with survival and gratification at the expense of human suffering and concern.

The denial of the psyche means a levelling-out of meanings and values, and represents an attack on the internal world, and the loss of an essential subjective grounding behind a merely executive ego. Freed from a sense of transgression, of the tragic, of something that arrests desire, we rush onwards without limit. This book, therefore is primarily concerned with exploring what happens when we take this path.

1 THE COMMON SENSE OF PSYCHOANALYSIS

I: THE PROCESS

Since the first formulations nearly a hundred years ago, psycho-analysis has become the dominant idiom in the way we talk about the human personality and social relations. Freud has become, as W.H. Auden put it, 'a whole climate of opinion under whom we conduct our different lives' (1939, p. 168). It is hard to imagine ourselves conversing without such common ideas as the Freudian slip, defences, repression, sibling rivalry, Oedipus and so on. Jung, although quite distinct from Freud in certain basic formulations, has also contributed to the common currency with such ideas as archetypes, persona, shadow and the collective unconscious. Adler has given us the 'inferiority complex', Otto Rank the 'birth trauma', and Reich the 'character armour' and our fascination with the orgasm. The somewhat pessimistic view of the human condition enshrined in psychoanalysis has struck a chord with us, much more so than the empirical models of humankind developed by academic psychology, the study of the human being as an object ignoring his or her experience as a subject. We could say that culturally psychoanalysis has become part of common sense – part of our practical understanding of ourselves and others.

The cultural ubiquity of psychoanalysis is in marked contrast to the small impact it has had in the treatment of illness. Here, the field is dominated by a biochemical, neurophysiological model with the development of potent drugs and the promise of the location of specific genes said to cause mental illness. The reaction against the all-encompassing biological view of human distress and illness has seen the growth of many so-called 'alternative therapies' which offer a more holistic approach. Under this umbrella have been popularised a number of 'humanistic' psychotherapies which tend to be eclectic. Psychoanalysis does not normally feature here either, although it is specifically concerned with the individual and freedom. In Europe it remains relatively isolated, treating only a tiny portion of those deemed to be mentally ill. The number of fully fledged analysts is small – about 450 in Britain, fewer than 50 in Ireland, mostly working in private practice, seeing people for between £10 and £50 per hourly session.[1]

In America, where psychoanalysis has tended to be subsumed into psychiatry, the scene is quite different. There are more than 3,000 practitioners and fees can be well over $200 per hour. But even here it has been reliably calculated that only one in 10,000 Americans is in analysis and that in some social and ethnic groups the figure is zero. Things have certainly changed since the heyday of analysis in the years after the war, when it was considered chic to use the jargon: 'she's *sublimating*', 'he's *repressing*', and so on. The help that analysts could give was greatly exaggerated, the profession was oversold. But although there have been lean years, there is now talk of a revival, with more and more people becoming disillusioned with the briefer therapies and the weekend cure-alls which address the symptoms without getting at the fundamentals. Much of the energy comes from the lay analysts, who in England have been permitted to practice since the 1920s, whereas in the States it is only in recent years that the American Psychoanalytic Association has begun to open its doors to non-medics.

There is much misunderstanding about psychoanalysis and in this chapter I would like to point to the common sense of the view expressed by Hanna Segal, a leading Kleinian analyst, that psychoanalysis should be the treatment of choice for *all* mental illness: in short, psychoanalysis should become the norm in therapeutics that it has become in cultural analysis. Many analysts would not take quite such a radical position on the efficacy of their work. But there is a belief that analysts have been taking it on the chin for years, in criticism that was often born of ignorance and misrepresentation. It would be ironic, says one analyst, if the field died because of the need to be anonymous. So there is a desire to reach out to the wider public and teach people about the realities of the discipline.

Let us, then, ask the question: why should somebody who is unhappy and has emotional problems seek psychoanalysis in preference to other forms of treatment? The answer is that analysis offers a radical and intensive examination of one's experience, and that during the process of treatment one's problems will come to be understood and that truth about ourselves will set us free. It is indeed a more radical therapy than other forms of 'talking cure', because it involves an exploration of three main areas. Firstly, the notion of the unconscious, with which we are familiar from dreams, slips of the tongue, jokes, hypnosis, certain drug states, phantasies, day-dreams and so on. Secondly, the concept of defence. Many types are described but all involve a partial blocking of strong unacceptable feelings from consciousness so as to avoid excessive anxiety. People start looking for treatment when their defensive manoeuvres are felt to be breaking down. And thirdly, we have the idea of transference. This is how we treat people in our current lives, often on the same unconscious model that we developed with our own parents in childhood. We have infantile expectations, anxieties, needs and wishes left over from childhood which seek fulfilment in the present day. It is the special situation of the analysis that highlights, brings into sharp focus these pressing infantile demands, and seeks to resolve them. This is the central task of an analysis – the resolution of the transference. In less radical forms of psychotherapy, the transference may be noticed but not interpreted. The 'positive transference' may indeed be mobilised, building up in the client the feeling that the therapist is the re-embodiment of the 'good parent' of childhood. This gives the client a feeling of confidence and belief that the therapy will help.

At this point a case history will help illustrate the process of an analysis. The patient was a woman aged 30, living at home with her parents. She was depressed and unable to do her work. She had various gastrointestinal symptoms and an inability to form close and stable relationships with men. She was seen by a male analyst twice a week for a number of years. She was close to her mother and could share all her feelings with her, but her father, although a kind man, was unable to get close to his daughter or to meet her emotional needs.

One of the first symptoms to give way was her inability to work. Some two years into the analysis, she was interviewed and accepted for a job. She phoned her analyst to tell him this. Instead of being delighted at obvious signs of progress, she was very angry. She felt sick all through the interview and cried all the way home on the train, then went to her GP and had a row with him, leaving him with the words: 'I hate all you men.' Later the analyst was able to point out that her inability to work was some sort of protest or living reproach against the failure of her relationship to her father. Getting a job would mean she would have to give up this grudge. During the next sessions there emerged strong angry feelings towards her father.

About three years into analysis she met a man called Brian who was clearly attracted to her. Then one day she said she realised that as soon as a man said he loved her she lost all feeling for him, and this was now happening with Brian, as it happened with other men in the past. She knew she was attractive to men. She must play up to them, string them along – it must be some sort of revenge, she acknowledged. With the help of her analyst she was beginning to make the connection between her childhood feelings of rejection by her father and her current behaviour with boyfriends. Instead of being rejected (passive) as happened in childhood, she was now the rejecting one (active). She was now in control. During this time she was treating the analyst sometimes suspiciously or disdainfully. She was annoyed by his remoteness and sometimes felt this to be a rejection. Again she was repeating with the analyst what she used to feel with her father.

Here we have the emergence of unconscious infantile longings and grudges from behind the defensive structure of an inability to work and make relationships. These longings tend to be acted upon both inside and outside the analysis. This is called the transference. The patient's analyst, GP and boyfriend all get the same treatment as was intended for her father. Her nausea and abdominal problems disappeared when she was able to vent her violent feelings towards men. On one occasion Brian said to her: 'We have so little time together, can't you be nice to me?' She felt physically sick and shouted 'No', and the sickness immediately went away. She described how she used to be at parties – feeling withdrawn and jealous of other couples. She would feel sick and have to leave to empty her bowels. But it was different these days, she said. Instead of symptoms it was feelings she had. These were mainly to shout abuse about her father. But this observation illustrates an important point: what were wholly unconscious and therefore inarticulate *symptoms* are changed during analysis into *feelings* that can be articulated and therefore can make themselves heard and be transformed. We might mention at this point that there is often an equation in the unconscious between feelings and bodily products. Infants tend to associate the expulsion of materials from the body with the evacuation of bad angry feelings and pain.

During the analysis this patient also experienced involuntary and irrational ideas: for instance, that if her mother died she would have her father all to herself. She mustn't think of her mother . . . she mustn't think badly of her mother . . . she mustn't be jealous of her mother. She began to feel guilty about thinking of her parents being separated. Another version was that she might go off on her own with a man who would want her and protect her. One day she said: 'It seems as if my mother is always interrupting me in some fantasy that I am trying to work out for myself.' And then later: 'It seems as if life with her consists of nothing more exciting than making jam and doing the washing-up.' She would think of Brian wanting her and of herself wanting to be with him, not in an adult way, more like a child wanting to be cuddled and comforted. This material points clearly towards the Oedipal longings which have lain mostly unconscious because they are mixed with desire and remorse, and in the case of this woman are particularly heightened by the failure of her relationship with her father.

It is important to stress at this point that technical terms are not used during analytic sessions even though they are used in the presentation of case histories. Also, interpretations are not delivered as dogmatic statements, but only as suggestions as to what might be emerging, and ideally only after sufficient clarification and accumulation of evidence. Transference interpretations are regarded as the most mutative. For instance, in the above example, it was only after the analyst had repeatedly been criticised for his failure to be kind and understanding that he was able to point to the possibility of the patient's re-enacting with him feelings that she had felt for her father. After a period of working through the constellation of feelings associated with her father, her analysis could be ended. At the end of this therapy and throughout many years of follow-up, this patient's eating problems had disappeared, as had much of her distrust of men.[2]

Having considered very briefly the three central elements in psychoanalysis – the *unconscious*, the *defences* and the *transference* – let us turn our attention to the way the analyst listens to the patient. Freud spoke of the analyst 'bending his own unconscious like a receptive organ towards the emerging unconscious of the patient' (1912a, p. 115). He spoke of the principle of 'evenly distributed attention', and used the analogy of the surgeon, 'who puts aside all his own feelings, including that of human sympathy, and concentrates his mind on one single purpose, that of performing the operation as skilfully as possible'. Such injunctions taken too literally and adhered to too strictly imply an analyst devoid of human feelings – an image quickly seized on by critics of psychoanalysis. But Freud was trying to make the point that the analyst does not intrude his or her own thoughts, feelings, ideas, advice or criticisms into the therapeutic space, but remains *relatively quiet* and inactive so as to allow the patient maximum freedom to construct his or her own transferential view of the analyst based on infantile longings and terrors; to create what the French analyst Pontalis calls 'the private theatre of transference'. It is a central tenet of psychoanalysis that we are constantly constructing the present in terms of the past. Outside the analytic situation, in the ordinary world, we get feedback that tends to correct and modify our unconscious biases. But inside the analytic session, there is no feedback, there is only space into which the patient can more fully create his or her pathological world view to the extent that its misperceptions become glaringly obvious and can then be interpreted.

Briefly, let us answer a criticism which follows from the above, that the analyst is a cold, aloof person and that this inhumanness is likely to be pathogenic in itself. Leo Stone says that while there are young, over-zealous analysts who do in some respects fit that caricature, 'I must state my conviction that a nuance of the analyst's attitude can determine the difference between a lonely vacuum and a controlled, but warm human situation' (1961, p. 22). That nuance he refers to is the basic desire of the analyst to help, to understand and to interpret – and 'to gratify a more "mature" wish of childhood, underlying and essential to the initial genuine viability of the analytic situation: a wish for tolerance and for sympathetic understanding, for help in mastering the baffling and challenging outer world . . . and most of all the mastering of a dark and mysterious inner psychic world' (p. 50). So it is only on this fundamental bedrock of human interest and concern that the analyst can create the free space for the elaboration and unfolding of the patient's psychical world. It is the patient's experiencing of this attitude on the part of the analyst that contributes to the 'working alliance' between analyst and patient (Greenson, 1967). The special way the analyst listens with minimal intervention allows the full psychical or internal reality of the patient to emerge. An important part of this reality involves the figure of the analyst, who will at different times become a feeding mother, a critical father, a helper, a trickster, a sadist, a torturer, a prison guard and many other guises that will be imposed by the transference drama. Therefore, by sensing what he or she is being made into, or the position he or she is being put into in the transference, the analyst can maintain analytic neutrality and can begin, if timely, to make interpretations in terms of the transferential dynamics.

The transference effects can change rapidly and can be of varying intensities. Sometimes the best guide for the analyst are the feelings evoked in her by the patient, the so-called counter-transference. Every transference evokes a countertransference reaction in the analyst. So the analyst must monitor her feelings towards the patient and contain them without acting them out. The demanding patient evokes a rejecting mother countertransference. That is, the analyst has a feeling of wanting to reject the patient. Sensing this, the analyst may be able to remain empathic with this patient, realising how painfully rejected at one time the patient must have felt. In another example, the analyst found herself feeling particularly fearful over a period of sessions with a well-mannered and courteous male patient. After a time she realised that she was unconsciously outlining the analysand's father, about whom the patient felt very bitter for his 'pathetic and cowardly' avoidance of the patient's severe mother.

The best-known example of transference is where the patient falls in love with the analyst. Freud discusses the erotic transference in his paper 'The dynamics of transference' (1912a). He was able to see that it was the analytic situation and what the analyst was re-presenting that evoked a buried childhood love. The analytic situation reawakens desire: the patient becomes a little child again wanting to be loved by an adored parent. The erotic transference is always present at some level, but it is the hardest to interpret. The heterosexual transference is less unacceptable to contemplate

than the homosexual transference, the interpretation of which is
strongly resisted by male patients in particular.

Hanna Segal, in an unpublished talk given in Dublin (1976),
points out that the way the analyst listens refers not only to an
intellectual openness of mind, but also a particular openness to
feelings, 'allowing our feeling and our mind to be affected by the
patient, to a far greater extent than we allow ourselves in ordinary
social intercourse'. We have to contain these feelings, and not act
on them and contaminate the analytic space. She gives an example
in which, in the first session, the patient had spoken about the
numerous ways in which she felt she had been a disappointment
to her mother and herself. In the second session she seemed acutely
depressed and spoke in a very quiet voice and described at length
how terrible she felt. She was depressed, felt dead, terribly weak,
she had an awful headache and so on. The analyst reported herself
as feeling very affected by this and wondered if she had done
something wrong in the previous session. She felt a pressure on her
to understand and try to help. In answer to a question, the patient
said that her mother used to have terrible headaches. The analyst
did not interpret the patient's identification with her mother, as
there seemed little point, but found herself wondering why she was
so affected by what was happening. 'I slowly came to realise,' she
said, 'that I felt *I* was a disappointment to her and to myself. I was
in the position of a rather bewildered child weighed down by a
mother's depression.' After an interpretation emphasising this
aspect, the patient went on to describe how she has 'perfect pitch',
and that she had been trained and encouraged and was gifted
enough to become a soloist, but that she has never been able to do
it. Instead she specialised as an accompanist. And apparently, when
her mother sang, she used to accompany her on the piano.
Apparently this patient had developed a perfect pitch for her
mother's depression and found a way of coping but only as an
accompanist.

To emphasise the point again: by listening and feeling and
accurately understanding the countertransference the analyst can
grasp in some palpable way the patient's psychical reality. By
feeling the anxious helplessness of that little girl trying to please a
perfectionistic mother, the analyst is able to make a useful
interpretation which has arisen out of an empathic conjunction
with the patient's unconscious.

Two more points should be made about the analyst's listening. Firstly, it is a listening to *everything* that is said and not said. It tries to be non-selective, not just listening for the transference. For instance, the patient says, 'I find you cold and aloof.' Now this will contain feelings from the past at the hands of people who were cold and aloof and it would be right to explore this. 'Who am I like whom you knew in the past?' Or, 'Who do I remind you of?' It is also right to acknowledge, not out of guilt or anxiety, but simply because it is true, that the analytic process *is* one-sided in that the analyst sets the fee (with some room for manoeuvre), the patient goes to the analyst, there is normally a set time per session, the patient is usually lying down and the analyst is sitting, the patient is revealing and the analyst is non-disclosing. The *reality* of the patient's relative inferiority vis-à-vis the analyst must be conceded when appropriate, as well as the necessary explorations of the phantasies which are inevitably evoked by the analytic situation.

Secondly, the analyst may fail to listen, and begin to act instead of interpret. If the analyst feels insecure with what the patient is saying or feeling, he is inclined to react defensively (Hinshelwood, 1985) perhaps using interpretations sadistically, or justifying himself, or being overly reassuring. Here the analyst is *acting on* his countertransference rather than analysing it. He is failing to listen. If this happens repeatedly, then the patient is put into a bind, trying harder and harder to get through to the analyst, trying to keep contact by becoming compliant, or breaking off in a state of some confusion.

II: THE MISUNDERSTANDINGS

Having dealt at some length with how the analyst listens and the rationale behind the unobtrusive analyst, let us consider a number of other misunderstandings that have arisen about psychoanalysis in the popular imagination.

First is the charge that psychoanalysis is not a science and therefore its assertions about the structure of the psyche have not been proved. It is true that psychoanalysis is not a *natural* science. Freud had high hopes that his 'Project for a Scientific Psychology' (1895) would be validated at least in principle by findings in neurophysiology. The 'Project' was abandoned, but the findings of the perceptual psychologists do corroborate basic tenets of psychoanalysis (see below). Psychoanalysis is a science in the broader sense of the word in that it accumulates knowledge by amassing evidence. This evidence cannot be obtained by controlled experiment, but only by piecing together clues in the manner of a detective or an archaeologist until one arrives at a conclusion that best fits the data. We cannot prove the existence of the Oedipus complex or the super-ego, but the burden of the evidence accumulated in thousands of cases points to their existence in psychical reality.

But to return briefly to the science of perception. The modern view is that the mind is an active process of forming and re-forming the world. It imposes pattern on the universe. Far from being a passive organ that receives the external world and sees it objectively without subjective contamination, it is selective, it organises, categorises and structures, and creates meanings. Psychoanalysis understands the mind in the same way. Patients come to analysis with an unfolding narrative which is what they have made of their lives, literally, what *they have made* of their lives. It is the task of the analysis to broaden and deepen the narrative, but analysts' minds are selective. This is why people say if you go to a Freudian analyst, you dream Freudian dreams, a Jungian, you dream Jungian dreams, etc. If you go to one analyst and later change analysts, then you find out different aspects of yourself in two different settings. Neither is invalidated; both are true. Both are scientific if one can get away from the kind of cultural terrorism that states that the only real science is natural science.

Second, one hears the charge levelled at psychoanalysis that it is all about the past and that this is irrelevant because it is the 'here and now' and the future that are important. The truth is that the analyst works in a circular fashion, interpreting the 'here and now' in terms of the past and back again, making both past and present more intelligible. We are of course working for the 'here and now' and the future, but we can only do this if we are freed from the compulsions of the past, the unfinished business, the misinterpretations and the excuses which have kept us ensnared in the past. Far from merely resurrecting old experiences for their own sake, analysis reconstitutes and brings vividly to life versions of those experiences, puts words on them; then and only then can they be given a secure place in the coherent and convincing life history of a person. As children we don't have words – the conceptual tools – to understand such basic feelings as rejection, hunger, jealousy, hatred, or guilt. Not being quite fully grasped and integrated, these early feelings return to haunt us in the present. An adult analysis will re-conceptualise and fully articulate these feelings and lay them to rest. Having re-entered one's own history in a creative and vital way one becomes much more aware of the significance and deep importance of the present. One wants to live awarely in that present, celebrate it and fulfil it.

A third general criticism of psychoanalysis is that it is too reductive. All human experience is reduced to sexual feelings, or the 'good breast' or 'penis envy' or some other unconscious infantile determinant. It is true that Freud's early discoveries were framed in a mechanical way, suggesting 'Newtonian' forces at work in the human psyche. The organising principle in Newtonian physics was gravity; while in Freud's psychoanalysis the psychobiological energy was termed *libido*. Libido energises the erogenous zones and can be displaced into any other activity. Our first experiences in life concerned our bodies – feeding, excreting, touching, taking in with our senses, kicking, moving, being cuddled. Freud suggested that 'the ego is first and foremost a body-ego; that is it is first derived from bodily sensations' (1923, p. 26). Many of the metaphors we use to describe experience still contain bodily sensations. We have 'gut feelings', we have to 'swallow our pride' or 'sit on our feelings', we feel 'uptight', we 'stick our noses into other people's business'. If we are worried about being found out, 'we cover our arses'. Like the woman in my first case history, we have experiences which 'make us sick'. From a sado-masochistic point of view, we can 'either screw or be screwed'. We can classify people on the basis of infantile phantasy, as 'suckers', 'arse-lickers', 'jerks' and so on.

Feelings, ideas and experiences are frequently, and when appropriate, interpreted along the lines of infantile prototypes. But the idea that infantile feelings *cause* adult problems in a tightly *deterministic* way, and that human experience is mechanically driven from the past, is a destructive over-simplification and denies the concept of the 'self as agent' which is central to psychotherapy. To be sure, there are infantile determinants to adult neurosis and psychosis, and psychoanalysis has indeed taught us how determined we are by unconscious forces, but that is only part of the story. What are our neurotic symptoms, caused by infantile traumata, trying to communicate to us and to others today? In other words, what is the *meaning* of our symptoms? Let us take the example of the woman in the first case history. Clearly her problem with men and her inability to get close to them in her adult life was caused by her bad relationship to her father. While this early trauma remained outside her awareness, she was determined by it and therefore unable to get close to men. On entering analysis she initiated a process whereby she could begin to make sense and discover the meaning of her symptoms and get free from them. (See Home, 1966 and Rycroft, 1968 for fuller discussion on 'causes' and 'meanings'.)

It is true that Freud did see everything as grounded in sexuality, especially in the early stages of his work. The reason for this was the he was attempting to discover what was repressed, and in those times it was the body and bodily feelings that were never talked about. What also needs emphasising here is that Freud's theory of sexuality was very broad, including not just genital sexuality, but oral and anal pleasure, pleasure sensations in the skin and in locomotion – in fact, any sensuous activity. He was interested in what we desire and what gratifies us. Later in his life Freud came to see the importance of aggression, and Melanie Klein spoke of primitive envy and sadism and the desire to make reparation. Later workers have felt that self-esteem was the central factor in psychological disturbance. So our archaic desires are not just based on sexual feelings, but must include a whole range of primitive drives and counterdrives to which the helpless human infant is exposed.

A fourth misunderstanding is that psychoanalysis can be understood and evaluated from the *outside*, whereas like many other experiences in life it can only be fully comprehended when one has *lived* the experience of psychoanalysis. Freud stated the view of the early analysts: 'we have been obliged to recognize and express as our conviction that no one has the right to join in a discussion on psychoanalysis who has not had particular experiences which can only be obtained by being analysed oneself' (1933, p. 69). This should now be regarded as a rather extreme view which makes analysis into a kind of secular cult into which one has to be 'initiated' and for which one has to learn a secret language. But it nevertheless remains true that psychoanalytic ideas have *not* been gained by direct and observable human behaviour in everyday life, but rather through observing and interpreting the 'internal' reality of experience. These data therefore are open to being dismissed out of hand by those whose orientation is towards what can be observed and measured. So Freud felt very concerned to protect his new discoveries from dilution and even ridicule from his friends and his enemies alike. He was clearly over-zealous in denouncing all those who didn't agree as resisting for unconscious reasons.

Psychoanalysis has survived, against the odds, and is indeed influential in many other disciplines. But it is worth emphasising that to understand the psychoanalytic process fully one needs to experience it at first hand. Many who have done so regard it as one of the central experiences of their lives, which as a result have become immensely more complex and meaningful. Coming into contact with a body of ideas through one's own lived experience and difficulty can be intellectually highly stimulating and provocative. But it is true that a broadly psychoanalytic view is held by people who have not been analysed, but who have come to see the appropriateness of psychoanalytic ideas through other disciplines such as literature, art and even religion.[3]

Fifth, a superficial reading of Freud has led to a widespread but misplaced assumption that the aim of psychoanalysis is to abandon defences and remove inhibition. In the early days of analysis, Freud used hypnosis and the 'pressure technique' to extract memories that were not easily accessible to conscious recall. He gradually came to realise that some force was operating that actually opposed the emergence of certain emotionally laden memories from the unconscious. He called this force *resistance*. What is called resistance in analysis refers to various defence mechanisms in everyday life. At first resistance was seen as an enemy to be got rid of so that the unconscious conflict could emerge and be resolved once and for all. But then, according to Laplanche and Pontalis, Freud 'realised that resistance was itself a means of reaching the repressed and unveiling the secret of neurosis . . . As we know, Freud held steadfastly to the view that the interpretation of resistance, along with the transference, constituted the specific characteristics of his technique' (1973, p. 395). So, far from stripping away the defences as some of the more action-orientated therapies advocate, defences are to be analysed and integrated into more conscious functioning. This view is clearly stated by Weiss:

> The patient's defences like his impulses are at first unconscious. Though they are part of the ego, they act beyond the control of the *conscious* ego. During analysis, they are brought under the control of the conscious ego and thus come to act in harmony with the other trends within the ego. They are thereby transformed from unconscious defence mechanisms to ego-syntonic control mechanisms . . . used by the ego to regulate (now consciously) the impulses warded off by the defences. (1967, p. 520)

Here is a brief example quoted by Weiss in the same paper. A 35-year-old man at the beginning of his analysis was unconsciously stubborn – so much so that he felt compelled not to co-operate with the analysis, yet was unable to experience his stubbornness and felt intense feelings of guilt and helplessness as a consequence. Later, as a result of the analyst's comments, the patient became more consciously aware of his stubbornness and was able to be more co-operative with the analyst. By analysing his anxiety and guilt about his unconscious stubbornness, the patient was able to gain some control over his defensive inertia. He was more able to be stubborn when he wanted to be, and co-operative when he wanted to be. He could now *use* this defence mechanism when necessary rather than *be used* by it. So analysis proceeds slowly, by modifying defences, making them more conscious, integrating them more with the forbidden impulses, and thereby overcoming some of the splits within the personality. To abandon defences completely would leave us in a totally vulnerable situation and would require urgent mobilisation of very primitive and violent defences which would greatly impoverish ego functioning.

. The sixth point of criticism is that people who go in for psychoanalysis are self-indulgent. They prefer naval-staring to action in the outside world. Any reading of the psychoanalytic case histories from Freud down to the present day will impress upon one the depth of the suffering, the sadness of lives crippled by mental illness. It is hard for people who are reasonably well adjusted to normal life to conceive of a person literally driven by anxiety – driven to work so hard that they get no rest; driven to avoid real contact with people lest they find some terrible weakness or flaw; driven to stem an ever-rising tide of hate and contempt directed towards others and against oneself. It is hard to conceive of a depression that leaves one feeling totally apathetic and lifeless. Most people are driven to analysis by their problems, partly conscious and partly unconscious. Anybody who entertained the thought of psychoanalysis as a way to some kind of self-improvement, as an interesting alternative to an evening class, would not stay the course unless they happened upon some real issue that had lain dormant. Psychoanalysis takes courage, initiative, commitment and a kind of dogged determination to get at the truth.

III: THE CURE?

Finally, we come to the vexed question of cure. Can psychoanalysis make people well? This is a very difficult question to answer and one that psychoanalysts are reluctant to get involved in. Since the advent of antibiotics in the 1940s, we are familiar with and have come to expect the complete cure of disease. That expectation extends to mental illness as well, but the fact is that many of the severe forms of mental illness cannot be cured whatever approach one takes.

Psychoanalysts will argue that it is very hard to measure *externally* changes which involve the *internal* world of the patient. Each psychoanalytic treatment is unique. It brings about changes in the direction of better functioning, increased harmony within the psyche, less rigidity and more freedom of action, increased self-confidence, less self-defeating and self-destructive behaviour patterns, more realistic aims and acceptance of failure, less denial and more honesty. Analysts speak of *changes* rather than cure – if we take that word to mean the abolishing of symptoms. Of course the deeper meaning of the word has to do with care – the care of souls. Curing is a method of preservation which prevents decomposition, like salting or pickling. Analysts have become more realistic about what they can do. Freud spoke of 'converting neurotic suffering into ordinary human misery', and of 'the capacity to love and to work' as being a rule-of-thumb notion of health. Once libido is going outwards towards work and in relationship to others, less is invested in *internal* conflict and psychosomatic symptoms. And in his paper on narcissism Freud made a point which seems to be central: 'we must begin to love in order that we may not fall ill, and must fall ill if, in consequence of frustration, we cannot love' (1914b, p. 69).

We say in our first case history that the working out of the woman's problem with her father enabled her to work and to begin to be able to love. Her unconscious frustration with what she perceived as her father's failure to love and understand her was making her ill. Again and again analysts will give examples of improvements of this kind – people for the first time able to relinquish incestuous ties and form new relationships; being able to work more creatively and fulfillingly. Underlying problems still remain in perhaps every case, but they are not of such a crippling force as those which consumed personal energy, leaving little for the external world.

We may well respect and believe individual analysts when they talk of patients getting better, but what about the method of treatment as a whole? We are still avoiding the question: does psychoanalysis get results in statistical terms? In a helpful survey of the literature, Fitzgerald (1987) has critically examined the results of a number of studies carried out to determine the beneficial effects or otherwise of various forms of psychotherapy. The most famous study was Eysenck's 1952 study, which concluded that psychoanalysis was no better than the passage of time. People get better in psychoanalysis at the same rate as they do outside it. He later reinforced his view with further evidence in 1960 and 1965. But his data were shown to be full of weaknesses. He overlooked a number of controlled studies of all kinds on the efficacy of psychotherapy. His figure of 90 per cent improvement for behaviour therapy did not include those who broke off treatment early, whereas for psychoanalysis he did include those who abandoned treatment in the early stages. His figures for so-called spontaneous remissions were calculated in such a way as to make them fly in the face of all clinical realities. For instance, his remission rates for alcoholics and psychopaths were 64 per cent and 75 per cent, and the suggestion that 66 per cent of those classed as neurotic get better if they are not treated is perhaps the greatest weakness amongst all his findings. Other, less biased studies have shown the spontaneous improvement rate for mental illness to be around 30 per cent, and the rate of improvement after all forms of psychotherapy other than psychoanalysis to be about 65 per cent. The overall rate of improvement for those in psychoanalysis was

83 per cent, which indicates strong but modest evidence in favour of psychoanalytic psychotherapy.

Furthermore, it is worth noting that more than half the psychiatrists and psychologists in the United States have chosen psychoanalysis as the treatment of choice from the range of therapeutic strategies available. One of those doctors, interviewed by Janet Malcolm, commented on the common and firmly held idea that

> what happens in analysis would have happened anyway – that people naturally change as life goes on and that analysts take credit for changes they aren't responsible for. I've had thoughts like this about my analysis and have had to stop myself. I've had to remind myself how rigidly determined our lives are – how predictable and repetitive, how encrusted and hardened, how resistant to change. If we had changed as easily as it's claimed, there wouldn't be people going to analysis at forty or fifty; they would have all changed naturally by then into wise, mature, moderately contented people. The young person whose life hasn't taken a course yet can deceive himself into thinking that his life has unlimited potential, although in fact he is already limited and determined . . . (Malcolm, 1982, p. 55)

2 LIMITS TO GROWTH

Having considered some of the basic principles of psychoanalytic therapy in the last chapter in broadly classical outlines, I want now to begin to situate psychoanalysis in a broader philosophical and religious framework. The aim is to bring back psychoanalysis to the heart of our understanding (or misunderstanding) of ourselves. Freud was a modernist and atheist in his thinking, but he established a theory of psychical reality and functioning, as well as a method of exploring that reality, which has certain resonances with religion and evokes for some a broadly religious interpretation, which as we shall see is both interesting and problematic. There are all sorts of dangers with this. In this chapter, I shall discuss some of these dangers and misunderstandings, and I hope in the process of this extended discussion to deepen our understanding of the whole psychoanalytic project.

THE ELUSIVE TRUTH

High in the mountains overlooking the bay of Corinth stands the spectacularly beautiful Delphic shrine, where Socrates was to find the inscription, 'Know thyself', which has become the central theme for psychotherapy in the modern period. Here the god Apollo gave counsel through his priestesses. Apollo is the god of enlightenment, reason and insight. He is also the god of healing and well-being. He gave guidance to troubled Greeks at a time in their history of great change and ferment, when, as in our time, the family and the old stability were crumbling.

The Delphic injunction to know thyself is central to the

psychoanalytic process. And in a certain sense it fulfils its obligation in this respect. But this knowing is a very paradoxical knowing. The truth which is discovered is constantly shifting and changing. It can never be pinned down like static information. It is lived experience which comes and goes. And sometimes patients will say in irritation: So, what have I learnt? What knowledge have I gained?

People come into psychoanalytic treatment in search of a cure for their emotional problems and ostensibly, therefore, to face the truth about themselves. But, as Freud repeatedly emphasised, the process is dogged at each stage and in every moment by resistance – resistance to knowing and remembering the very material that would lead to truth. The word used to describe the process of acquiring truth – apprehension – means on the one hand to lay hold of something with understanding, and on the other to anticipate in anxiety and dread. Here is the fundamental human dividedness with respect to truth contained in language.

For Freud and for psychoanalysis, the Oedipus complex remains central. Oedipus is a metaphor for a certain dread which connects our desire unconsciously with foreboding, with indebtedness and guilt. It stands for a fundamental ignorance or amnesia about our origins. During analysis this metaphor is endlessly reworked, encountered and rejected as an ever-present nodal point. Frequently it appears in dreams and fantasies that create anxiety: for instance, some patients have the strong endopsychic perception that someone has been murdered. Oedipus blinds himself on realisation of his own truth, which was inscribed in him in the prophesy of the oracle, perhaps partly by identification with the blind seer Teiresias, and partly in the realisation that when he could see, he was blind. We must understand here that Oedipus is exemplary. His actions are not to be explained away by the fact that he was greatly traumatised at birth by being abandoned. Psychoanalysis understands Oedipus as a universally *structuring* phenomenon that causes a dividedness in the human subject with respect to knowledge, freedom and desire.

SIN AS SEPARATION

New Testament writing, like psychoanalysis, equates truth and freedom. In John 8: 32, 34: 'You shall know the truth and the truth shall set you free . . . everyone who commits sin is a slave.' Here the connection is evoked between sin, ignorance and unfreedom. Paul Tillich, an existential theologian greatly influenced by psychoanalysis, speaks of sin not so much in terms of wrongful acts, but as being in a *state* or *condition* of separation, of being separated from a certain fullness of Being. Clearly post-Oedipally, this is a permanent occlusion. Tillich says: 'Our sin is the great all-pervading problem of our lives . . . perhaps even the word sin has the same root as the word asunder. In any case sin is separation. There is separation among individual lives, separation of man from himself, and separation of all men from the ground of Being' (1949, p. 156).

Being ignorant of and estranged from ourselves, we endlessly repeat past patterns, encircling some primordial formative moments in our earliest childhood inscribed for ever in the unconscious. Freud links our failure to remember our past with repetitions in the present: 'We may say that here the patient does not *remember* anything of what he had forgotten and repressed, but *acts* it out. He reproduces it not as a memory but as an action; he *repeats* it, without, of course, knowing that he is repeating it' (1914a, p. 150).

He goes on to give a number of examples. For instance, the patient does not remember how hostile and dictatorial he used to feel towards his father, but instead repeats this pattern of behaviour with authority figures. Or in another case, the patient does not remember that as a child he was intensely ashamed of certain sexual activities. But he makes it clear that he is ashamed of the psychoanalytic treatment to which he has submitted himself, and does his utmost to keep it a secret.

The blind repetition of behaviour that often one knows to be destructive to others and to oneself is this state of sin. It is just these repetition compulsions that bring people to psychoanalysis. They hope to *re-member* and *re-collect* – literally bring the separated parts back together, to overcome the split between consciousness and the unconscious. The theological concept of sin takes on a whole new meaning when viewed in the light of psychoanalytic insight. Sins are much more than a list of forbidden acts, when one realises that these acts are committed in a state of alienation and separation. Making the links with the present and the past tends to overcome the sense of being a slave to compulsions. The process is never complete, and therefore sin is never overcome completely.

As Tillich points out, sin and ignorance are conditions of our human existence, of our finitude and of our culture. They are givens in the human situation:

> The counsellor and psychiatrist can help, but can he make us whole? Can he give us salvation? Certainly not if we are not able to use our freedom and if we are conquered by the tragic conflicts of our existence. None of us is isolated . . . Health and illness are fighting with each other. How can we be whole if the culture is split within itself, if every value is denied by another one, and if every truth is questioned? . . . How can we be whole if we are connected with people who are in discord with themselves, in hostility against us, or if we have to live with individuals, groups or nations who are irreconciled and sick? This is the situation of all of us, and this situation reacts on our personal life, disrupting the concord we may have reached. The reconciliation in our souls and often even in our bodies breaks down in the encounter with reality. (Tillich, 1956, p. 181)

Psychoanalysis can liberate us from our neurotic trends and splits and increase our personal power and freedom, but we are still inevitably left in a state of separation and ignorance which is a condition of our existence and of the reality of our world. Freud implicitly recognised this when he said to one of his female hysterics, Elizabeth Von R., that he only hoped to transform neurotic suffering into ordinary human misery.

MODERN SAVIOURS

There have been many inside the psychotherapeutic movement who have not heeded the wisdom and modesty of this statement. There seems to be an ever-present tendency to idealise one's own form of therapy and to imply that the client's problems will be solved. A recent television series on psychotherapy implied as much in its introductory remarks. It showed people crowded in busy city streets and on commuter trains. People were walking fast with deadpan expressions. The voice-over wondered whether all these people were happy or not – perhaps they had hidden emotional problems, or patterns in their lives that they would be rid of? The ensuing group-psychotherapy session, psychodrama in this case, shows the way these problems are worked on. The therapist assumes and is allowed to assume a very powerful role in directing participants to act out and dramatise very early anxiety situations, and the clients comply in the hope that by re-experiencing those early fears they might now find more adult, creative solutions. There is no doubt that this form of psychotherapy can be helpful. What is at issue is the role of the psychotherapist. In the transference (which is at no point commented upon or analysed by either the therapist or the clients) the therapist becomes that all-powerful parent of early childhood who will make everything well. The regression to the infantile position in the clients can be beneficial, but it can also be dangerous, with the loss of critical faculties and the over-valuation of the therapist and the method. One sees clients sometimes becoming just like their therapists, apparently assertive and confident, even using the same manner of speaking! Former problems are denied or minimised. A highly evocative phantasy has been re-stimulated: namely the possibility of fusion with the all-powerful perfect parent of childhood. Under the illusion of their phantasies, the clients believe that there is no need for 'ordinary human misery' – a new life is there for the taking. In a modern and secular sense they regard themselves as saved.

An endless stream of popular psychology books suggests that you should 'build warmth and trust', 'expand your consciousness', 'tune into yourself and your family', 'conquer your fears', and so on. Important figures in various branches of psychotherapy have become charismatic and powerful and their methods become offered as panaceas. One thinks of Janov's assertion that 'Primal Therapy is like neurosis in reverse . . . once the major defence system is broken, the patient has no choice but to get well' (1970, p. 103). For Perls (1973) it is living totally in the 'here and now'. For Maslow (1971) it was 'self-actualization' and the 'peak experience'. For Reich (1927–33) and the neo-Reichians (Boardella, 1976) it is the release of bio-energy. Rogers speaks of how the therapist cares for his client 'in a non-possessive way . . . in a total rather than conditional way . . . The term we have come to use for this is unconditional positive regard' (1961, p. 62). We may be warned that there are indeed difficulties on the way to growth, but if you are prepared to work on yourself there are vast resources to be tapped. Such optimism sends a certain type of person from one therapy to another in search of the elusive fulfilment of the primal phantasy.

The incorporation of some aspects of Eastern mysticism into

psychotherapeutic strategies has further complicated the issue; for now there is the possibility of overcoming the narrow egoic view of the world. Studies in altered states of consciousness (see Tart, 1975) and the use of mind-expanding drugs opened up new and transcendental experiences for those willing to experiment. Zen and Taoism offered a philosophy which apparently contradicted the dominant Western values accorded to the ego – analysis, manipulation, exploitation and control over the world – in favour of 'making this so-called mystical consciousness the normal everyday consciousness' (Watts, 1961, p. 46).

Rama, Ballentine and Ajaya (1976) have brought together Eastern thought and Western psychotherapy into a new synthesis which is challenging and stimulating. A central figure, Patanjali, who wrote the Yoga Sutras over one thousand years ago, identified five basic causes of human misery: (1) *Avidya* (ignorance), (2) *Asmita* (limited self-concept), (3) *Raga* (attachment), (4) *Dvesa* (aversion), (5) the fear of death. These afflict the so-called neurotic and the so-called normal person alike. Yoga does not concern itself with whether or not a person is sick or well, but beckons its practitioners to higher states of consciousness and self-awareness. It is not concerned with correcting a maladaptive ego, but with transcending the limited view of the world that the ego provides. We might say also that psychoanalysis is not about adaptation to the world either. Most analysts would welcome the expansion of consciousness, the increase in self-esteem, the loosening of neurotic attachments, the decrease in phobic avoidance, and the greater acceptance of death which a successful analysis can provide, but it is true to say that psychoanalysis is concerned with the concrete and not with the mystical. In fact the mystical flight from the concrete may be just a case of avoidance!

It is a question of degree. To think that we could attain all knowledge, that we could accept the world totally, that we could overcome all attachments and overcome the fear of death itself – in short, give up the egoic view of the world – is a dangerous illusion. According to one study conducted in England, in certain altered states of consciousness which are frequent but fleeting occurrences for many people, we can attain an egoless state in which we feel in touch with the cosmos and experience 'the peace that passeth all understanding'.[1] The widespread interest and practice of various meditation and contemplation techniques bear witness to both the human need and the great psychological and spiritual renewals that can occur in experienced and disciplined practitioners. But we return, and indeed we must return, albeit refreshed and healed, to ordinary consciousness with its daily tasks and decisions and tensions.

But reaching towards the blissful annihilation of selfhood and the consequent devaluation of the material world and the world of human need and aspiration represents a denial of the anxiety of human existence – the anxiety which is essential for a creative work. To quote Rollo May, quoting Paul Tillich:

> Mysticism does not take seriously the concrete and the doubt concerning the concrete. It plunges directly into the ground of Being and meaning, and leaves the concrete, the world of values and meanings behind. Therefore it does not solve the problem of meaningless. In terms of the present religious situation this means that Eastern mysticism is not the solution to the problems of Western Existentialism, although many attempt this solution. (May, 1974, p. 97)

This analysis gives the lie to the belief of the Human Growth movement that people who expose themselves to the appropriate training techniques derived from various forms of psychotherapy and Eastern religious systems can attain greater and greater growth and self-fulfilment. We go to 'group encounter', and then we go to 'advanced group encounter', we become more 'growthful', more liberated. The error is in treating human potential as if it had no limits at all. In contrast, psychoanalysis is unique amongst the range of psychotherapies in asserting the essential incompleteness of the human condition. Our desire is destined for only a partial satisfaction. There will always be a lack. There is the longed-for complete satisfaction and the endless search for it, but it is always disappointing and insufficient. To be conscious is always to be searching for something that one never finds.

There is an ever-present retrogressive tendency to deny such a 'castrated' view of ourselves and to reach for total satisfaction and to deny the coexistence of the constructive and the destructive, to deny ambivalence and the universality of conflict and tension. Freud indeed struck the most profound blow of all to human narcissism (following on from Copernicus and Darwin) by establishing the extent to which we are governed by unconscious forces.

THE EGO-IDEAL

Jonathan Hanaghan, the founder of psychoanalysis in Ireland,[2] developed a radical Christian psychoanalytic viewpoint:

Reverse the process of driving out all but idealistic thoughts. Undefended, receive yourself unto yourself, the high, the low, the unselfish, the selfish. Only as the pressure of the powers of darkness make themselves felt as *your* impulses and *your* desires will you realise that at *your* soul's centre rage the cosmic and transcosmic conflicts. Only then will you feel as helpless as a little child: only then will you yearn for help. That yearning is your prayer uttered or unexpressed. It brings you into a state of simple spiritual needful dependence, a relation which is akin to a baby's relation to its mother. Accept it as the highest wisdom. Do not put the darkness of your human understanding between you and the love of God . . . Do not prevent this truthful experience that will authentically come to any person truthful and brave enough to explore within. (Hanaghan, 1957, p. 165)

Hanaghan was a Christian as well as a psychoanalyst, in that he believed psychoanalysis was both healing and saving in the full religious meaning of those terms:

When Freudian psychoanalysis is more fully understood, it will be seen that psychoanalysis is ultimately concerned with a cosmic and transcosmic conflict. For according to Freud, *value* enters into mental illness; value rooted in the spirit of man . . . A sufferer is not a lone person, with an illness, but a lover entangled in his utmost deep with father and mother, brother and sister, husband or wife, with school and college, with factory and workshop and the wide world. (1966, p. 110)

Clearly he regards the psychoanalyst as a mental healer: 'Whilst training broad and deep is necessary in mental healing, love, patience, tolerance, courage and abiding are as necessary. Mental healing is essentially an atoning work bringing the sufferer at one with himself, his family, his people, and with humanity and the universe' (p. 111).

Hanaghan held a meeting each Saturday night in his house in Monkstown, South Dublin, in which he spoke about the religious dimension to psychoanalytic work. It was not enough just to have the analytic sessions without considering the unique aim and direction of one's life, the question as to what one was to *become*. Hanaghan taught that we are aided in our search by another faculty of the personality, apart from the id, the ego and the super-ego. He called that faculty the ego-ideal,[3] and it expresses the inner freedom of the self seeking its own higher fulfilment. The Quakers call this the inner light and others the Holy Spirit within. Hanaghan clearly distinguished the ego-ideal from the super-ego. The super-ego is tyrannical and carries the castrating voices of the ancestors, whereas the ego-ideal is a still small voice inviting us (rather than commanding us through fear) to become what we essentially are. The ego-ideal is fleshed out by our identification with those encouraging, helping, enabling parents, teachers and other significant adults.

For Hanaghan, man is spirit. Therefore, the imagination is central and primary:

> All good and evil proceed from personal response to the primal presentations of the imagination. Imagination is nearer to man's spirit than is his body or his thought. Through imagination evolution or devolution (the descent into evil) declare their veiled purposes . . . Evolutional purpose declares itself imaginatively as *Vision*, devolutional purpose, imaginatively as *Phantasy*. Thus through imagination is the cosmic conflict between good and evil made manifest to man-spiritual. (1957, p. 60)

It is the visionary aspect of the ego-ideal that enables people to choose the creative solutions, make the productive decisions, to move forward to become what they truly are. The super-ego makes us do things because we are afraid or guilty; the id tempts us to short-cuts and immediate gratification, while the ego (which in this case Hanaghan calls the actuality-ego) is the pragmatist, attempting to balance all the demands. It is only the ego-ideal that has the overview, the transcendental view, and can stand outside the limited and tedious demands of everyday life and render some decisions infinitely more valuable than others.

Talking of his work as a psychoanalyst (1962), Hanaghan says:

> Again and again I have been able to heal by appealing to this Ego Ideal and calling forth the libido to invest the Ego Ideal more and more. Let the libido invest the Ego Ideal so that you love your ideal self more than yourself, you love what you hope to be even more than what you are. (1973, p. 5)

Hanaghan is quite unequivocal in many of his statements:

As you know, the majority of psychoanalysts have no interest in religion. They are so fascinated with their own science that they don't press beyond it. I press beyond it . . . The central factor in the analyst's healing is the analyst's capacity to love. And by love I mean the spiritual capacity to give another person utter freedom of heart to say and to feel what they like without condemnation. (pp. 9, 10)

Hanaghan's original contributions to the interpretation of the New Testament and to Freudian thought have not yet been widely disseminated. During his lifetime he preferred to work and to give talks rather than write. Ludovic Kennedy said of him (after doing a television programme with him), 'He gave what was in his heart, freely and fully. I count it a great privilege to have met this man.' Hanaghan had an ability to get to the centre of a person. He was a man of primordial energy and charisma. He possessed genuine healing powers and helped many people through psychoanalysis, charging fees only according to their ability to pay. He took many people for little or nothing. He strongly challenged the narrow hypocritical religious attitudes of conventional Christians of that time with his own inspired fusion of Freud and Jesus. Many came to hear his talks on Saturday nights and went away feeling more deeply the meaning, the beauty and the significance of their lives.

The concept of the ego-ideal is both mystical and concrete. Most analysts would work with some preconscious notion of integration and progress towards a self-fulfilment for their patients. But Freud warned against having preconceived ideas as to how the patient might get well: 'He should withhold all conscious influences from his capacity to attend and give himself over completely to "unconscious memory" . . . He should simply listen and not bother about whether he is keeping anything in mind' (1912a, p. 112). If one's mind is directed towards a solution, that of drawing the libido into the ego-ideal; if one believes that the aim of human nature is ultimately to be directed towards and to find its own ideal, then surely the essential freedom of the analytic enterprise is jeopardised. Instead of analysing, one is unconsciously suggesting a direction – a direction which is one's own view of the Christian ideal. Hidden countertransferences in the analyst are going to be acted out instead of being subjected to scrutiny in the analyst's own self-analysis. There is an ever-present danger that the analysis will be short-circuited in favour of the ideal. One is reminded of the fact that the resistance of the patient and of the analyst is always ready to seize upon a centrifugal attitude to avoid the essential work of the analysis. If patients know that their analysts have strong feelings about spiritual ideals then they will be inclined to eclipse perverse elements within themselves, however much they are told to 'free-associate'.

There is a profound wisdom in adhering to the psychoanalytic technique as directed by Freud in his papers on technique and as elaborated by others. Modifications to the classical technique have come about in response to the difficulties encountered in managing psychotic or borderline patients who do not themselves have the capacity to contain conflict, whose self-structure is so weak that they need a lot of support before analysis can begin.

But to speak of 'the analyst's capacity to love and to heal' makes him or her into too grandiose a figure, indeed puts too great a pressure on him or her to *perform* as a lover or a healer or a saviour of the patient. There is a great danger of analysts' identifying with these archetypes as a defence against their own helplessness in the analytic setting. Many analysts are themselves wounded people, who have come to some sort of self-acceptance and reconciliation through their own personal analysis and training analysis. It is all too easy for them to don the mantle of healer to avoid further pain and self-analysis. In the extreme case, one could identify oneself with Jesus on the cross and take all the hostility from one's patients, analysing it back to them as *their* problem while never having or wanting to look into one's own countertransference attitude.

There is a danger for both the analyst and the patient in following too closely the ego-ideal, in that both can become resistant to further self-analysis; and herein lies the perennial difficulty for all human beings – that, as Ronald Laing says, we seem to be capable of endless self-deception. That we need to have ideals goes without saying: there have to be goals and values to which we are orientated. But the ideals are in a dialectical relationship to the incoherence and chaos of the unconscious. Both must be kept alive for the sake of vitality. Once unity is achieved, or believed to be achieved, we have illusion. John Sturrock, writing on the work of the French psychoanalyst Jacques Lacan, states:

> This moment of self-identification [during the mirror stage of infancy] is crucial, not because it represents a stage on the way to 'adulthood' or 'genital maturity', but because it represents a permanent tendency

of the individual: the tendency which leads him throughout life to seek and foster the imaginary wholeness of an 'ideal ego'. The unity invented at these moments and the ego which is the product of successive identifications, are both spurious; they are attempts to find ways round certain inescapable factors of lack (*manque*), absence and incompleteness in human living. (Sturrock, 1979, p. 122)

The spurious unity of the ideal ego is echoed in Vedantic teaching by the concept of *Maya*, which is roughly translated as the veiling of reality or the relativity of reality. It is often translated as 'illusion'. Our knowledge of the world and of ourselves is limited and is based on denial. The specific focusing of consciousness means that the totality of reality is lost. In the memorable words of St Paul:

> whether there be prophecies, they shall fail; whether there be tongues they shall cease; whether there be knowledge it shall vanish away. For we know in part and we prophesy in part. But when that which is perfect is come then that which is in part shall be done away . . . For now we shall see through a glass darkly; but then face to face: now I know in part; but then shall I know even as also I am known. (1 Corinthians 13)

We see only in part. This is Martin Buber's 'I-It' relationship:

> Man travels over the surface of things and experiences them. He extracts knowledge about their constitution from them; he wins an experience from them. He experiences what belongs to things . . . We are merely following the uneternal division that springs from the lust of the human race to whittle away the secret of death. Inner things or outer things, what are they but things and things! (1958, p. 5)

This is the task-orientated consciousness in which we spend most of our lives. But we can *participate* in what Martin Buber calls the other primary relation, the 'I-Thou', in which in brief moments, face to face, we see the world in its totality, in which the subject–object split is overcome and the eternal breaks into the finite. Buber describes an incident when he was eleven years of age, spending the summer on his grandparents' estate, when he stole into the stable unobserved to stroke the neck of his pet horse. He says that what he experienced that one time was deeply stirring:

> I must say that what I experienced in touch with the animal was the *Other*, the immense Otherness of the Other, which however did not make strange . . . but rather let me draw near and touch it . . . it felt like life beneath my hand, it was as though the element of vitality itself

bordered on my hand . . . palpably the other, not just another . . . yet it
let me approach, confided itself to me, placed itself elementally in the
relation of a Thou to a Thou with me. (1947, p. 42)

But he goes on to say how he became *conscious* of his hand stroking
the horse and the I–Thou relation dissolved back into the I–It:

> I can elicit from these experiences only that in them I reached an
> undifferentiable unity for myself without form or content. I may call
> this an original pre-biographical unity and suppose that it is hidden
> unchanged beneath all biographical change, all development and
> complication of the soul. (Buber, 1947, p. 43)

We can enter into this I–Thou relation, but we can never *possess* it
as part of ourselves. If we have a religious sensibility we count
ourselves small in relation to God. It is God alone who possesses
truth. God is Being itself, from which we are ever excluded in our
finite existence.

ON THE WRETCHEDNESS OF THE PATIENT AND THE CHRISTIAN

Christianity stresses the recognition and confession of sins. In other
terms, we forgo omnipotence, we accept a certain castration, an
incompleteness. We can assume at some level our position as
separated or alienated. We feel at a loss, or we feel *the* loss, the pain
of loss, as conceived of when we talk metaphorically about the loss
of the breast. This loss has an inescapable feel of anguish or
depression about it. But it is the assumption in some difficult and
paradoxical sense of this brokenness, of this subjection by life, that
characterises both the true Christian position and that of the patient
in analysis. Both have to let go an imaginary omnipotence, without
any guarantees of tangible gain. The Christian may not be saved,
and the patient may not be cured. In both there is an
acknowledgement of sinfulness, which as we indicated earlier is a
structural condition of our existence, as well as, in psychoanalytic
terms, an awareness of the infantile and primitive nature of
unconscious phantasies. Both require a certain faith in goodness
without proof, a certain belief in the process without any prior
givens.

Naturally, in the face of this we recoil back into greatness, into omnipotence away from the horror and abjection (to use Kristeva's term). At the simplest level this is just a requirement for functioning, for living. We need to assert ourselves and our authority and not be humble and small. This is part of our self-preservative instincts, as Freud called them. However, in a more malign way this omnipotent pulling back from subjectivity can assume a more totalitarian position. This is the position of the Pharisee, the moral majority, or the guru, the position of those who identify themselves very fully with and put their faith in an ideal ego. They create total systems, total beliefs that have the potential to destroy. With great irony we can say these people have no need of forgiveness or the presence of the analyst. They are in no need of food, help or sustenance. Forgiveness is there, it always is before anything we do, but they have no need of it.

THE PARADOX OF SUFFERING

The New Testament praises the poor, the halt, the lame, the sick and the sinner, which to our eyes seems perverse. Yet it seems to assert that these people are more attached to life than the rich, the well and the good. In a similar way, in analysis, the injunction to free-associate, to let oneself go, to be open and unselective, makes us come upon disturbance, anxiety and dread, a sense of our own fragility and weakness. This has a deepening effect, a homeopathic effect, adding a third dimension to life. But this is impossible to understand from a positivist point of view and there can be no justification for these claims. To think in terms of redemption through suffering – or analysis, for that matter – seems to justify all kinds of subtle oppression and reverses all our humanistic aspirations to equality and health.

Perhaps there is an insoluble tension here between the position of subjection and the position, roughly speaking, of the ego. We are somehow existentially always caught in this tension, and the psychoanalytic and the Christian perspective, in the sense that I am using both, is fundamentally important and the most difficult to grasp – namely the idea that something actually good can come out of a toleration of suffering.

Beethoven was thirty when deafness struck, and during the last eighteen years of his life he was not able to hear any of the music he composed. He felt compelled to live as an exile and even contemplated suicide. Yet a year later he completed the *Eroica* symphony – a work that brought a whole new dimension into European music.

Charlie Parker, the co-originator of 'bebop' and modern jazz, produced his highly original and lyrical music during the 1940s and '50s. And yet all through this time he was fatally addicted to heroin and alcohol. He lived only for his music, which is still as fresh and evocative as ever, across the years and all the later developments in contemporary music.

The psychoanalytic world has been greatly enriched by the work of Victor Frankl and Bruno Bettelheim, both of whom were forced to endure suffering in the concentration camps and were later to emerge as leading educators in the psychoanalytic movement. Frankl developed his existentialist approach, which he called logotherapy, to help people to develop their own values and meanings even in the face of unalterable suffering, in the camps themselves.

> I spoke of the many opportunities of giving life meaning. I told my comrades (who lay motionless, although occasionally a sigh could be heard) that human life, under any circumstances, never ceases to have a meaning, and that this infinite meaning of life includes suffering and dying, privation and death . . . They must not lose hope but keep their courage in the certainty that the hopelessness of our struggle did not detract from its dignity and meaning. I said that someone looks down on each of us in difficult hours – a friend, a wife, someone alive or dead, or a God – and he would not expect us to disappoint him. He would hope to find us suffering proudly – not miserably – knowing how to die. (1946, p. 83)

It was Bettelheim (1967) who used his experiences in the camps to develop an understanding of how some children can come to be deeply traumatised:

> In the German concentration camps I witnessed with utter disbelief the non-reacting of certain prisoners to their most cruel experience. I did not know and would not have believed that I would observe similar behaviour in the most benign of therapeutic environments, because of what children had experienced in the past. Like others who have worked with autistic children, we were again and again confronted with a parallel blotting out of all pain. (1967, p. 57)

But suffering is not always so ennobling: often it just leads to wastage and more wastage. Often in an analysis one can trace psychopathology which has never been resolved through several generations. For instance, one patient's tense anxiety states, which would lead to insomnia and a terrible relentless driving of herself, could be traced back to her father, and then to his mother who was experienced by him as severe and castrating. It was also turning up in her eldest daughter, whom she described as highly strung. The same or similar behavioural features and states of mind could be seen throughout four generations, without much change for the better. Doubtless such pathologies are at least in part inherited genetically, but that doesn't alter the point that suffering is not necessarily regenerative. Very often suffering leads to more suffering, as part of an endless compulsion to repeat.

Those of a more Jungian persuasion would perhaps tend to think in a religious way, in terms of death and rebirth as part of the individuation process. But perhaps to think in these terms, as an analyst at least, is rather too optimistic, even dangerous. What does happen in analysis is that both the patient and the analyst wait and wait, and it is only later, after perhaps many years, that one realises that there has indeed been change. But it is not necessarily the change that the patient had sought on entering analysis.

And for some patients there is suffering before analysis, and more suffering during analysis, and there is no discernible breakthrough, no change or rebirth, only a negative therapeutic reaction. This might be because the patient was not suitable for analytic-type therapy in the first place, and should not have been taken on. Or, and this is less likely to be admitted, the analyst's interpretations had acted as a subtle and constant undermining of a fragile ego, an ego that should have been shored up by a more supportive psychotherapy rather than being subjected to the rigours of an analysis.

Also there are those patients who cannot risk cure or help. They feel that they do not deserve to be helped. Instead they deserve punishment and the analyst can unwittingly become the new punitive agent. One analyst reported on a patient whom he had seen for two years twice a week, who was always most co-operative in the analytic work. Yet the sessions lacked any life, anything that could be called personal in Winnicott's sense. Then the analyst commented (to a colleague) that the patient never ever looked at or greeted the analyst at the door. There wasn't a flicker of recognition, even after long breaks in the treatment such as holidays. The patient later reported that he had felt he must suffer if the analysis was going to be any good to him. This was the reason, he said, that he avoided any mutuality with the analyst. Of course there were other reasons, but the point here is that his need for suffering, for punishment, for not being cared for, was dominating the treatment, and had been a persistent, yet mute, repetition in the transference.

Certainly both the patient and the analyst suffer during the course of an analysis. The analyst experiences something of the patient's early anxiety states, partly due to the patient's projection, but also because of the inevitable reactivation of his or her own childhood disturbances and anxieties. Furthermore, the analyst wants ultimately to help and cure people, and the patient's suffering is a constant reminder of how difficult this is. This must be the reason why analysts write papers and talk to each other so much. It is often not that they have anything especially new to say, although there are always exceptions; it has much more to do with an abreactive process which seems to be necessary when one is called upon for so many hours each day, over many years, just to hold and contain sometimes intense conflicts and feelings.

It is very difficult to comment on suffering without seeming to glorify it. But I think the true Christian position and the psychoanalytic position have much in common. It was well put for us by Charles Melman in an unpublished talk in Dublin. He said that if a managing director comes to you for analysis and when he is on your couch as an analysand, he still wants to remain a managing director – that is, in the position of master – he is not yet in analysis. He is alienated. He thinks he is complete in himself. He wants to be in charge and order you around. But the Christian and the analytic view, as has been stressed in this chapter, is that this position is illusory and imaginary. In Christian terms, one has to accept (confess) one's sinful state. In analytic terms we must accept the fact that we are castrated. Clearly, in this less alienated state, in this more truthful position, we will suffer, but the suffering carries with it a potential, an openness, a creativity, a possibility for change in an unknown direction.

ON BECOMING A CHILD

In a lighter vein, the New Testament injunction to become 'like a child' is a common theme in all psychotherapy. In the psycho-analytic process there is a constant cross-referring from the present to the past and from the past back to the present. Winnicott (1971a) stressed that psychoanalysis, whether with adults or with children, took place in that intermediate area of two overlapping fields of play. For adults this was free association. For children in therapy it was the 'squiggle game' (1971b). What is called for is the simplicity of beginnings, of a return to those developmental impingements where we began to become less than ourselves. Some psychother-apists use play or painting as a form of therapy as an attempt to reinhabit that world of simple reverie which is the opposite of the compulsive 'fun' of much adult leisure.

To many, and this is true of both adults and children, play is too simplistic and naive, it is not productive enough for the obsessionally inclined. Or the fun that we are supposed to be having, and these days there is much more of it, becomes something which is not play. This fun is often too close to our instinctual life, too excited, for us to be actually able to experience it. Play requires little but a capacity to experience experience. Having fun requires gadgets and much money, but close by is boredom. Play is central to the development of the self, not only amongst human children, but also among mammals generally. Free association is a form of play with, and on, words and analysts' interpretations are their contributions to the game. It is a serious game which will enable patients to reinhabit their own experience and to begin to live a life which can feel more real, be more genuine and seriously pleasurable.

BRINGING DIVISION

I have come to bring division. From now on five members of a family will be divided, three against two and two against three; father against son and son against father, mother against daughter and daughter against mother, mother against son's wife and son's wife against her mother-in-law. (Luke 12: 52, 53)

... If anyone comes to me and does not hate his father and mother, wife and children, brothers and sisters, even his own life, he cannot be a disciple of mine. (Luke 14: 26)

This is a very clear statement, a very truthful statement, without pretence. It clears away the punitive super-ego embargo on hate. It implies that hatred is necessary and fundamental for life. To acknowledge hate and bitterness is to be close to life. If we are too much in the domain of the ego, we can pretend with profound insincerity that we don't hate, but if we are subjects and therefore in subjection, we will and must hate. Hatred is fundamental to desire.

Freud said: 'Hate, as a relation to objects, is older than love. It derives from the narcissistic ego's primordial repudiation of the external world with its outpouring of stimuli' (1915a, p. 139). Omnipotent hatred is our first response to life – that is an absolute rejection of the world with all its otherness and difference. This is why analysts like Winnicott and Kohut have emphasised the mediating role of the mother and father in protecting the infant (via primary illusion) from the total shock of the external world.

For Freud ambivalence of feelings – that is love *and* hate – is universal. Both love and hate are always present in varying degrees, but one emotion is often repressed. Coming from a broadly sentimentalised Christian or secular tradition, analysts, like parents, may be tempted at times to feel that they love and care for their patients or children. Perhaps Winnicott had this in mind when in 1947 he wrote about the analyst's need to be conversant and familiar with his own hatred. He set out a whole series of reasons why a mother will hate her baby. In both the case of the mother and the analyst, acceptance, tolerance and *conscious* knowledge of her own hate, mean that she will not act it out destructively. The New Testament clarification here on hate seems to be saying this: hate that is known can be thought about, spoken about, symbolised or sublimated; hate that is unknown and repudiated becomes very destructive.

We may think we have liberated, in a certain sense, attitudes to sexuality, but our attitude to hate is quite different and repressive. In a culture where everyone tries so hard to be happy and well, perhaps there is a need for a place to reflect and to talk freely. Analysis is one such space where one can speak freely without being helped or cared for *too much*. One can have the freedom to be depressed or enraged *over a long period*, or be silent, or negative, or whatever, without feeling compelled to 'work on it'. Mindful of how much rage has to be repressed, and mindful of how much depression exists, forcibly hidden under the glitz, and how little private space is left uncolonised by a sort of manic consumerism, the analytic space may yet prove to be an invaluable one.

In a very difficult paper, Winnicott describes how rage actually creates reality: 'it is the destructive drive that creates the quality of externality . . . The object is in fantasy always being destroyed. The quality of "always being destroyed" makes the reality of the surviving object felt as such' (1969, p. 93). When hating or murderous fantasies *don't* do the damage in reality that we *fear* they might do, we can feel hatred and rage more safely. This means that we can go at life in a more full-blooded way, not so over-anxious lest we hurt someone. The capacity for hate therefore is a developmental achievement which only comes about in a facilitating environment. Again, in 1947 (p. 202), Winnicott wrote, 'It seems to me doubtful whether a human child as he develops is capable of tolerating the full extent of his own hate in a sentimental environment. He needs hate to hate.'

The availability of the facilitating environment, which must survive and absorb these destructive attacks, is what is very much in question in modern culture, an issue we will take up in the next chapter. If there is no stable and reliable other who is *seen to be unharmed* in spite of being murderously attacked in fantasy, then the eventual fate of these primitive feelings may have much more to do with real destructiveness.

THE QUALITY OF AGAPE

Love 'beareth all things, believeth all things, hopeth all things, endureth all things' (1 Corinthians 13: 7). Most analysts, for very good and very sensible reasons, would avoid the use of the word 'love', except in the ordinarily accepted erotic transference sense, or in the sense that a parent loves his or her child. The word has become so hopelessly debased and sentimentalised in our period that we have good reason for never using it. I have tried to stress in this chapter the difficulty of using these 'ultimate' words like love, healing, truth, and the like. They contain so much power that they can be used for manipulation and deception. They become invaded by unconscious significations and turn into their opposites. Consequently, they easily lead to inflation, to a totalisation of the therapy, and a very dangerous regressive adhesion to gurus. They also can facilitate simplifications and banal platitudes about the therapist's role. Nevertheless, it is perhaps important to situate psychoanalysis within the Western tradition, and clearly we must try to examine how the analyst's role is at least some species of a modern version of Christian love, however problematic such a notion is. Tillich was in no doubt:

> It is indeed important to know that theology has had a lot to learn from the psychoanalytic method the meaning of grace, the meaning of acceptance of those who are unacceptable and not of those who are the good people. On the contrary, the non-good people are those who are accepted, or in religious language, forgiven, justified, whatever you wish to call it. The word grace which has lost any meaning, has gained a new meaning by the way in which the analyst deals with his patient. He accepts him. He does not say 'You are acceptable', but he accepts him. And that is the way, according to religious symbolism, God deals with us; and it is the way every minister and every Christian should deal with the other person. (1959, p. 124)

Furthermore, analysts have themselves suggested that love – and they mean, in effect, the *agape* quality of love – is what is required in the analytic setting. I have already made reference to Hanaghan. Ferenczi (1929) advocated that the analyst should provide that love and tenderness of which neurotic patients in his view had been deprived. Alexander (1956) indicated that the analyst should provide a 'corrective emotional experience' to undo the effects of bad parenting in the early years. Balint (1952) wrote about 'primary love', Winnicott (1965) spoke of the 'holding' of the patient in analysis, Bion (1967) of 'containing'. All these point to the *agape* quality in love. They all require of the analyst an ongoing patience, reliability, endurance, a willingness to be used (Winnicott 1969), a capacity to wait, and so on.

However, there are definite limits; the availability of the analyst is not unconditional. We do have the safeguard of the 50-minute hour. We see our patients for only a few hours a week. It is part of the great wisdom of psychoanalytic technique that our caring of the patient is 'dosed'. It is implicitly acknowledged that as analysts we can only give of ourselves effectively for short periods. But there is on the contrary an implicit and often an explicit demand from patients and sometimes from analysts themselves, that we give *all* the time. But the boundary is there, enshrined in the process itself, that saves the analyst from emotional exhaustion, should he or she be inclined to follow the narcissistic ideal of the analyst as lover. The reality is that the analyst can only *tend* to embody these *agape* qualities for short periods and for a specific purpose, in order to be a witness (Khan, 1983).

So the analyst is 'selfless' in this *agape* sense for only relatively short periods of time, and even this selflessness is distinctly ambiguous. For the acceptance that Tillich speaks of is not to be confused with Roger's 'unconditional positive regard'. For all the apparent passivity of *agape* love, there is an active desire, a concern, a concrete participation with the other, in the form of interpretative interventions and, occasionally, affirmation of important life events. The analyst's role is a human version, as has been stressed all along, a limited and always imperfect participation in *agape*.

However, I think it is important not to duck this question as to the relationship between the historic *agape* and the work of the psychoanalyst. Without an attempt at situating psychoanalytic therapy within the larger context of the Western tradition, there is a danger of psychoanalysis being lost and subsumed as a small branch of medicine. On the other hand, too easy an assimilation into a religious tradition also carries dangers of a facile reduction of the analyst's role as some version of saintly love. As we go into this, we shall see that *agape* and the analyst's participation in *agape* are not ultimately reducible to words. We can describe the analytic technique for the purposes of instruction and training, but this is only preliminary – the analytic function cannot of necessity be simply and adequately defined. The analyst and the patient both participate in something that is beyond language, which is unnameable, which is utterly open and other.

But let us come back to the concrete, and ask this basic question: what is the analyst paid for by the patient? The patient has to pay, but what is he or she actually paying for? Is it for the analyst's interpretations, or the insights that might be offered into the patient's life? Or is it for the analyst's care and concern? It cannot really be for these alone, for the analyst may make only a few interpretations, and after all, the care and concern offered are not unconditional. This care and concern, as I have stressed, are limited and circumscribed in time. In fact, let us be specific: the analyst inflicts a number of deprivations on the patient. The patient is mainly restricted to fixed sessions; he is denied knowing about the analyst's own life; he has to pay, including paying for missed sessions; he has to refrain from physical contact with the analyst, restricting himself largely to words while lying on a couch (although this is not always the case); and he has to avoid talking about his sessions in the outside world. It is a peculiarly human, fallible and necessarily incomplete form of care, to say the least. The fees that the patient pays must be sufficient to safeguard the analyst's countertransference from contamination by his own resentment. For the patient to pay too little would inevitably arouse hostile and resentful feelings in the analyst, which would inevitably spill over into the analytic space. From the patient's point of view, paying an appropriate fee is often burdensome, but it does leave the person free of a sense of indebtedness or obligation to the analyst. The person is then free to use the analytic space without guilt – at least, without guilt arising from this source. The fees, therefore, clearly and correctly benefit the analyst and enable him to do his work. And from the patient's point of view, the sessions are free from a sense of debt.

But patients will still ask the question: 'What am I paying you all this money for?' The analyst does not answer this question directly, because it is a very good question, and so much will lie behind it. But for the purpose of our discussion here we must formulate some response, especially as we are talking about some human form of love. Would it be true to say that the patient is paying for the genuine professional help that the analyst gives, for the reliable support that the patient experiences in living and being able to continue to live a difficult life amidst considerable suffering? Yes, this is definitely true, and it is often not appreciated just how valuable this long-term support really is, and just how genuinely cost-effective it is, in terms of keeping people out of hospital and enabling them to continue functioning at home and at work. But as I have indicated above, this support is to a certain extent ambiguous, because the analyst is not especially helpful in the ordinary sense, and also is supportive only in quite an unobvious way. Generally speaking he does not respond to direct demands for help and support. He does not respond to the patient's immediate needs for affirmation, for answers to his questions, for advice, for help, for relief from suffering. Such is the enigmatic role of the analyst. He is a shadowy figure. He is human without many of the conventional expressions of humanness. It is easier to say more clearly what he should not do than to say what he actually does.

However, we might formulate an answer to this question of what the patient is paying for, in this way: the patient pays for the presence of the analyst. He pays for the bodily and human *presence* of an other. As I indicated in the last chapter, and will develop a little further here, the analyst is very much present, and his largely silent presence is highly evocative.

Freud, in his work *Inhibitions, Symptoms and Anxiety* (1926), details the sources of anxiety which are experienced as specific losses, as separations that we negotiate with great difficulty, and never completely, as we are maturing. First, there is birth and the primary experience of helplessness – the loss of being contained by the mother. Then there is the loss of the breast – the giving up of some exquisite experience of total satisfaction. Next there is the feared loss of the penis, which represents the loss, among other things, of a precocious sense of power and completeness. Then there is the feared loss of parental love and support, and its corollary, the fear of loss of love of the super-ego.

What is evoked in a very poignant way by the space, the silent presence of the analyst, are all these losses, with which we must come to terms in at least some sort of way, and which we must work though, if we are to have access to our own desire. A gulf, a mystery is opened up, a potential space, and our question is: what does this presence of the analyst mean? The whole viability, the creativity of the analytic process, it is argued, hinges on the quality of this absent presence of the analyst.

And the presence of the analyst, this continual and reliable presence, participates in a religious symbolism. As Le Gaufey indicated in an unpublished lecture in 1991:

> Beyond the word in the prayer: presence. In the quiet silence of love, as well as in the harping on of hate: presence. This word is the classical naming to signify that something has to be taken into account without any hope of equating it to any quantity of words.

The patient, then, is left on his own in the presence of another, who is both remote and absent in nearly every ordinary sense and yet very much present and available. In Lacanian psychoanalysis, which represents perhaps an extreme of inscrutable remoteness, the analyst occupies the position of the Other, with a capital 'O', to designate his ungraspable and unnameable role. He is just beyond all the patient's expectations from ordinary others, ordinary egos, and represents that radical Otherness, that essential separation, which the patient must confront continually if he is to begin to live a life, his own life, as distinct from a life compulsively compliant with the desire of others. Lacan states clearly that the analyst must not accede to the patient's seductive demands for love and attention. Otherwise, both analyst and patient will become locked into an illusory struggle, repeating an incestuous relation in which the child's desire was to be the exclusive object of its mother's desire. Yet desire we must, but the Lacanian point is that we can only approach desire through speech, through formulating our needs – always and inevitably incompletely – in language. 'It is precisely because we cannot approach it [desire] except by way of some demand, that once the patient approaches us and comes to us, it is to ask something of us, and we already go an enormously long way in terms of engaging with, of clarifying the situation by saying to him simply: "I'm listening".'[4]

In another, yet related, sense, the analysts of the British Independent tradition would appear less inscrutable, being at times prepared to close the gap, where the pain of the loss feels so great that a maternal management may be temporarily necessary to save the person from disintegration. But here also the analysis proper depends on maintaining the 'transitional space', the 'period of hesitation' elegantly described by Winnicott (1941) in which desire is born. Here the presence of the analyst is construed primarily as a waiting presence.

Slightly different again is the Kleinian emphasis on the interpretation of unconscious phantasies – particularly those directed against the maternal object, the vengeful attacks on the mother's body, the destructiveness aimed at destroying what is good yet unattainable. Klein postulated, as we shall see more clearly in the next chapter, that the human infant makes violent imaginary attacks on the mother's body because it is extremely anxiously driven by enormous instinctual needs for food, attention, warmth and so on. It is the analyst's toleration and interpretation of derivatives of these envious and greedy attacks, his survival, his non-engagement in hostile countertransference reactions, which are part and parcel of his role as a 'container' for the patient's so-called evacuative communications via projective identification (Bion, 1962). The notion of container which has been so widely accepted and helpful for analysts in understanding what they are trying to do, is the Kleinian version of the presence of the analyst. This is another version of the analyst's representation of *agape*.

In one sense, and very practically, the analyst's role can be adequately defined in broadly humanistic terms, as Greenson (1967) has adequately done. Why try to go beyond his reasonable and all-inclusive explanation for what the analyst should be trying to do from day to day? But, in another important sense, by defining so clearly and precisely our analytic work, we are led to a premature *closure* of all the important questions, questions which must be left open and unanswerable, although we constantly attempt answers. Technique, yes, we need good technique, but there must be a 'beyond', a going beyond at every point if the analytic project is to have life and be evocative.

In this chapter I have moved from the over-simplistic notion of psychotherapy as a knowing of the self, or growth of the self, to a consideration of the insoluble paradoxes that challenge at every point such an essentially narcissistically-bound knowing of oneself, whether as a patient in analysis or as an analyst who believes he knows too well what he is doing.

IS PSYCHOANALYSIS A RELIGION?

Behind the ambiguous silent presence of the analyst, who in Lacanian terms is in the inscrutable position of the Other, or who in the British tradition is some version of a mother in a state of reverie, does there lurk God? In view of the arguments being advanced here, this question is extremely important. For many analysts, the answer would be an emphatic 'No!' or the question would be regarded as irrelevant. But, as I have noted, the power that some have assumed in the psychotherapeutic movement has amounted to a God-like position, both outside the psychoanalytic tradition and, we must also say, within it. And for some patients, clients and analysands, psychotherapy has become a kind of religion. As I have indicated in the previous section, the analyst does re-present and participate in, in an ambiguous, paradoxical and limited way, the *agape* quality in love. But the stress must always be on the word 'participation'. The analyst is participating in a process which allows the unconscious to speak. He or she is always working with what is beyond ordinary discourse, trying to hear, in that evocative phrase of Lacan's, 'the discourse of the Other'. To say that this Other is God is too easy, too simplistic, too limited, unless we have a notion of God as being ungraspable, unrepresentable, always beyond.

There are many within the Catholic religion, for instance, who have taken to psychotherapeutic training and methods to facilitate their work. Nuns and priests attend counselling workshops to undo the repressions and taboos of a more ascetic era. There is a flourishing publishing industry that unites psychotherapy and religion. But as far as psychoanalysis is concerned, we must maintain the *separateness* of the discipline from religion on the one hand and medicine on the other, while acknowledging that psychoanalysis can contribute to both, both methodologically and theoretically. The dangers of the absorption of psychoanalysis into one tradition or another are immense. Freud was at pains to maintain this separateness. The issue at stake is the unconscious, which unseats all compromises and disrupts all definitions. Any attempt at taming, organising or adapting the unconscious, which may be expedient and necessary, and indeed essential socially and personally, is not psychoanalysis in the purest sense. Other psychotherapies have been co-opted to serve various social needs with great success at least from a certain standpoint, but psychoanalysis as a theory and practice must continue to protect itself from any dilution.

It is the paradoxical nature of this book, that on the one hand it seeks to affirm the unique contribution that psychoanalysis can make and has made to human freedom and understanding, and yet on the other is calling for a concern over the untrammelled expression of freedom in society. Psychoanalysis has shown that 'the self' is a construct, that it can essentially form only on the basis of containment, of the holding or the mirroring of a fragmented infant by significant others, normally parents, so that destructive elements are rendered more manageable and emotionally tolerable.

In the next chapter we will see how just this process of self-cohering is put in question by the conditions of modernity.

So, to return to the question, psychoanalysis is not a religion, although as I have stressed it participates in an enlightened religious tradition, which stresses tolerance, rationality, responsibility and a search for honesty and truth. It enables moral action to proceed from a more centred self. But this centredness can only ever be relative. Analysis fosters a centredness, but no analysis is ever complete. The centre is never found. Also, we must make it clear that of course there are other ways to proceed towards centredness; analysands or analysts have no monopoly in this respect. But so much of what purports to be moral action (religious or secular), as we will see in the next chapter, proceeds increasingly from de-centred selves – selves alienated in self-contempt or self-inflation, based on a denial and hatred of life, indeed a love of death. Psychoanalysis, it must be clear, cannot *command* moral action. It does not seek to force change. It can prepare the ground, but moral action itself must proceed from a religious – in the broadest sense – conviction about ultimate meanings, choices and values which have to be struck, in spite of not knowing.

Psychoanalysis can only be understood, therefore, as a *preparation* for living, which remains incomplete and open, but which holds out the possibility, for each participant in the process, of developing his or her unique human idiom (Bollas, 1989).

3 CULTURE: A MAINLY
KLEINIAN PERSPECTIVE

I: INTRODUCTION: DIVIDEDNESS

A person reports the following experience:

I was in my home town walking down the main street looking in the
shops. There was no need to, there was nothing I wanted to buy. But I
had a vague feeling that I wanted something. I wanted something new:
some new gadget or toy that might cheer me up. I could walk round for
two or three hours like this going into one electrical shop after another
all selling the same Japanese stuff. I looked at radios, walkmans. The
shops were full of merchandise; it was coming up to Christmas. All the
televisions had the same man talking and gesturing simultaneously. Out
in the street it was crowded with shoppers. People with bags and
buggies. Occasionally someone would bump into me and push past and
walk on. It would make me very angry so with the next two or three
people I would stick my elbows out deliberately to give myself extra
space. Sometimes they would tell me to 'watch out', but mostly they
were in such a hurry to consume that they ignored me. I would feel
disappointed in a way. One young girl in her twenties was pushing a
baby which was crying and pulling another child who was protesting
and trying to pull her in the other direction. She was jerking his arm
furiously. I felt sorry for her, as I walked on.

Nobody knows anyone here. We are all independently walking around
doing our business. I thought of statistics and market shares; individuals
don't count, only the quantities they consume. I imagined someone
having a heart attack and people gathering around, but nobody knowing
the person. Later in a shoe shop I saw a white skinhead with torn faded
jeans arguing impatiently with a beautiful young Asian girl who was
serving him. She looked cherished, even over-protected, while he
looked vandalised as if he was in some war of his own making.

Then I remembered how this street used to be with family businesses and names on the shop-fronts that never changed, where people spoke to each other. I used to go round with my father and people would speak to him. You always went to certain shops: this was called loyalty. People didn't have much money so they didn't buy much. Each shop was different; some had their own peculiar smell. Always somebody spoke to you, spoke to me, knew my name . . .

Consider another report of a session with a man in his early thirties, who is described in the case notes as polite and well-mannered, somewhat narcissistically aloof and possibly violent underneath. He had regularly been 'beaten up' by his very aggressive father and older brother. He is divorced, and he is not quite sure why that happened. His wife left him. He agreed they probably were not suited and he didn't think he loved her. He was now having relationships with three separate women simultaneously – two of whom, according to him, were unhappily married. He was sure that he didn't love any of these women, yet he was planning to get away permanently with one of them to a foreign country. This is what she had wanted so he was going along with it. He comes to the session late:

> Well, I finally resigned my job today. I made the decision over the weekend, although it was under pressure from Liz. She says she's sick of waiting for me to make up my mind. She wants to go away with me to X and it has to be sooner rather than later. Anyway, I have to get out, make a new start. Only, I know that Liz will treat me, dominate me, in the same way as my wife did; she's already doing it. But what the hell, she's a nice girl. But I don't think I really love her; but I don't know what that word means. I have to get out anyway. I can't keep up this façade (loving several women at the same time) any longer. The strain is enormous. Each one thinks that she is special. God! I just have to leave. It's now or never.

There is something of a pause. Then he continues:

> Yes, I do seem to be attractive to women. I have been thinking over what you were saying about my loving women as possibly having a sadistic element behind it. Perhaps I want to break up marriages. You could be right, who knows, but I certainly don't do it deliberately. I am flirtatious with women in a sort of socially acceptable way. It's not my fault that they are in unhappy marriages.
>
> I couldn't believe it, how many people came up to me when word got around that I was leaving and said they would miss me. I never knew I was appreciated and admired. But the sense of freedom from the grind . . . it's an appalling system that condemns us to work as tiny atoms in that vast machine. It's insane. And all the stress diseases –

people of my age with ulcers and hypertension . . . and divorces! Ha! It's mad, and what's it all for? I deliberately chose to have a small car – a little car – it serves me just as well.

You know, last year I was in France on holiday, staying in the university campus. A funny thing happened which is kind of symbolic, it makes me laugh when I think of it. We were sitting having breakfast in the cafeteria, and these poor Algerians who basically have nowhere to live loiter around the campuses in the summer months doing a bit of begging and stealing. Well, a long lanky bloke comes up to our table. He doesn't seem to bother with the others. He asks me for francs. So I give him some small change from my pocket. He goes away and comes back later and asks for more. He says he has not eaten for many days and he needs money. 'You rich people,' he says, 'can afford it.' This time I make an effort to search myself, and then tell him I have no more money. He's going to stick on to me like a leech, so I refuse and turn to my companion. He pulls my shirt at the shoulder and looks into my face and mouths obscenities about the bourgeoisie, how we are all trapped, that money possesses us. Why not be free like he is and self-determining? Then he asks for money for food. When I refuse again, he gets steadily more abusive and shouts curses at me . . . how we are mean . . . how we are blind . . . how we keep money for ourselves and let the poor starve. Eventually, some of the cafeteria staff ask him gently to leave. He does so as they lead him by the arms; he is walking backwards shouting at me all the time. Outside he bangs on the glass window and you can still hear him shouting as he wanders off into the hot sun. The staff came up to me and apologised and said there was nothing they could do. He does this all the time. People sitting nearby looked over at me and smiled sympathetically, relieved it wasn't them this time.

But the whole episode left me thinking. It's like a portent. He chose me. It is as if he knew something about me that I didn't know myself. And now here I am free, like he is! Well not quite like he is, but there are similarities . . .

Very soon after this session, he did emigrate with Liz, thanking me for the help I had given him. He felt he had a good grasp of his central problems in relation to work and women. For my part, I felt that I had made very little impact on his problems and in fact I had not managed to get him to see that there was a problem!

VARIOUS PSYCHIC SPLITS

The first example, Brian, and the second, Jim, both demonstrate in an apparently normal way the sort of splitting and alienation that was being considered in the last chapter. In both examples there is a pervasive sense of anomie and deadness. In Brian there is a split between present and past: the present is bad, unfeeling, uncaring; the past is benevolent and good. In Jim, all badness is located outside, 'in the system', while he himself is supremely attractive to women, largely unaware of his narcissistic coldness. In this chapter, we want to look in an extended and varied way at the consequences of our dividedness, the cultural significance of Freud's discovery of Otherness within us, which psychoanalytical theorists have been working with in these last hundred years. We can understand the divided subject and the nature of the divide in many ways.

Freud conceived of it mainly as repression (*Verdrangung*) which separates the unconscious from the conscious/preconscious systems. Otherness resides in the unconscious, the repressed unconscious, which as Freud indicated is the hidden repository of our forsaken yearnings, urges and losses which constantly seek re-emergence and transference into daily life. Freud was aware of other defence mechanisms, perhaps prior to repression. It was left mainly to the Kleinians to explore other conceptions of this human divide. For Klein, thinking in terms ultimately of psychotic mechanisms, it was *splitting* that was to be her main focus.

However, the term splitting (*Spaltung*) has had a very old and varied use in psychoanalysis and psychiatry. Freud and Breuer noted the dual personality – the splitting of consciousness – in certain hysterical states. Bleuler used *Spaltung* in the process of that condition he termed 'schizophrenia'. Splitting appears again particularly in Freud's work on fetishism and psychosis. What was new was that whereas repression was seen as a split between psychical agencies, the ego and the id for instance, in a horizontal fashion, splitting was seen as a vertical fault-line. Here the split was *within* an agency – a split within the ego itself. In pathological splitting there is no dialectical relationship between the split-off elements. In this sense splitting is more severe and primitive than repression, where at least the links with the repressed elements are maintained, however tenuously.

I will now discuss at some length Melanie Klein's conceptions, before looking at the wider cultural implications of her discoveries.

MELANIE KLEIN – THE PARANOID-SCHIZOID POSITION[1]

It was Melanie Klein's work with young children and very disturbed adults that led her to formulate two very early developmental stages through which all children pass, the residues of which remain within the adult personality. We tend to regress towards these residues when under stress. The first and most primitive stage is called the *paranoid-schizoid* and it involves a fundamental splitting.

The newborn human is utterly vulnerable and in the beginning needs total care. It has a very low toleration for anxiety and therefore anything that disrupts its stability beyond a small margin is experienced as frightening. Hunger, frustration, pain, anger are all disruptive in this way. Being unable to contain these strong feelings, which are felt to be bad and dangerous, the baby gets rid of them, by projection, into the outside world. The baby is split into a good self, where everything experienced as good is kept within, and a bad self, which is denied and projected into the outside world. This radical splitting of the self tries to ensure that the good is kept separate from the bad. The good self and all the good things it gets tend to be idealised as a reassurance against the badness outside. The trouble is that the splitting is only partially successful and the bad things are felt to be threatening and likely to reinvade at any moment. These persecutory anxieties are the basis for many of the 'irrational' fears of small children. The dark is feared because the reassurance has gone and one anticipates the return of these monsters.

The splitting involves the parents as well. The good mother who gratifies and comforts the child is idealised and retained within, while the frustrating and angry mother appears in dreams and fairy stories as a witch – a frightening figure who means us harm. The bad image of the father is the giant or the ogre who has great strength and can inflict great punishment. Clearly the images of the witch and the giant are far more dangerous and persecuting than the reality of those normal parents who sometimes fail to meet their children's needs. Why should the parents be recast in such extreme and dangerous forms? Jung explained these images in terms of archetypes which are part of the collective unconscious. But Klein's view is that the images of the parents become massively distorted by the baby's own rage, which is projected into the parents. Clearly the more angry the baby, the more frightening the image of the parent.

In the story of Hansel and Gretel, it is ravenous hunger that drives them to destroy the house made of food. Their 'badness' is located in the witch who wants to fatten up Hansel in order to eat him, and to have Gretel consumed (eaten) by the flames. In other words, the witch comes to contain the destructive and therefore split-off and projected elements of greed and intense hunger. The children are innocent and the witch is filled with badness and evil intent. Whereas, in *Jack and the Beanstalk*, the Ogre who chases Jack down the beanstalk and nearly kills him is not just a punitive figure, but a terrifying cannibalistic giant who contains the little boy's projected greed. As the little boy once wished to possess and destroy in a greedy way the Ogre's possessions – his money, his golden eggs and the harp – the Ogre turns on him with the same magically destructive power. The Ogre is only destroyed when Jack gives up the magical thinking symbolised by the beanstalk. He cuts the beanstalk down as the Ogre is climbing down after him. He stops having and projecting magically destructive thoughts and therefore there are no longer any magically destructive ogres.

In *Little Red Riding Hood*, we meet a nice girl who on the face of it wants to take food to her grandmother in her house in the woods. She is unaware of her split-off sexual desires; she wears a red cloak (meaning passion or menstruation) and she strays from the path (of virtue) to pick flowers. She actually gives the wolf directions as to how to get to her grandmother's house; it is obvious that she (unconsciously) wants to do away with the grandmother – who represents a mother figure who stands in the way of her more primitive sexual desires. The wolf symbolises all the animalistic tendencies within ourselves and is made to carry Red Riding Hood's unacknowledged desires, which eventually consume her. Unaware and innocent of the power of her sexuality, she projects it onto the figure of the wolf and it eats her up!

It is not a coincidence that in each of the three stories referred to, the feared danger is of being eaten up. It is those primitive cannibalistic desires of the infant that are most feared and repressed and therefore likely to be projected onto figures in the outside world. It is because the infant endows these feelings with magical power that these monsters assume such frightening proportions.

Together with the primitive defences of splitting, denial and projection, the paranoid-schizoid mode of experiencing does not see people as people, with needs and concerns like one's own. People are seen as split up into parts – so-called 'part-objects' – that are to be used purely to satisfy one's immediate needs. Experience is narrowed down so that initially one sees the breast, not the mother, and the penis, not the father. For instance, the mother is to be exploited for what she can give in terms of food and nourishment: she can be attacked and robbed of her food and goodness. Similarly, the father can be attacked and robbed of his power symbolised by the penis. There is no concern or indeed perception of the parents as being hurt by these activities and there is no feeling of guilt. There is the primitive precursor of guilt, however, that is, the fear of retaliation and being invaded.

Before leaving this theoretical outline of the paranoid-schizoid stage of development, it will be important to emphasise the role of the environment in determining whether and to what extent the child grows through this stage to the next developmental horizon. Clearly, if the parents *in reality*, as opposed to phantasy, are rejecting or more than normally frustrating or retaliatory, then the paranoid trends within the personality are going to be greatly enhanced. The primitive phantasies may be confirmed by the reality of the child's experience and it will not have accumulated enough good experience to move on to the next stage.

MELANIE KLEIN – THE DEPRESSIVE POSITION[2]

The next stage of development described by Melanie Klein is the so-called *depressive position*. If the child stored up enough affirmative experience during the early stage, then the tendency will be towards integration rather than splitting. Instead of splitting off and disowning the bad parts of himself he will have the confidence to tolerate them better, to realise that he can both love and hate. He sees himself as a 'whole' person now, not split into the good self and the projected bad self. He sees his mother also as a whole person – the good and the bad mother are the *one* person. The mother who feeds and gratifies him and the mother who withholds and frustrates are the *same* person.

The main anxiety during this time is the so-called depressive anxiety – the fear that the child has damaged his mother by his destructive and aggressive feelings. It is the same anxiety that appears in depressive illnesses. The depressed person or child is frightened by the believed harm that his vengeful phantasies have had on the person he also loves and needs. These feelings mobilise the wish to repair the damage, to restore the person to life and wholeness. So just as his destructive impulses were believed to have caused the damage, so there is the corresponding belief that his loving and creative impulses can make good the damage. Klein refers to this rebuilding work as reparation. It is reparation that allows the child to rebuild the world shattered by his own impulses. If reparation succeeds then the child gains in confidence and the belief in his own goodness. He acquires the capacity to love, to be concerned about others, to acknowledge that he contains both good and bad feelings. If reparation fails then he is thrown into depressive despair and will tend to regress towards the earlier paranoid-schizoid position.

During this phase of development the child is getting more in touch with external reality. If the *real* mother does survive his magical destructive attacks, then the power of these destructive phantasies is considerably diminished. If on the other hand the mother retaliates, then the feared power of these impulses and their badness is confirmed and the child feels persecuted. Again, if the parents are not available to the child then he is thrown back on his phantastic inner world. It is a time when parents are tested. The child tries out his destructiveness to see if the parents survive! It is a time when he wants to hate the parents to see if they can stand it. And it is a time when he gets very worried that he might have done some permanent damage. Of course, if the parents do actually get sick, divorce or die, then the child blames himself.

During this stage of development, the child discovers his extreme dependence on this mother, and goes through intense feelings of fear and loss, mourning, pining and guilt. These are very real feelings and imply a considerable depth in emotional development. Bowlby describes the grief that very young children go through when separated from their mothers in residential nursery settings. He quotes Robertson's 25-year experience:

If a child is taken from his mother's care at this age [1½ to 3 years], when he is so possessively and passionately attached to her, it is indeed as if his world has been shattered. His intense need of her is unsatisfied, and frustration and longing may send him frantic with grief. It takes an exercise of imagination to sense the intensity of his distress. He is as overwhelmed as any adult who has lost a beloved person by death. To the child of two with his lack of understanding and inability to tolerate frustration, it is really as if his mother had died. He does not know death but only absence; and if the only person who can satisfy his imperative need is absent, she might as well be dead, so overwhelming is his sense of loss. (Bowlby, 1980, p. 10)

One can see in this empathic statement how the child feels a mixture of sadness, grief and rage – a yearning for the mother to return and a fury at her not doing so. This is perhaps an extreme version of what happens to normal children in the depressive position. For normal children have to let the mother go. They have to accept psychological separation as well as physical separation in non-traumatic doses. It is thanks to Bowlby's work that children are no longer left in hospitals in states of utter depression surrounded by well-meaning strangers. But it is the central task of the depressive phase of development that a mourning of the parents be gone through in early infancy. The child has to let go the earliest attachments that involve intense loving and hating. It has to recognise the mother (and father) as *out there*, as separate individuals who have lives and feelings of their own, who are available but not exclusively for the working through of these feelings. The child must then become active in rebuilding the world that it in phantasy believes it has destroyed. By its creative efforts it can help the parents outside, and rebuild its shattered inner world and establish good helpful and encouraging figures within, who will sustain it when the external figures are absent.

Winnicott speaks of the 'capacity for concern'. In this state the child acknowledges guilt, but can hold onto it in full expectation of an opportunity to make reparation for it. 'To this guilt that is held out but not felt as such, we give the name "concern" . . . if there is no reliable mother-figure to receive the reparation gesture, the guilt becomes intolerable, and concern cannot be felt. Failure of reparation leads to a losing of the capacity for concern, and to its replacement by primitive forms of guilt and anxiety' (1963a, p. 82).

The pain of depression can be so great that the child (or depressed adult) cannot face it and make reparation, but instead tries to escape the pain altogether, invoking the so-called 'manic defence'. Unable to face the grief and mourning, he denies all these helpless feelings, denies that he is dependent and assumes a triumphant contemptuous attitude to the world. He is supremely in control. Nobody can touch him. He achieves this pseudo-freedom at the expense of his internal world. He has to deny the shattered nature of his psyche and pretend that all is well. It is a precarious existence and one that requires the person to move ever faster and faster lest he come at last to feel the inward grief. The manic defence is not confined to those with manic-depressive psychosis, but is a much more generalised defence against the whole cluster of feelings that surround helplessness, dependency, guilt as well as loss, grief and depression. Winnicott, in a paper simply called 'The manic defence', speaks of the 'flight to external reality from inner reality . . . the denial of *sensations* of depression – namely the heaviness and sadness – by specifically opposite sensations, lightness, humorousness, etc. The employ-ment of almost any opposites in the reassurance against death, chaos, mystery, etc., ideas that belong to the *phantasy content* of the depressive position' (1935, p. 132).[3] This blanket denial of the inner world leads to a rather shallow personality who lacks depth and sincerity. Winnicott gives the example of the extrovert book of adventure, in which the author tells of the acting out of a childhood day-dream which perhaps was, and still is, a flight from personal reality. The story is gripping and full of incident and excitement, but one is left with a light-weight feeling, and turns with relief to an author who can tolerate depression and doubt!

Let us return to the cases of Brian and Jim mentioned at the beginning. Brian inhabits an anonymous world which is a reflection of his experience with his parents, who he felt ignored him. It is now the world that ignores him and is impersonal. The reference to the man who might have a heart attack is Brian's fear that he might collapse into depression, but the fact that nobody knows him – understands and supports him – makes this very frightening. The argument in the shop is also the split within him – the cherished Asian girl who is the part of him who was loved and known is radically separated from the angry skinhead at war with himself and self-destructive. It is this separation of the 'good' and the 'bad', characteristic of the paranoid-schizoid position, which gives this story its pervasive sense of estrangement. His nostalgia for the old family business – literally that business that went on in the family – when people were known as individuals, points to a store of good experience which, together with a therapist who is empathic enough, might be able to sustain him through his collapse into depression. Then, instead of having 'a vague feeling that I wanted something . . . something new, some new gadget or toy to

cheer me up', there might be a feeling of liveliness, commitment
and fulfilment.

Jim is more aware that he is avoiding some central problem in
his life, namely, his incapacity to love and feel deeply. These
women who love him, love his phoney surface self which he knows
is a façade. At another level he feels persecuted by people who can
dominate him, like his ex-wife and Liz, and like the Algerian in
France who demands money from him. The fact that he feels this
experience as a portent shows how precisely it parallels his internal
world. He feels he deserves punishment for his 'badness', which
has an echo of his treatment at the hands of his father. Only when
he is sufficiently punished by giving up a good job and going away
with a woman who dominates him and whom he doesn't love, will
he feel free. This freedom is illusory; it is only a matter of time before
there is renewed persecution. His inner badness is so bad in the
eyes of his internalised father that he cannot face it, and instead
condemns himself to endless flight.

II: CULTURAL EXTREMES

In this section, we will look at some aspects of contemporary
culture at considerable length, using these nodal developmental
points developed by Klein and others.

It will be clear from the foregoing that there is a developmental
line which goes from the paranoid-schizoid position, through the
depressive position, to what Winnicott calls 'mature dependence' –
a sense of mutual concern, a capacity to feel feelings, an
acknowledgement of vengeful and destructive feelings, which can
to some extent be modulated, sublimated, dreamed about, spoken
about and narrativised, rather than acted upon blindly. There is
obviously nothing inevitable about this developmental process. In
fact it requires certain conditions which may no longer obtain.

But we must emphasise as well that these Kleinian concepts are
perhaps better understood as 'positions' rather than developmental
stages. They are nodal points to which we return both in health and
pathology. Paranoid-schizoid and depressive phenomena can be
observed at all levels of intensity and severity. In health, we can
oscillate between relatively benign disintegrated states (paranoid-
schizoid) and integrated ones (depressive). This is what Bion

(1963) felt to be the basis of the creative process. On the other hand, in pathology we can feel degrees of persecution and terror in the disintegrative phase, akin to the infantile situation, and a degree of depression which freezes life in a flat parody of integration.

I want to use these conceptions, these models, in a creative way, as a basis for thinking about contemporary cultural developments. Like many other psychoanalytic terms, they are best used to evoke further thinking rather than explanation. They are to be used in Bion's sense as tools for thinking with, as empty containers in search of meaning, waiting to be fleshed out by new realisations.

What will be crucial for the discussion in this section is our general psychoanalytic understanding that human identity is constructed in a social milieu through object-relating. Clearly the quality of that environment, the existence or not of essential supportive facilitating conditions, will be reflected in the stability of that selfhood. And what most theorists of modernity agree on is that the achievement of some *coherent* selfhood has become increasingly problematic. Psychoanalysis, however, is well placed, first, to show how social conditions structure internal states, and second, to supply criteria by which modern social experience can be evaluated.

THE CRUMBLING OF THE OLD ORDER

The Polish historian Leszek Kolakowski spoke of the change that occurred in the late Middle Ages, when

> the old order began to crumble. Religion, philosophy, art and politics which were somehow part of a unified order created by divine wisdom, this cosmos gradually began to break-up. And this is precisely what Modernity is about, the crumbling of this order, the *separation* and *autonomization* of various sides of human activity, or varied forms of culture . . . the growth of rationalism. (1986, p. 18)

Here we have the origins of the cultural *splitting* in modernity. The old social structure, with its sense of interconnectedness, its mutual obligations, its solidarity was to begin to fall apart. With the beginning of modern capitalism, the individual was increasingly left alone. Everything depended on individual effort with no security to be found any longer in traditional status. For the poor of the cities this meant growing exploitation and impoverishment. For the new middle classes the role of capital and the market assumed a new force. The role of the market in the old medieval world had been relatively small and was well understood, but now nothing was predictable. Everyone was a potential competitor. Not being wealthy like the Renaissance capitalists meant having to live in perpetual insecurity.

Freed from the shackles of the feudal system and from bondage and subordination, modern individuals emerged in their own right, now to choose their own way in the world and increasingly their own meanings. While this was an immense liberation, it brought with it the dangers of hubris and disorientation. The most radical characteristic of modernism is the decision to live without God. Since the beginning of human culture, man has always experienced, known and understood himself in relation to supra-personal presences, whether these be the gods of the ancient world, or the one supreme God of the major monotheistic religions, Judaism, Christianity and Islam. Now humanity has to be its own sole witness, and God is dead. We live in total isolation in the immensity of the universe – a state to which Martin Buber has referred as 'cosmic homelessness'.

Modernism is a historical process that developed slowly over three centuries. It crystallised its identity at the end of the last century. In the twentieth century the bubble has burst. In the words of Yeats: 'Things fall apart, the centre cannot hold . . . the best lack all conviction, while the worst are full of passionate intensity.' The essentially schizoid nature of modernism is being made manifest.

VERSIONS OF REALITY

With the passing of some overarching view of reality as ordained by a religious system, with an 'incredulity towards metanarratives' (Lyotard, 1979), and with the modern and postmodern deconstruction of meaning and values, we are left with versions of reality and unreality, and a widespread confusion between the internal and the external.

We live surrounded by images. The image more than anything typifies contemporary culture. Surveys in the United States showed that people spend as much as fifty hours a week in front of the television set. With the advent of multi-channel television, it is rare for children, in particular, to watch a programme right through from beginning to end. With the remote control in hand, they can 'channel-hop', keeping an interest in only fragments of programmes, and mainly in special effects. Gone is the idea of the development of a story, of a sequence of events that unfolds. Instead, everything is fast-moving, things jump out of corners, everything changes rapidly amidst noise and pulsation. Surveys have shown that children spend more time watching television than any other single activity.

'Reality' is increasingly created for us. Our perception is no longer innocent. We tend to see what has been pre-structured for us by the media, by advertisements, videos and so on. The image, in every sense, forms us. Even our images of nature, which we might think have escaped this domination, inevitably call to mind commercials for hair shampoo, breakfast cereals, or fast cars on lonely roads. We see a sandy beach and think of tourist development and suntan oils. Likewise, sexual intercourse, for a long time banned from direct portrayal on the screen – a small concession to privacy – is now explicitly imaged for us. Even this area of our lives is constructed for us!

The world increasingly takes on an hallucinatory character. It is difficult at times to separate fact from fantasy. Crime programmes about real crimes insert exciting dramatic reconstructions of the real events. Revolutions and wars become news 'stories' which unfold under the eye of the video camera. Journalists risk their lives to bring us these stories, which are barely distinguishable from entertainment. But these stories are real events, agonising for the human participants, who will be photographed in their suffering to give the story a human dimension. There are degrees of suffering that one must show, for instance, when making videos to stimulate charitable donations. A sick child is worth much more than an ailing old woman. Images of hugely successful, hugely wealthy entertainers, giving their services 'free' to vast audiences, are interspersed with images from Africa of starving children and emaciated cattle. These images are inserted like commercials to stimulate a 'real response' from the public. The response is huge. But what is the response to? Our delight with the music and the whole glamourous event? Our belief in our own generosity and that of millions of others, in that 'now we are really doing something'?

Is it a response to guilt, a simple assuaging? Or is there some reality that comes across in these terrible images?

News-gathering increasingly becomes news-making. The power of the media to inform, literally to form and shape our thinking, in an age where images can be transmitted worldwide, is of concern amongst some journalists. How they select material, the language they use, what they leave out, and so on, can alter or even determine the course of events. Reporting can no longer be considered a neutral business.

Propaganda, we know, is blatantly part of totalitarian systems, part of the crude manipulation of history to exclude contradictions. Young people from former socialist countries have said that they always knew they were being fed lies. They just didn't believe anything that they were being told from the official media. We in the West have a different problem: we believe often that we are being told the truth. But, as Chomsky (1991) has pointed out, this 'truth' also serves the interests of corporate capitalism, which has increasingly come to mean American imperialism. So our versions of reality are certainly more varied and sophisticated, but all the more deceiving in their ability to colonise and manipulate our inner space because, unlike our Eastern counterparts in earlier decades, we have no adequate defence against them. Chomsky, however, perhaps underestimates the ability of the Western media genuinely to inform people: many instances of investigative journalism have turned up truths which have shaken governments.

In this context also, we should note biases or fashions that amount to an unconscious self-censorship, or at best a lack of openness to conflicting interpretations of culture in our media. What is not fashionable will not easily find its way into journals, periodicals, books or university faculties. For instance, sociology is dominated by a feminist viewpoint; psychiatry is dominated by a biological viewpoint; 'the troubles' in Northern Ireland are dominated by a republican viewpoint; economics is dominated, especially now, by a capitalist perspective. This is part of the splitting that inevitably occurs in a frenetic culture, where increasingly each special interest group competes for its own language and imagery. I will refer to this again in the next section.

In our age of global communications, of rapid transmission of images and stories around the world, we can call up almost any kind of entertainment at will. We can see programmes made at great expense and technological skill – shots of wildlife, for example, that might have been immensely difficult to capture – and yet we have no awareness of this. Programmes featuring death, disease and war, which might move us for a time, are abruptly followed by a late-night chat show, and thus meanings and differences tend to collapse. In the free market of air-time, a shot of a bombed-out suburb has to compete for space with commercials, for the postmodern idiom celebrates its freedom to 'pick'n'mix'. We have to become in Baudrillard's terms a centre that can switch for all networks of influence.

As Jameson (1991) has noted, this newly created decentred subjectivity is akin to schizophrenia. The masses of fantastic images, messages, hypes have a fragmenting effect on the inner world, destroying the past for the intense emotionality of the present. The gap between high art and popular culture narrows to nothing. Random music, computer verse, guerrilla theatre, packaged nature, artistic commercials and commercial art, commingle equally and freely with new low-cost reproductions of the classics in what is now a democratic and populist demystification of the so-called pretensions of high modernism.

The beleaguered self, struggling to attain coherence, depth, or perspective, in short, to attain to the depressive position, is invaded and split by these often brutal, contradictory and confusing images of reality. They create an inevitable pressure to regress to a paranoid world of confusion. Alternately excited and terrified, we can be overwhelmed and forced to retreat into an agitated boredom and apathy. In this state, we require more feeding, still more consumption, to fill up the alarming emptiness created by the lack of sustained and coherent meanings. To a certain extent multi-channel television fills this demand. It is easier to watch television than it is to do almost anything else. The programmes, the images, the commercials are exquisitely and expensively crafted. They contain no errors or imperfections of any sort. Everything is done with the viewer's gratification in mind. The image creators make an extreme effort to feed us, while the viewers passively absorb, without being aware of this discrepancy.

This passive–receptive attitude characterises the earliest stage of infancy and creates or unleashes an insatiable demand for more. Along with this regression has come the inevitable instinctual de-fusion of the life and death instincts. We note therefore an increasing appetite for violence to which the market has responded with illicit movies – part of a worldwide trade in pornography – depicting scenes of such brutality and perversity that progressives and conservatives alike are shocked and dismayed. But people turn away in horror less and less from such images. The defences against these regressive tendencies are being broken down by the exposure of children and adults to violent imagery in the media generally.

Apologists still argue that children have always been exposed to violence, for instance, in fairy stories and folk tales. These stories do indeed have a violent component, but the child is required to *construct actively its own mental image*. There is no *imposition* of a violent image, alien, strange and shocking. Second, the cruelty in fairy tales is always *in context*. The giant is slain because he is so powerful and frightening. Evil is punished. The good and the ugly are juxtaposed in a way which is congruent with the child's psyche. Cruelty in these stories has always enabled children to accept and integrate destructive phantasies – to come to know them in a *symbolic* way. When the wicked stepmother leaves home, the child is delighted and can feel mostly unconsciously its hatred of a frustrating mother, while leaving the real mother relatively unharmed. Bettelheim's book on fairy tales (1976) points to the psychological function of fairy stories, and how they help children cope with conflict and *imagine* solutions. Third, fairy tales are known to happen in another place and another time; they are part of an inner reality, rather than part of the external world.

Seen in the light of postmodern trends, Klein's depressive position might be conceived of as a small island of privacy and of relative peace from this fragmenting schizoid imagery. In our time this is a precious, yet precarious, developmental achievement, which must be seen as a sanctuary for the self and its capacity to relate to other selves. It is only from this position that one can begin to understand, experience and enjoy the world. It means the difference between decentred ruthless consumption, and the *real* experience of coherent living in a vital world – alive with possibilities and potentialities.

THE LOSS OF HUMAN SOLIDARITY

Let us move on to consider a related issue, namely the collapse of communal life, which has been a feature of the modern period.

Since the end of the fifties, we have witnessed the progressive weakening of working-class movements and the gradual fragmentation of the body politic into a variety of special interest groups that no longer define their political objectives in terms of a better society, but rather in terms of narrow self-interest. This process was inevitable, but our oldest political wisdom indicates to us that a sense of community is a human necessity and that one pole of our psychic health depends upon that involvement and commitment *outside* of ourselves. However, the remarkable successes of consumer capitalism since the Second World War in buying off workers' discontent has eclipsed organised and effective protest.

The political concerns of the post-'68 white middle class have centred around feminism, anti-racism and green issues. But during this time we have seen the emergence of a new marginalised proletariat of unemployed. At particular risk are immigrant workers from former colonies and poor economic migrants, who suffer frequent racial attacks from the white working class and stricter immigration controls imposed by governments. No new political structures have been developed to incorporate the excluded. Furthermore, there is no common language among political groupings on the Left. As Ignatieff points out:

> One of the characteristic political conceits of the sixties and seventies was the feminist claim that only women could understand the grievances of women, as blacks were the only ones who could understand the experience of racism. This is the politics of solipsism, which gives up in advance the task of bringing blacks and whites, men and women, together. (1986, p. 17)

The emerging confidence of the Right since the end of the seventies accelerated a process which had started much earlier. People were to turn away from anything labelled 'public', which has become synonymous with inefficiency, wastage and bureaucracy. The New Right appealed to the people – including, it now seems, to those behind what was the Iron Curtain – over the heads of political theorists, the old paternalistic consensus politicians, apparatchiks, guardians of restrictive practices and party hacks. There was a whole radical new language of freedom and initiative. This was clearly a liberation in both personal and economic terms, which in many ways parallels the postmodern conflagration discussed previously.

Suddenly acquiring wealth and making a profit was no longer something to be slightly embarrassed about. To make money and to show it was a good thing. A leading city broker was recorded as saying: 'I don't think we should apologise for being rich. I'm proud of it.' The new breed of entrepreneurs was aggressive, restless, urban technocrats, 'interested in money to the point of obsession', says one. 'Let us make a million and we'll strive for ten . . . there's a lot of ego in it, when you get all fired up it's like a drug.' Margaret Thatcher was the leader of this revolution (or she was the right person at the right time) and she lasted long enough to affect all other political groupings, perhaps permanently. Even some on the Left now talk enthusiastically of the market.

But our attention here must focus on the personal and psychological consequences of this revolution. In the recession of the early eighties, a new career pattern was born. There was less and less to go round, so the trick was to work harder and longer. It was the young who were most suited to cope with the frenetic pace of technological advance, the new electronic money markets, and it was they who went to work in finance and advertising, the new sunrise industries and the professions.

But what does this aspiring lifestyle mean in personal terms – this image, this façade, the ostentation, the excess, the abundant proofs of potency, and, in particular, work and more work? Firstly, we must say that such an exotic style generates envy, consciously or unconsciously. This is an open or hidden intent on the part of these young aspirers. It generates envy amongst the middle-aged, the elderly, the poor, the marginalised, the disabled – in short, all those who for one reason or another cannot live in that way, or cannot make that sort of money. Envy, as Klein (1957) has clearly explained, is the most deeply repressed of impulses, hidden behind all manner of reaction formations and rationalisations. We will return later to the emergence of envy in spite of repression. The account which follows attempts not to follow the path of envious deprecation.

We must note the liberation of creativity that has marked this lifestyle, the liberation of energy and the breaking through of constraints. But the hyperactivity, the mania, the ruthlessness, also reveals a deadness, a death of the self. We can say this with some confidence because the evidence is there in psychotherapeutic practice. We see the flight from inner reality which is part of the paranoid defence against depressive anxiety. We see it in the poor, broken or non-existent relationships. We would see it in the compulsive hard work, the burn-out and the psychosomatic symptoms as an unconscious punishment, a severe punishment, for the equally unconscious, but very visible gratification of infantile demands. This extreme driving and forcing of the self often seems like a desperate attempt to try and *get a real feeling of existing*.

The evidence is also there outside the consulting room in the community. The lifestyle of these new rich is ostentatious and shallow. It has little to do with true creativity, which as Bion (1962a) has shown involves an encounter with paranoid-schizoid anxieties, an immersion in chaos to achieve a new integration. Instead we see a severance, a cutting-off from human concerns which allows the unrestrained release of infantile strivings involving narcissistic omnipotence and exhibitionism, which is now unsituated, ungrounded, and therefore very unstable. The effect is, as Zygmunt Bauman has suggested, 'an eviction of human concerns from politics . . . [which] has promoted freedom as the right not to be bothered by public affairs' (1988, p. 36). The plight of the poor, the aged, the mentally ill, of all these vulnerable groups cannot be acknowledged by the new aspirers because these disadvantaged groups *represent* the split-off, denied, vulnerable side of themselves which they must continuously disown. So we witness greater disparities between rich and poor. People no longer feel guilty about condemning poverty: it is the fault of the poor themselves. There are new polarisations as splitting increases.

The old-style 'one nation' conservatives believed in the super-ego, that is, in a paternalistic authority rooted in a traditional morality instilled by parents, teachers, the church and the rule of law. But with the breaking of the social contract, the New Right, as Christopher Lasch suggests, 'either seek to enforce moral and political conformity through outright coercion, or they take the same libertarian view of culture that they take towards economics, asking that everyone enjoy the freedom to follow his own self-interest' (1984, p. 201).

Let us pause for a brief case illustration. John was a successful accountant with a big firm. Someone had suggested analysis to him, and he seemed motivated to come because, as he said in the first interview, he did feel something was missing in his outwardly glamorous life. He agreed to come twice a week. Mostly he talked about his loneliness: he was 32 and single with no long-term involvements. He spoke openly but in a detached way about his paranoid anxieties, about his appearance, his masculinity, his latent homosexual feelings and phantasies, and his desire to live an exotic lifestyle abroad. He ignored all the analyst's comments. One day he came smoking a cigar. He asked the analyst for a light. The analyst didn't smoke. He was annoyed, but carried on to recount a dream: he was on a train – a fast intercity train; there were few people in his compartment and they all appeared to be made of wax. I suppose they were dead, he said. Outside, it was winter, but there was one tree which seemed alive. He could tell this because it was green while all the others were grey. He had no associations and no idea what the dream meant. When the analyst pointed out that the one green tree in the dream perhaps indicated that there was some hope, the patient laughed loudly – 'Hope, what do y' mean hope?!' He laughed again, and said he didn't believe in dreams anyway. However, when the analyst gradually, over many sessions, attempted to interpret the omnipotent imaginary nature of this lifestyle as a cover for an inner deadness, the patient paid for his sessions and never returned.

John's severance from his feelings could perhaps have been handled better by his analyst. John left because his omnipotent defences were being exposed. His mocking laughter was an evacuation, an expulsion of all potentially depressing concerns about his life, his loneliness and hidden fear of emotional reality, his loss of solidarity with himself and others.

THE SPIRAL OF FEAR

A generalised sense of paranoia pervades modern culture. The loss of human solidarity, the split within the self and the split between the self and others, has led to a private and public suspiciousness on a greater scale than ever before. Higher real incomes, the massive increase in consumer spending – shopping is one of the most preferred leisure activities – has led to a corresponding paranoid fear, both real and imagined, that what we have will be taken away from us. Unconsciously, acquiring desired objects carries with it the retaliatory fear that they will be taken away again.

Consequently the private security business has been a growth industry in recent years. The number of those employed by private security firms in Britain now actually exceeds the total size of the police force. It is estimated that as many as half the companies across Britain employ private security guards. Many of these guards are poorly trained, and themselves have criminal records. The police indicate that they are under-staffed and that without greatly increased recruitment they are unable to stem the rise in crime. Within the last twenty years there has been a fourfold increase in violent crime.

Psychoanalytically speaking, we might say there has been some de-fusion of the instinctual life brought about by the breaking of the social contract. A destructiveness has been released. Kohut explained this phenomenon in relation to individuals: 'If the self is seriously damaged, or destroyed, then the drives become powerful constellations in their own right' (1977, p. 122). And he takes an analogy from physics. An atom remains stable as long as it remains intact. As soon as you split the nucleus, immense amounts of damaging energy, nuclear energy, are released, out of all proportion to the size of the atom. So for Kohut, the cohesiveness of the self is all-important. By extension, a fragmented society releases disproportionate amounts of energy, unbound and potentially dangerous.

Feelings of helplessness are induced by rising crime statistics, and we are inclined to lock ourselves into our houses, workplaces and offices with security devises, alarm systems, vicious dogs and the like. This is the culture of retrenchment: each against the other. With the loss of historical continuity and the collapse of the public domain, we limit our horizons to consideration of our own and our children's survival. We protect ourselves and watch out for the other. Our personal and professional relationships are especially affected. Whereas formerly we emphasised obligations, now we emphasise 'rights'. Our social relations have become intensely legalistic. We can no longer rely on the goodwill of the other. As Christopher Booker put it, 'legalism has penetrated right down to the smallest details of our lives. People (as for instance the garage that mends one's car) are no longer motivated by the pleasurable desire to do the job properly, but only by the sullen faced desire to do the minimum that is legally necessary in return for the maximum reward that can be legally exacted' (1980, p. 53). The law can always be invoked, and new laws continually created, in order to protect us from each other. Erikson's (1950) first stage of human development, 'trust versus distrust', which parallels Klein's paranoid-schizoid position, characterises the emotional climate. 'Our society', says Lasch,

> far from fostering private life at the expense of public life, has made deep and lasting friendships, love affairs, and marriages increasingly difficult to achieve. As social life becomes more and more warlike and barbaric, personal relations, which ostensibly provide relief from these conditions, take on the character of combat. (p. 69)
>
> . . . In some ways middle class society has become a pale copy of the black ghetto, as the appropriation of its language would lead us to believe . . . The increasingly dangerous and unpredictable conditions of middle class life has given rise to similar strategies for survival. Indeed the attraction of black culture for disaffected whites suggests that black culture now speaks to a general condition . . . The poor have always had to live for the present, but now a desperate concern for personal survival . . . engulfs the middle class as well. (1979, p. 129)

Before moving from the personal and social to the international political scene, in the next section, let us pause and introduce a new theoretical variant on the Kleinian psychoanalytic formulation of paranoia, but one which supports and deepens it. For this analysis, I am indebted to Charles Melman.

Paranoia can be considered as being essentially linked to our representation of space, because spontaneously our way of representing space is a Euclidean one. This has been our natural geometry for centuries. And we continue to think according to the rules of this geometry. There has been an attempt by rationalism to link the rules of thinking with the rules of geometry. But Euclidean geometry is based on the existence of *closed* figures, that is, an isolation of what is inside a circle, for instance, from what is outside it. There is an *absolute* boundary between the inside and outside.

Psychoanalysis, and in particular Kleinian psychoanalysis, shows us also that the fundamental way in which our primitive ego is constructed is on the Euclidean principle. We can conceive of the ego as a circle with a defined inside and outside. The primary narcissistic phantasy is that all goodness is located inside the circle and all badness is located outside. As we indicated earlier, in discussing Kleinian notion of the paranoid-schizoid position, the earliest configuration of the ego is essentially a paranoid one, and it is to this primitive logic of the fundamental cut – the cutting-off of the inside from the outside – that we are inevitably drawn.

This is very different from the representation that is given for example in the *Book of Kells* (a ninth-century manuscript in Trinity College, Dublin), because space is represented there as a weaving, or as a fabric. If the surface is represented by a weaving then what at certain moments disappears and goes outside, returns inside again. In a weaving or texture there is no cutting, and what has been excluded (repressed) can return. But in the Euclidean model, what has been put outside must remain outside. We will have to be very vigilant so that what has been put out does not come back in. In the *Book of Kells*, there is a representation of St Mark with the lion. He himself is a weaving, and not only is the weaving going through his body, but he himself is entirely woven.

Why do we represent space in the modern period in this Euclidean way? It is linked to what Lacan (1949) has designated 'the mirror phase'. The child sees itself in the mirror as a closed form, at a time in its infancy when it is suffering from an almost total psychical and physical helplessness. It is delighted with its image of completion and seizes upon it with jubilation, as a way of narcissistically overcoming its helpless dependency. From then on it sees everything *outside that form* as devalued, and therefore threatening. Klein, as we have seen, says more or less the same thing. The child introjects everything that is good, and projects the bad. But this is a paranoid conception of the world, to think that you are good and everything outside is bad. This is the very source of paranoid thinking.

However, Lacan shows us that clinically there are complications. Because that image with which I identify myself, that image which is going to become my own and constitute me, is essentially the image of *an other*. This is to say that my self is constituted by an other. It is an other who is in me. And this is why as a subject or as a self, I am always a little bit of a stranger to my own ego, which has been structured by this other. So the very principle of paranoia, which is the feeling of being intruded upon by another, is realised in the very nature of the structuring of the ego. So that, in normality, I have an ego that is constituted on a paranoid principle. It is the other who is in me, and there are times when I can find myself completely detached from this other inside me, for instance, when I want to hit out at or destroy that other. I might strike someone who appears to be very like me, and I will also unconsciously hurt myself, as in the case of Lacan's Aimée (1932). This was a patient who tried to stab a famous actress. The patient, Aimée, Lacan tells us, was in fact trying to hit out at her own ideal ego (her perfect mirror image), and she arranged things unconsciously so that she herself would be struck at the same time.

These ideas of Lacan address a fundamental problem: namely, the quest for being and the need for a specific localised identity, subjecthood, or sense of self. Lacan, following Freud, shows that the very basis of our identity is otherness, the image of an other. In other words, the ego is above all a social agency. We saw firstly that what is bad is pushed outside, but now we see that what is bad, in the sense of false, goes into the very fabrication of the ego. I can continue to put it (the image) outside, but it is within the ego because it is the ego itself. With the introjection of the image of an other, all the problems of miscomprehension and misperception of the world will be found inside us. And therefore, in a fundamental sense, the self can never be sure of its own identity, because the closer we get to it, the closer we get to the image of an other.

What conclusions can we draw from this? We can say that what is outside of the ego, that is the unconscious on the one hand, and the external world on the other, is considered threatening. What is different to the ego is considered as menacing. Anyone who is not like me, for whatever reason – their colour, their religion, and so on – poses a threat to my ego.

What is more interesting is that the person who is *like* me, the one most like me, is as intolerable as the one who is different to me. This seems at first to be paradoxical. But it relates to the problem of the split between the ego, formed in the image of the other, and the far more enigmatic and elusive subject (which is unconscious and therefore unfindable), and our fundamental uncertainty as to which of these at any one time constitutes the self. Which is the one to be recognised, to be valued, to capture the desire of another? Here is the fundamental *intra*-psychic rivalry, which is endlessly replicated culturally. This is the problem of the intense rivalry between siblings. Analogously, you get within all groups the phenomena of splitting and schism, the division of people who are alike. So people who are alike are going to look for a *little* feature, or a little trait of difference, in order to put outside what is inside. This is why the great religious, political and national movements, including the psychoanalytic movement, where initially a certain unity is realised, always end up being broken, divided and split.

So this view of paranoia, which situates it normatively in the structuring of the ego during the mirror phase, has become especially relevant for the analysis of contemporary culture. We have noted the increasing incapacity of the social fabric to contain and integrate the drives. The modern social fabric has become to an extent 'unwoven'. The fear released has left us more exposed and unable to feel necessarily depressed and concerned. We are then less able to mitigate, mask and work through some of the fundamental misperceptions of the early ego into the more mature 'weaving' of a more integrated self, where the subject and ego remain split, but there is a knowledge, tolerance and emotional understanding of this predicament.

We must now turn to look at examples of how these issues, the fundamental problems in the initial structuring of the self in the modern period, have worked themselves out politically and historically.

MASS PROJECTIONS

Here is part of a television play by Les Smith, broadcast on Channel 4 (*Rear Window*, 21 September 1991). A middle-aged Vietnamese woman is on a empty stage, alone and seated. She has been crying.

> I never thought that the Americans would come to our village. I thought we were immune from them. But one morning they did come. We could hear the helicopters in the distance. We have to send all the young men away, because the Americans think all the young men are enemies. Then we have to send all the old men away, because they will shoot them too. We must send the women away, because they have done terrible terrible things to our women. But some people must remain in the village, or the Americans will burn it to the ground. They have bombed us and wrecked our crops. They have shot women and children, even young babies. If you are frightened, we say that you must go and hide in the rice paddies. But if the Americans come upon you there, you must not run, as the Americans will shoot you if you run, because they will think that you must be a fighter. If you are carrying anything, they will

shoot you because they will think it is a weapon. So try not to be carrying anything, and move only slowly or keep still. Don't look scared or they will shoot you. Look happy and smile, but don't smile too much, or they will think you are laughing at them, and they will shoot you . . .

David Shukman, a BBC defence correspondent, revisited Vietnam and described his visit to the War Crimes Museum.

It was situated in what was once a grand old colonial home, the grounds of which were crammed with tanks and artillery pieces. On the verandah, where flower boxes may once have been, was a collection of rocket launchers, shells and machine guns. Inside, room after room was lined with photographs of American GIs at their worst, beating Vietnamese, dragging them or sitting on their severed heads. There were graphs illustrating America's spending on the war. There were copies of USAF charts marking the zones where defoliant chemicals had been sprayed to lay bare the Vietcong hideouts. Beside them were pictures of the injuries people had suffered during these sorties. And, placed almost carelessly on a shelf near the door, was a jar containing a deformed foetus. A caption said it was the result of chemicals. (1988, p. 20)

We must think about the *image* of America – the image which is always the image of perfection, it is the ideal and triumphal image. But what is the fate of that which falls outside of this big image? For what falls outside the image has been excluded and is therefore not known. It is the other who is made to carry the excluded elements, which are the instinctual drives, the helplessness, the incoherence, the badness, the deformity. We are thinking here of the process of *projective identification.*[4]

There are films of recent years (Adair, 1989) that have begun to question this image of America. But, to date, there has not been one film made of the Vietnamese experience – of the American alter ego, of the American other, of everything that America, in its image of itself as the policeman of the world, is terrified of. But what is outside always threatens to return. And when the GIs returned home, they were not welcome, because they were now contaminated with that otherness. Some made an adjustment back into civilian life, but others, painfully and tragically aware of the atrocities that they had committed in the name of America, committed suicide or took to the forests and hills to lead strange and marginalised existences.

Norman Mailer said of the war in Vietnam that American culture contained so much destructive rage that it had to export it, and Vietnam, during that period of the late sixties and early seventies, became the focal point for the massive discharge. More high explosives were dropped on North Vietnam during those years than were dropped in the whole of the Second World War. And for every one ton of explosive used by the Vietcong, the Americans used one thousand tons. In terms of projective identification, this represents a massive faecal evacuation of destructiveness – a splitting attack which has the aim of destroying and totally controlling the other.

The Balfour Declaration of 1917 gave Britain's support to a Jewish homeland in Palestine. Although this decision was recognised as problematic, the civil and religious rights of the Palestinian Arabs were to be protected. The Anglo-French declaration of 1918 also promised the Arabs independence if they supported the Allies against the Turks. But, as Fisk (1990) has meticulously documented, these promises were not meant to be kept. As far as Balfour was concerned, Zionism was far more important than the fate of 700,000 Arabs. And then the guilt about the Holocaust virtually guaranteed the creation of Israel in Palestine. The Arab armies that invaded the new Israeli state were driven out, together with well over half a million Arab Palestinians whose homes had been in that part of Palestine that was now Israel. Fisk comments: 'The result was inevitable. While the Jews of Israel exulted in their renaissance, the Arabs of Palestine left in despair. From the camps of Europe, those who had avoided the execution pits and the gas chambers had at last reached the Promised Land about which their cantors had sung at Auschwitz' (1990, p. 17).

The Palestinian Arabs who fled to neighbouring territories ironically believed that their exile would be brief. They took their front-door keys, legal documents, deeds of ownership to property, maps of their orange groves and fields, identity papers, in the belief that when the hostilities were over they would be able to return and resume normal life once again. But in the years that followed their vacated homes would be reoccupied by Israeli settlers or be torn down, the developers would move in, whole villages would be erased from the map, whole areas renamed.

So, by the arguments being developed here, the Palestinians, these dispossessed people, in the years following 1948, were forced to carry a suffering. A suffering that was a loss of everything. This suffering was a *passing on* of a much greater suffering that originated, as far as recent history is concerned, in the death camps of Europe.

The Jews of Europe (and others) were brutally forced to carry the split-off, impure, perverse elements that had to be excluded from the *pure image* of the Aryan race. As such, as an excremental remainder, they had to be eliminated in a manner which was perhaps unique in the history of human massacres. So much has been written about the Nazis and the systematic, scientific orderliness of the slaughter of six million Jews. A million children were among those killed. Such a mass traumatisation cannot possibly be absorbed, assimilated or symbolised, but instead will be repeated. The original projection from the Nazis is carried, without being psychically processed, and now *re*-projected into the Palestinians, who, in the same way, but on a much smaller scale in terms of numbers at least, will be the new remainder.

The Israeli invasion of Lebanon in June 1982, and in particular the massacre of Palestinians, mainly women and children, in the camps at Sabra and Chatila in September 1982, can be seen as just such a repetition. The massacre was carried out by the Christian Phalange militia with tacit Israeli support. The Phalange of Pierre Gemayel was created after he had visited the Olympic games in Berlin in 1936. He was very impressed by the authoritarianism of the Hitler Youth. He is quoted in Fisk. 'I saw then this discipline and order. And I said to myself, why can't we do the same thing in Lebanon. So when we came back to Lebanon, we created this youth movement' (p. 65). His youth movement blossomed. After Hitler's fall, the Phalangist movement died out across Europe, but it survived in Lebanon as a brutal private militia, and later became the close ally of the Israelis. Here, we can see how Israel's identification with the aggressor was complete. They were to help in every way the fascist-inspired Phalangist elimination of the Palestinians in the camps.

Israel invaded Lebanon in 1982 with a massive force in order to destroy the Palestine Liberation Organisation (PLO). By the end of the second week of the invasion, the Red Cross was reporting 14,000 killed, the vast majority of them civilians, and another 20,000 wounded. The Israelis used cluster bombs in civilian areas, and phosphorus, which causes terrible burns. They attacked Beirut from the air, flying low as there was no resistance, no missiles or anti-aircraft fire. They bombed West Beirut indiscriminately and repeatedly for weeks, killing about 4,000 people. The Israelis' final military casualty toll was 500, only 3.5 per cent of the Lebanese and Palestinian total. However, this figure was to rise in the years following the invasion. Of course, the war in Lebanon bore absolutely no relation to the Second World War in scale. Yet on the level of individual atrocities, the Sabra and Chatila massacres stand alongside similar outrages in the Second World War (Fisk, 1990, p. 389).

What of the much-vaunted moral *image* of Israel? 'Purity of Arms' was the slogan of the army in 1948. Their purity is to be contrasted, in their minds, with the 'Palestinian scum' which must be eliminated. But it would be inappropriate to apportion blame naively here. The PLO did pose a military threat to Israel, but our purpose here is to illustrate the terrible consequences of destructive omnipotent projection, the consequences of drawing the paranoiac circle and the alienation which always follows the image of perfection. Israel's own critics speak, and in so doing, point up the universal danger. Amos Oz comments:

> After Lebanon, we can no longer ignore the monster, even when it is dormant, or half asleep, or when it peers out from behind the lunatic fringe . . . It dwells, drowsing, virtually everywhere, even in the folk singing guts of our common myths. Even in our soul melodies. We did not leave it behind in Lebanon, with the Hezbollah. It is here among us, a part of us, like a shadow, in Hebron, in Gaza, in the slums of the suburbs, in the Kibbutzim and in my Lake Kinneret – 'O Lake Kinneret mine, were you real or only a dream? . . . ' (1990, p. 23)

This monster represents that unassimilated trauma that is so threatening that it must be evacuated, and yet the evacuation is only partially successful, for behind the idealised view of Israel lurks this capacity for real destructive vengeance.

Consider also the Israeli journalist, Michael Elkins:

> We can go on like this recreating and reflecting the existing images of each other, and reflecting these reflections – endlessly and hatefully – as in a hall of mirrors. The result will be that all of us – Israelis, Palestinians and Arabs – will be locked into endless and bloody agony in a hall of mirrors of our own creation and from which there is no exit.
>
> Or we can begin by adopting a certain integrity – a certain generosity – in the use of language.

That's not too hard. It's the easiest of hard things that must be done if we are ever to come to peace with one another, and so with ourselves. (*Jerusalem Post*, 13 November 1983)

THE DENIAL OF DEATH

Another consequence of our modern domination by and fascination with image, with surface, with phantasy, with here-and-now immediacy of experience, is the loss of our capacity to acknowledge death. As we have already mentioned, the image stands for perfection, for completeness, for omnipotence and the denial of any lack.

During the sixties and seventies, it became clear that the way we lived caused some of us to die unnecessarily early. The sensible thing to do was to stop smoking, cut down on alcohol and fats, start exercising, eat properly and so on. In the light of this knowledge, an unprecedented concern, amounting to a hypochondriacal anxiety, has arisen about our state of health. Health food shops abound, alternative medicine, and so-called health fascism, which is the health equivalent of a moral reformism. The new puritans are proud to have curbed their excesses and they believe their reward will be a long life, in this life, not the next. And with the decline in belief in an afterlife, this life and longevity in it have become all-important.

The fact is that many more people are living to quite advanced ages, keeping going in spite of physical and sometimes psychological deterioration, kept alive by new medical treatments, in a world where there is less and less of the social nexus that used to make old age worthwhile. We can now have longer lives, in the same way that we can live better lives materially, that is, have more and more goods and services. But the same question arises and it is the question of *quality*. What do we have all these things for? These questions become especially highlighted and poignant when the loss of the social, which we have noted as one of the characteristics of modernity, means that old age can become a terrible isolation where people have only the radio and television for company. An existence in relative comfort is undoubtedly an enormous material advance on former generations, but not much of a life, just carrying on surviving because there is no way out. We note also an increasing exploitation of the aged by some private concerns who have been required to step in to fill the gap left by the run-down in public services.

Alan Bennett's monologue, 'Soldiering On' (1988), is about a woman approaching sixty, who has just lost her husband. She keeps up appearances in a world of acquaintances, trying to ward off hurt and the terrible pressing awareness that in reality her daughter is mentally ill ('It can occur in the best regulated families' [p. 75]) perhaps because of something (sexual) her father Ralph did to her when she was young. Also, her treasured son Giles says she has a 'liquidity problem', and gets her to sign away her money and eventually her home, requiring her to move to a little off-season holiday flatlet. Throughout all this she maintains a dignity, an English dignity ('although the church [Ralph's funeral] was an absolute choker' [p. 71]), thinking of what Ralph would say: 'Come on Muriel, you're a widow lady, you've got time on your hands. If anybody's in a position to roll their sleeves up, it's you' (p. 75). She speaks in clipped phrases to cut off intense feelings:

> [Giles] doesn't like to come down, says it upsets him. Don't know why. Doesn't upset me. Miss the tinies. Not so tiny. Lucy'll be twelve now . . . I'd seen myself as the model grandmother, taking them to Peter Pan and the Science Museum. Not to be. Another dream bites the dust. My big passion now is the telly box . . . [but] I wouldn't want you to think this was a tragic story . . . [*pause*] . . . I'm not a tragic woman . . . [*pause*] . . . I'm not that type. (p. 79)

All the hidden problems of modernity become manifest during old age, when the narcissistic supports, by which more than ever life is lived, fall away. Ego functions deteriorate and physiological systems fail. In such circumstances, the old person will have to be able to draw on some very supportive *internal* object to avoid depression and bitterness. Indeed, there are those elderly who have retained their vitality and are remarkably un-bitter about their failing powers. For them, life is still a blessing and they live out of some endless inner resource. But for many, living in a world that hopelessly exceeds them and daily shocks them, life becomes a secret curse and there is no way out, because, in our period of radical absence, we have lost the capacity to give death meaning. Death is just a terrible *unspeakable* end, which is always present as a nothingness and totally devoid of meaning.

It was the Victorians who repressed sexuality, but today we are obsessed with sexuality and repress death. Sex is used defensively and almost compulsively as proof against ageing and death. As Rollo May put it:

> As long as you can hang onto the virtue of individual potency, you can laugh in the face of death . . . The drive to repress the awareness of death falls with particular weight on Western man, because of his reliance on the myth of potency, which has played a central role in Western man's struggle for identity since the Renaissance. (1969, p. 107)

Saul Bellow notes the *unconscious* power that death has over the way people manage their lives:

> Take something like modern erotic life. If you omit the death factor from it, you don't know what's going on, you can't see it. But, you know, if you are a perishable subject and it is going to be all over within a certain time and you glory in your vigour and you want to collect as much sensual pleasure as you can, then you proceed with a certain urgency which only death can explain. (Quoted in Bourne *et al.*, 1987, p. 23)

Death is unspeakable and ultimately unsymbolisable. To pretend anything else is to trivialise it. Death is infinite, beyond all human imaginings. In Lacanian terms – and this is implicit in all psychoanalytic theory – death exists in the dimension of the Real. This dimension of the Real is outside of human comprehension. Lacan describes it as unassimilable, as 'an appointment to which we are always called . . . but which eludes us' (1964, p. 53). He speaks of it as the failed encounter. The Real is forever 'en souffrance', which means in suspense, in abeyance, pending. 'It is the real that governs our activities more than any other and it is psychoanalysis that designates it for us' (p. 60). In 1920, Freud developed his theory of trauma, the repetition compulsion and the death instinct, and realised that 'the pleasure principle' did indeed have a 'beyond'. Traumas occur in the Real, they are accidental, yet their residues are caught up in our lives and we compulsively repeat and repeat them without knowing why. We are unable to get rid of them yet unable to assimilate them. These traumas, which overwhelm the psyche, are like little deaths, representatives of non-being on the borders of signification and meaning, insisting on being represented, yet remaining elusively unrepresentable. It is with this 'outsideness' of the Real that psychoanalysis is essentially concerned. The traumas with which it deals are the traumas of infancy and childhood, the psychic floodings of our origins, of our insertion into a world that is utterly Other.

Psychoanalysis can therefore be seen as reversing a dominant trend in postmodern culture, namely the avoidance of death. A recent comment by Christopher Bollas, during a Dublin lecture in 1988, to the effect that psychoanalysis was essentially a preparation for death, is paradoxical yet crucial, because we normally think of analysis as about being more, about some kind of increase in one's life, not a reduction. But the same point is made by the Jungian analyst James Hillman (1975), when he says in effect that the way we practice psychoanalysis should relate events to death, and not necessarily to cure. The question he poses is: what does death, our own death, do to every moment in our lives? He asserts that the tomb must touch our talking and connect what we say and do with death.

Psychoanalysis is thus a modern form of initiation. Analysands are encouraged to regress, by lying down and free-associating, by suspending their normal historically determined consciousness. By being directed to pay attention to their dreams and phantasies and other formations of the unconscious, they come to encounter intimations and re-editions of those traumas. They come upon the tragic. Roy Schaffer says: 'Analysis raises the melodramatic and the pathetic to the level of the tragic and so changes the atmosphere, quality or dignity of an entire life' (1983, p. 192). This is an initiation.

In a culture without ritual, we have lost opportunities to symbolise death. Gone are the adolescent initiations of pre-industrial cultures described by Eliade (1957); although it must be true that much adolescent risk-taking, experimentation with drugs, and the like must represent a kind of self-initiation in the absence of the formalised ritual. Adolescents, like anyone else, have to come close to death in order to feel real and alive. But to a large extent, the rituals of births, marriages and deaths have lost their sacramental character, to be marked instead by a flat bureaucratic and legalistic efficiency. Ritual was the way in which we were able to situate ourselves in the cosmic order of things. This brought a sense of unforced humility, a sense of knowing one's place and accepting limitation. Gone too is the sense of the tragic such as we find in a Tess, or a Bathsheba Everdene or an Anna Karenina, or in the marriage feast in *The Deer Hunter*, before the boys go out to Vietnam, for instance. Gone, for that matter, is the peasant brutality that we would find in Zola, or the mad schizoid extreme of a Raskolnikov.

Psychoanalysis has shown what writers, for instance, have always known, how desire has to be continually marked by death. The only way a life can be constituted is by reference to a death. If you avoid death you miss life also. Freud highlights this essential point three times in his writing. He retrieved the Oedipal myth, which had been forgotten since Sophocles' time; so that now we link desire to the death of the father. In *Totem and Taboo* (1912–13), he showed that the relationship of a couple is organised by the murder of a father. And in *Moses and Monotheism* (1939), he created a myth which is the murder of the primal ancestor – which is strange, because it is historically untrue: the Jews did not kill Moses. But perhaps Freud was trying to underline the importance of symbolising death, and the need to *link* the enjoyment and excitement in life to a primordial murder.

So is it a question of establishing a place for death in our own life, so that death is no longer a trauma that comes from the *outside*, from the Real, but is woven into the fabric of our lives? Should we be trying to bring about a sort of rational human control over death? This is ultimately an impossibility, as we cannot gain a symbolic *control* over death. Death counselling, bereavement counselling can help, psychotherapy can help, but death remains utterly Other. It is our ignorance of this in modernity, our belief that we can do without it by abolishing it, that paradoxically makes life lifeless.

We can, however, affirm a particular type of resistance when it stems from a vitality that absolutely acknowledges death, while fighting against it:

> Do not go gentle into that dark night,
> Old age should burn and rage at close of day;
> Rage, rage against the dying of the light.
>
> (Dylan Thomas, 1952, p. 159)

This represents a determination to live, a love of life, because there is an implicit acknowledgement of the finality of death. But the denial of death, our refusal to take it on board, or our belief that we can somehow tame, control or eradicate it (a belief to which some forms of psychotherapy can play up), lead to a denial of life and courage too. Life then is led in a linear, rational fashion with control and much good sense, but no depth and vitality.

Klein's depressive position refers to an essential *mourning*, to a sense of the tragic, to a sense of joy which accepts the impermanence and fragility of life. Without this process, which has become lost in the frenzy and hype of postmodern culture – there is no place that is silent any more – death remains totally in the Real. It is banished from life, and so therefore is vitality lost from life. Desire is vapid: at once everywhere and nowhere. Life becomes a flat existence, and death always threatens to return.

DEATH RETURNS – THE APOCALYPTIC MOOD

Part of the fundamental instability of postmodernism is, as I have indicated, the denial of death, and now we will note a simultaneous anxious preoccupation with death and destructiveness. We are filled with catastrophic expectations. Crisis follows crisis. We live with the threat of global pollution, the destruction of the rainforests, the loss of a hundred species every day, famine, nuclear suicide, and the slow insidious spread of AIDS. On the personal level, we live with hypochondriacal anxieties and an anxious concern about our physical and mental well-being. Having abolished death, we fear its return from the dimension of the Real. Death like a foreign body comes at us from the outside and in a global way. Let me illustrate this, on the individual level, with two brief vignettes.

A woman was admitted to hospital having taken a serious overdose. She described her life as being quite normal and uneventful until her first pregnancy, when she became depressed. She had had two miscarriages before the birth of her first baby girl and had had a number of other children in fairly rapid succession. Throughout all this time she had been depressed, she now admitted, and her own brothers and sisters had been encouraging her to seek help, but without any response on her part. She insisted that she had had a normal upbringing in a large family. But on one day, she recalled, she arrived home from school, to be told that her mother was dead. She had died suddenly that morning in circumstances that were never explained to her. In fact her mother was never mentioned again in the family and she was never told how or why her mother had died. Her mother's place was taken by a number of aunts. She related these events in the same flat monotone. She could not recall thinking about her mother again in the subsequent years.

The trauma of her mother's sudden death was completely abolished. This patient had had no opportunity to symbolise or in any way mourn her mother's catastrophic departure. So the question for this woman is: what did it mean for *her* to be a mother? In terms of her experience, what is a mother supposed to be like? And we might make a response – a response that this woman was not able to make or in any way to comprehend and keep *within* her mind. Instead it was a response destined to be *enacted* through her: a mother is someone who dies and vanishes without trace. It was only when she herself became a mother that the answer to her own unconscious question *happened to* her. It could not be answered by her, but only through her. She was overcome by depression and felt compelled to end her life.

A man in his early forties, very competent in his work, tried to kill himself, by taking an overdose of aspirin, and then driving to X. It transpired that as a young boy he remembered being taken forcibly by his mother at night out to X, after she had been badly beaten up by her alcoholic husband. In her great distress on this journey, the mother had said to her terrified son that she would have loved to kill herself. This man, as a little boy, had abolished the unthinkable thought, and it only returned to him as an act in the Real. During the suicide attempt, he described himself as feeling supreme and omniscient. He felt that he was acting from outside the realm of human affairs. It was only when he thought of his own children that he decided to seek help. At that moment, when he thought of himself as father, he regained his position within a symbolic universe and therefore within life.

Similarly for postmodern culture, if it is true that we are unable adequately any longer to think, imagine, and contemplate death – the essential connection between life and death – are we then inevitably condemned to act it out? Does death, insofar as it has been excluded, assume horrendous proportions in the Real? The history of this century, this fratricidal century, would bear this out. Without the sense that human freedom and desire must be touched by death, which is the basis of our morality, then there is theoretically and practically no end point, no limit to human action. The field is wide open to all manner of mass perversion.

In particular, we might consider as a good example modern

scientific discourse and its elimination of human subjectivity. It is modern science to which we have to look to see most clearly the return of death. Its pursuit of the rational, its domination of the human reality has always made it the vehicle by which death must return. Positivism has triumphed over all forms of metaphysical thought, now deemed irrational and unscientific. As the Critical Theorists of the Frankfurt school were pointing out in the forties and fifties, modern culture was becoming increasingly dominated by 'instrumental rationality', and as Marcuse (1964) clearly indicated, science is inextricably linked to the creation of the means of mass destruction.

Yet the modern humanist conscience with its benign optimism cannot conceive of radical evil. With its tolerance, its high-mindedness, its democratic traditions, it has lost the language with which to understand this radically excluded Other, which arises as if from another universe, with its *fatwa*, its jihad, its pogrom, its legitimate targets and its surgical strikes. It is the very naivety and complacency of such thought that facilitates the return. And it is the experienced shallowness and limitedness of much that passes for life in a rich and successful country like Britain that makes young men prepared to go off and fight in the Falklands or the Gulf. At least here they will experience something Real.

THE GHOSTS OF RELIGION

This century has been the century of failed utopias. Many people put their faith in the Russian revolution and communism. Marxism offered not only a total explanation of life, but it also held the key to history. It was therefore immensely attractive, because it identified itself with social justice and with the liberation of oppressed peoples. Fascism was also attractive to some, as it promised a way out of decadence and offered its adherents the possibility of a new order founded upon discipline, racial pride and nationalism.

No less important were the educational and child-rearing utopias (explored in more detail in Chapters 5, 6 and 7) that were to be brought about by giving children freedom at home and at school to develop without interference – only then would there be no more hate, conflict and war. It was and still is argued that aggression is *created* in the family, and results in its being endlessly exteriorised in later life. Remove coercive controls and guilt and you remove the sources of aggression, and the essential goodness of the human spirit will be manifest. Alice Miller is perhaps the most recent exponent of this dream. Closely related was the dream of personal liberation – the throwing off of the shackles of bourgeois convention and the remnants of guilt associated with religion. This was in part a revolt against the mechanisation and dehumanisation of life in newly industrialised countries, and a return to romantic ideals. It showed itself most strongly in the arts and changing sexual mores.

The scientific and technological dream, to which we have already referred, was that progress in human existence would occur primarily through reason. Scientifically controlled, people would become rational and sensible. To become like this, they needed to live in a rationally ordered environment. And so there developed a whole new architecture. According to Hughes, 'from 1880 to 1930 the language of architecture changed more radically than it had done in the previous four centuries. The ideal of social transformation through architecture and design was one of the driving forces of modernist culture. Rational design would make rational societies' (1980, p. 165). The new Internationalist style of modern architecture was to be functional, geometrical and technological, with no ornamentation. New futuristic cities were planned to house rational people. Steel, reinforced concrete and sheet glass were to be the new materials. Le Corbusier dreamt of the 'vertical city bathed in light and air'. He hated the chaos of the old medieval city with its randomness and overcrowding. Instead he dreamt of giant avenues designed for rapid transport, and high-rise blocks with green spaces. One of Corbusier's aphorisms was 'architecture or revolution', because the widespread feeling was that violence was created by living in a bad environment. One expert on the mood of that time said, 'we were all thoroughly of the opinion that if you had good architecture, the lives of the people would be improved; that architecture would improve people, and people would improve architecture until perfectibility would descend on us like the Holy Ghost' (Johnson, quoted in Hughes, 1980, p. 165).

Many of these utopian notions have collapsed under the weight of their own internal contradictions. However, new ones will be born. The political socialist utopias have been dramatically unmasked and exposed in a way which could scarcely have been imagined. Fascism, at its extreme represented by National Socialism, was defeated, yet is by no means dead as modern forms of anti-Semitism and new forms of nationalism emerge. We note also the rampages of the Red Guards and the fanatical extremes of Pol Pot in Cambodia. Apartheid crumbles as an ideal of separate racial development. The Iranian revolution, on the other hand, represents the very significant re-emergence of a religious fundamentalism.

Permissiveness at home and in school has led to a breakdown in authority and a pervasive loss of impulse control, a theme which we will take up again later in Chapters 6 and 7. The dream of overthrowing bourgeois conventions has happened at unknown human cost. The divorce rate at the beginning of this century was 1 in 500, whereas now it is 4 in 10. The number of children born outside of marriage has risen from 1 in 25 to nearly 1 in 4, during that period. It is an open question whether or not this 'liberation' has increased the sum total of human happiness.

The promise of science and technology used in the service of man has been marked, as we have noted, by the emergence of its destructive potential. In July 1945, the first atomic bomb was exploded in New Mexico. Oppenheimer, the leader of the team that created the new weapon, said that they had invented death. In 1953, Watson and Crick unravelled the structure of DNA, paving the way for man to alter the genome of living organisms. This has already been done with viruses and bacteria. The consequences of this sort of omnipotent behaviour, this playing God, are at the very least alarming. Our technological domination of nature poses a threat to the natural environmental cycles which have evolved over billions of years.

However, none of these utopian ideas is dead. But what sense can we make of them? How can we contextualise them? Clearly the question of utopias is also the question of ideologies. Of the more important ideologies cited above, we can note a spectrum from the pathologically fanatical to the mature vision of a better future. We must keep this spectrum in mind in the following discussion.

At the pathological end, as Freud noted in *Group Psychology and the Analysis of the Ego* (1921), individuals in groups can lose their super-ego inhibitions and thereby act out formerly repressed unconscious impulses. This happens in obedience to the new authority, who represents a new father and becomes the group ego-ideal to which everyone submits, giving up their individuality. This process creates uniformity, which overcomes the problems of rivalry and envy. Freud notes how common this is:

> We are reminded of how many of these phenomena of dependence are part of the normal constitution of human society, of how little originality and personal courage are to be found in it, of how much every individual is ruled by those attitudes of the group mind which exhibit themselves in such forms as racial characteristics, class prejudices, public opinion, etc. (1921, pp. 122–3)

The question of weakness and the willingness to surrender one's identity to the group is crucial. Chasseguet-Smirgel (1984) takes an idea of Didier Anzieu (1971), that the group experience is similar to the dream experience. The group is imagined as this magical place where all our wishes can be satisfied. According to Anzieu, in the group dream there is a threefold regression: to primary narcissism; the loss of the ego and super-ego; and the re-fusion of the id with the primary object.

For Chasseguet-Smirgel, the group leader is more of a powerful mother imago than a paternal one. In fact the powerful hold that the group ideology can have over us is due to the fact that it promises us a way out of the difficult paternal universe. The group becomes for its members the substitute for this lost object – the almighty mother, the good breast, the healer of narcissistic injuries. All the privations, losses, competition, castration anxiety, etc. encountered during normal development are magically removed. The group illusion heals all these wounds. The leader of the group promotes the regressive re-fusion with the primal mother. With this mother everything is made possible, and as Chasseguet-Smirgel points out, the leader of the group 'may be compared to the pervert's mother who makes her son believe that there is no need to wait and grow up in order to take the father's role' (1984, p. 61). There is no need for delay and difficulty. Ideologies magically remove obstacles and privations, which are related to the prohibitions imposed of necessity by the father during the Oedipal struggle. Ideologies, in the extreme, promise a world without the father.

The killings and the atrocities associated with fanaticism can be ascribed to the removal of the paternal super-ego, and also to the desire for immediacy: everything likely to hamper the success of the ideal must be eliminated. Ideology also involves splitting and projection of the bad into the outside world. The group becomes one vast omnipotent idealised ego with which each member can merge. The loss of individuality created by the donning of a uniform is more than compensated for by the spreading of the omnipotent ego over the whole mass. Group members may be far apart geographically but they feel united by the great cause. Anyone who threatens the utopian group illusion is identified and killing is instigated at the behest of the ego-ideal. Even those who are just not part of the group may also have to be eliminated, for their presence also threatens the group illusion. It therefore becomes very difficult not to join a group, partly because, in the extreme, one might be eliminated, but more generally because one will be isolated with no ego support.

Lacan linked the proliferation of ideologies and utopian notions with the decline of patriarchy, with the decline of the paternal imago, and with the father during the modern period, as lacking, weak, humiliated or a sham. 'It is this lack [of the paternal imago] which, as explained by our theory of the Oedipus complex, exhausts instinctual energy and vitiates the dialectic of sublimation. Impotence and the utopian spirit are the sinister godmothers who watch over the cradle of the neurotic and imprison his ambition' (1938, p. 46).

When we have found *the cause*, the *great idea*, we have come to the locus of the Other, which means we have come to the centre of everything, and we believe like the paranoiac that everything proceeds from us, that everything happens because of us. In this position, which is the absence of a position in the symbolic humanly constituted reality, we have disappeared as a subject. We are above, outside and beyond human reality. Therefore, from this position, we can commit *in*human acts.

When we have to deal with people who have found 'a cause', or who have become subsumed in an ideology, it becomes very difficult or impossible to converse with them. I will briefly cite a particular instance – a fairly benign one – of this *disappearance of the subject*. The person I have in mind was brought up in what he described as a middle-class, materialistic, business-orientated family in Northern Ireland. Depressed by what he felt was the banality of this upbringing, he almost consciously set about finding some ideology that would satisfy his craving. Firstly, he discovered a mystical–psychotherapeutic group that explained all human suffering in terms of body-tension, using techniques derived from Reich. He became convinced that body work was the solution. All his conversation returned to this theme. However, he became disillusioned after about a year. And he changed dramatically from being almost lost in a cause, to being a person again with whom one could be convivial. Then after a brief illness, he turned to running as the solution. He trained excessively and took part in many marathons, and as he said later, his whole life was 'consumed' by running. He dropped that, only later to devote himself completely to macrobiotics; and so the list goes on. In between being taken over by these 'causes', he would regain access to his subjectivity: he would be tolerant of his own and others' frailties, he would regain his lively sense of humour and become open to his work and the many cultural activities in which he had always had a great interest. But in his utopian phases, he was intolerant, abusive and disdainful of others outside his group. Speaking with him, one felt one was not speaking to a person. He was inaccessible and impervious to the needs of his colleagues and family. Former friends described him as cold, hard, even frightening, unrelenting and boring at times in his pursuit of the cause.

We can trace in this person, who is very typical of our period, the movements between subjectivity and asubjectivity, as experienced concretely by those who were close to him. We can see the search for the omnipotent ideal, which is pre-Oedipal in character, because when it is found the subject disappears. Subjectivity can be willingly surrendered when there is the prospect of (re-)entry into an imaginary perfection.

From the psychoanalytic point of view, it is the father who must, of necessity, bring about the separation of the mother and child. It is the father (not necessarily the real father) who demands that we give up this absolute pleasure, this ideal union, the perfect simplicity. He insists on the Law and the giving up of everything that is totally satisfying. From this point of view, the point of view of our blissful time with our mothers, we face a terrible and continual sense of loss, a loss of something that perhaps it wasn't necessary to lose in the first place. We will feel forever tempted to throw over this oppressing world of father in favour of a return to what is totally pleasurable and promises total success. This, as we have seen, has been the dominant trend in the modern period. But this regressive return to the mother, to which we are all seductively drawn, involves us in a submergence and a terrifying loss of self. It is the father who situates us as a subject, as separate self, in relation to the world. It is the father who will help us to tolerate a certain unbearable sense of separateness, loneliness and isolation, which follows on from his interdiction, and which we will never totally accept as reality. We will always feel that we are missing something. Post-Oedipally, we are now forced endlessly and creatively to rediscover the object of satisfaction. Desire is then kept perpetually on the move in search of the ideal, but with no hope of ever finding it completely. It is this castration which, in health, prevents us from ever finding *the cause*.

The Mexican poet, Octavio Paz, spoke of our inability to bear the emptiness left by the break-up of the old order. The Christian tradition, as we have noted, gave people a framework in which they could become reconciled and find some meaning in their defeats. Suffering was somehow understood to be part of a larger order. With the loss of the old Christian order, there is no longer any meaning to be found in defeat. Suffering is just suffering and it leads to nothing and is unredeemable. It leads to the void and a craving for substitute systems, which offer illusory answers to the problems of existence. 'This is when the ghosts of religion appear. The emptiness can be filled with caricatures such as communism or fascism or total ideas, or with sects, all this flowering of superstitious selves in the Western world' (Paz, 1986, p. 18).

In summary, we must emphasise the distinction, therefore, between the authentic religious position and the ideological extremism which reveals all the *violently paranoid splits* of the modern period. The former implies a reconciliation with our internal world, rather than a manic flight from it. It entails our entry into the depressive position, with the consequent painful loss of omnipotence and perfection. We wish to make reparation, but this creative work must be essentially grounded in the post-Oedipal acceptance of the paternal universe, which transcends us. The only illusions which can then be tolerated are not totalising 'Brave New Worlds', but realistic possibilities which can be worked for.

4 FEMINIST OUTRAGE

In the last chapter, we considered the increasing fragmentation of modern and postmodern culture, the crumbling of the old order, the loss of a frame of reference, and the pervasive and accelerating tendency towards splitting, denial and projection. Here we will consider the impact of these phenomena on our closest personal relationships. The crisis in our culture is most clearly marked in the relationships between men and women.

The effect of the re-emergence of the women's movement into popular consciousness in the last two or three decades has been to shatter the post-war myth about the nuclear family and to expose painfully the conventional hypocrisies of sexual relationships and the family. A new generation of educated young women takes for granted the new freedoms that their mothers fought for and their grandmothers would have been shocked by. However, the pace of change may have outstripped the culture's capacity to cope.

Psychoanalysis has made a major contribution to this debate. The Freudian position has always been controversial, but Freud was one of the first doctors actually to listen to his women patients, and psychoanalysis, through the work of the early women analysts such as Karen Horney, Anna Freud and Melanie Klein, has provided an important cultural space where women have been able to define and explore their subjectivity. Here I want to examine in a limited way the feminist polemic itself, its validity, its agenda, its possible unconscious determinants, its revolutionary effects. So much so far has been written and said, but here I want to concentrate on some of the emotional repercussions of feminism.

The political ferment of the sixties and seventies has died down as women feel increasingly free to explore the new options unencumbered by guilt or disapproval. To be a single parent, or a working mother, for instance, is now quite normal. But there are many problems and the issues are still hot, with some on the Right becoming increasingly hostile to the women's movement. Much political discussion centres on sexist attitudes and the desire to minimise or eradicate the differential conditioning of boys and girls at home and at school, which, it is argued, has been the cause of male domination in the past. We have expected boys to be tough and independent, while we assume girls will be soft and dependent. What we need to do, it is argued widely, is to make girls capable of being assertive and independent and make boys more sensitive, and the inequalities will disappear.

Some important issues are missed in these arguments. Firstly, there may be, after all, an *innate* difference, genetically determined, in the psychological predispositions of the two sexes. This argument will not be addressed here. Secondly, it seems that *all* cultures have *structured unequally* the male and female sexual identities. There has to be difference, and there has always been inequality. Juliet Mitchell says:

> I'm pessimistic in the sense that I think that all societies have to construct some way of symbolising sexual difference . . . And we don't know of any societies in which that difference doesn't also have a degree of deference in the relationship . . . Meaningful difference has implied some sort of hierarchy hitherto. And that's my worry, that's my pessimism. I can't envisage a society in which sexual difference will not be in some way symbolised. (1987, pp. 71–2)

This argument will also be left to one side.

Thirdly, there is the question of the *dynamically repressed* unconscious, infantile sexual phantasies and impulses, and the question of how these powerfully charged emotions and the equally powerful defences against them find expression in adult roles, and how they influence the dynamics of sexual politics. This contribution is frequently missed or overlooked, and it will be explored here mainly through the work of Freud and Klein, as their contributions are regarded as central. Firstly, however, feminist cultural analysis must be understood in outline.

CRITIQUE OF PATRIARCHY

Feminism is essentially based on the realisation that gender divisions in culture are not fixed and immutable. Indeed they can be subverted, and the stereotypes of women as passive, submissive, masochistic and emotional can be changed. If women have been constructed on the negative, inferior side of the sexual divide, the side of man's repressed other, for whom *her* difference preserves *his* own natural superiority, then feminism radically contests this. It also cancels the idea of woman as naturally complementary to man, who is the norm, her role being to complete him.

As is well known, modern post-'68 feminism in Britain and America was deeply hostile to Freudian psychoanalysis. Feminists identified social, economic and cultural factors as the causes of oppression. Putting it simply, in the first instance, feminists sought to deny sexual difference and compete with men on equal terms politically, economically and culturally, concentrating on learning and developing a strong sense of identity, advocating androgyny and the wholesale rejection of an essential feminine ideal. They argued that we are all human beings and we should all have equal opportunities. There should be a sharing round of so-called male and female attributes. In practice, that meant that masculine values were held up as the norm for which both sexes could strive. For instance, Nancy Chodorow suggests that sexual inequalities would disappear if men learned more equal roles. Feminine traits were rejected and there was a lot of intolerance to any departure from this feminist norm.

More significantly and perhaps more interestingly, other feminists not only recognised sexual division but *celebrated* difference. French feminists like Julia Kristeva, Luce Irigaray, Hélène Cixous, Marguerite Duras, and American authors like Adrienne Rich and Mary Daly advocated separatism for women, struggling with the inadequacy of language structures based largely around male significations, which could not express the otherness of woman's experience, as essence beyond language, as beyond representation, as subversive of the symbolic order, as silence. Owens quotes Cixous: 'One is always in representation, and when a woman is asked to take place in this representation, she is, of course, asked to represent a man's desire' (1983, p. 344). Luce

Irigaray says: 'Investment in the look is not privileged in women as in men. More than the other senses, the eye objectifies and masters. It sets at a distance, maintains the distance . . . The moment the look dominates, the body . . . is transformed into an image' (Owens, 1983, p. 342). The prohibition bears mainly on woman as subject, for there is no shortage of images or representations of women. But in being represented, their subjectivity is negated, they are already spoken for.

Cixous and Irigaray have proposed an image of fluidity and multiplicity of feminine sexuality which is presented as another order, as something radically distinct from and freer than the dead weight of the father-ordained post-Oedipal female desire. Female desire arises directly from the body; its rhythms and its movements subvert the rigidities of the masculine order, reclaiming an alienated world of vital fullness and desire, in repudiation of a desire originating in a lack. Cixous and Irigaray set up a romance of femininity, flowing, subversive, reproachable, in place of the recognition of an alienated reality of fragmentation and loss. These post-Lacanian writers go on the offensive against Lacan and his scandalous statement in Seminar XX that 'Woman does not exist' suggesting that Lacanian theory is a defence against desire, a mode of repression that makes full desire impossible. As Cixous says: 'I don't want a penis to decorate my body with . . . living means wanting everything that is, everything that lives, and wanting it alive. Castration? Let others toy with it. What's a desire originating in a lack? A pretty meagre desire' (1976, p. 262).

Feminism is at the centre of the debate about patriarchy, the grand narrative or the metanarrative, and the whole question of image and representation in the Western tradition. It is about exposing a system of essential male power that authorises certain representations while blocking and invalidating others. The existence of feminism, with its insistence on difference, forces us belatedly into a reconsideration of the hegemony of the phallo-centric universe which was implicit in high modernism. Insofar as postmodernism deconstructs modernity, feminism gives it its political and radical edge and a new vigour, as distinct from the pessimism, the sense of irredeemable depletion and fragmentation in cultural theorists such as Jameson and Baudrillard.

If women are marginalised, they are now, as Owens says 'in the middle of the margin' of a new avant-garde. A specifically feminist practice is emerging in nearly every area of cultural activity, with the recovery and re-evaluation of previously marginalised or underestimated work. There is the elaboration of a feminist voice, insistent on difference as a testimony to the plurality of the times, which also includes many other marginalised groups – blacks, ethnic groups, gays, anti-imperialists, regionalists, ecologists and so on. But this forced coalition with 'others' suppresses plurality within the movement itself, as there are multiple internal differences within feminism – essentialist, culturalist, linguistic, Freudian, anti-Freudian. Furthermore, the emphasis on difference, plurality and otherness can relegate or re-marginalise women, assimilating them as merely an indicator, a marker, or another representation of difference.

So much for feminist theory, which can be seen as elitist and removed from the actual lives of women. Closer to home, we might say, it is indeed still women who support the family on an emotional level, who cope with most of the chores, who tie up the loose ends, who cope with the demandingness of young children – women now more than ever isolated on housing estates and depressed. In spite of equal pay legislation, women are still under-represented in top jobs, and over-represented in the low-paid, part-time, non-unionised, temporary sector, doing menial work such as cleaning and catering. Women are over-represented in the helping professions, facing all the demands and health problems of a culture in exhaustion and turmoil.

Coincident with the rise in consumer capitalism in the fifties and sixties went the universal degradation of women, who were used to sell every type of consumer product. In supplements and magazines, particularly pornographic magazines, women were used to satisfy the masturbatory fantasies of men to a greater degree than ever before in human history. Lessening of censorship and taboos generally led to ever more violent and explicit movies depicting violence and rape of women. And perhaps, most significant of all, are the violent attacks on women in the home, child abuse, and the attacks on women in the street and neighbourhood. It is not safe for women to go out alone at night, and into some areas, by day or night.

It is in the mass media where these feminist issues are being exposed and the war is being fought, where real fear and anger are expressed on a daily basis, in newspapers, magazines, on access radio, television and so on. This has become the greatest social issue, arguably taking more air-time, more column inches than any other. The social and cultural ramifications of this insistent political onslaught are obviously immense. We will touch on some of these later.

Finally, we might note that in a global context, men are indicted. In a world where men have held power, they are also held responsible for war, the military industrial complex, the worldwide wastage involved in the trade in arms – the old men who send the young men to war, the men who develop technology for mass destruction, who plunder (mother) earth's resources without concern for the environmental consequences. The feminist critique of millennia of patriarchy is complete.

CONSCIOUSNESS HAS BEEN RAISED

The result of the feminist cultural analysis has been the mass politicisation of women.[1] More than ever before women are aware of their secondary and inferior position. With the advent of mass education this century, women (and men) are no longer ignorant. Women's minds have become emancipated, their consciousness has been raised. Feminist literature developed a populist style in the late sixties, which was hardly surprising, considering the orgy of exploitation of women as sex objects in the previous decades. Germaine Greer's book, *The Female Eunuch*, was an instant success on its publication in 1970 and that of the paperback version in 1971. In roughly twenty years we have come to a position where many women are saying what originally the educated few had discovered. Teenage and younger girls are aware of sexism and challenge the assumed dominance of their brothers. What the earlier feminists fought for in terms of easier divorce, contraception and abortion are now accepted as natural and normal by their daughters. This new awareness amongst increasingly large numbers of young educated women in the better-off parts of the world is primarily an awareness that women have *choices*. They do not have to become wives and mothers. They do not have to look to men to find approval and affirmation. They can work and follow a career. They can work and share the child-rearing. Or they can choose to stay at home as they always were expected to, but on terms of equality with the man, no longer a slave but as an equal. Or women can choose to live without men, or live together, or live alone: the possibilities are endless. There is a trend towards choice, although many women still find many of these options closed for one reason or another.

MALE NARCISSISM SHATTERED

The relations between the sexes have become radically altered. How have men coped with the onslaught on their position? In earlier times men were 'gallant'. While having power over women and blacks, white males disguised their ascendancy by becoming their protectors. Women were put on pedestals while still being regarded as fair game amongst males together. But this attitude, seen psychoanalytically as a defensive reaction formation against sadism, did protect women and lessened the worst effects of male exploitation. With feudalism and paternalism now swept away the sexes stand face to face; their deeper motives can no longer be veiled by what are now considered to be hypocritical conventions and obligations. Progressives would not share Philip Reiff's view that 'hypocrisy is a precious thing in any culture. It may help build up those habits of avoidance that swerve us from honest but head-on collisions with one another' (1966, p. 49).

As women saw the connection between sentimental adoration and male supremacy, men could no longer claim to be their protectors; men's ascendancy became less and less tolerable, and men have been thrown into some confusion. Some men assert their domination more directly in violent fantasies, occasionally acting out these fantasies in rapes and muggings. One study showed that the treatment of women in films has increasingly shifted from reverence to rape. Men no longer treat women as ladies. Even women who want to retain the social conventions of the past find it increasingly difficult, because now they *should* regard themselves as 'liberated'. Faced with the challenge to their potency, men can become more 'macho' – an evocative word that has something to do with being mechanical and includes a cluster of attitudes and defences. Feelings are split off from thought and behaviour, and as a defence against weakness the man becomes more aggressive, more intrusive and more controlling. His concern with his performance completes the analogy with the machine. One study of children showed that when feelings of helplessness are close to the surface, little girls characteristically tend to cry and ask desperately for help, while little boys become angry and throw things.

Melanie Klein's view of a regression from 'whole objects' to 'part objects' is relevant here. Instead of treating women as people with needs and desires of their own (whole object relationship), men have regressed to seeing only 'tits, bums and fannies' (part-object relationship), which is the appropriate way for a little boy to use his mummy in the first year of life. This regression is characterised by extremes of feeling and less control of impulse. The massive hard-porn industry may defuse some of the intensity and needs of the regressed male, or it may focus attention and libido and facilitate regression. The violence behind the façade of machismo looks tough, acts tough, but in reality it is pseudo-strength, an omnipotent phantasy which for a time seems to offer triumph over the enemy. It is always in danger of collapse, and this is when the barely concealed violence erupts as a desperate last-ditch effort to hold on to some shred of self-esteem. Male narcissism, for so long based on the belief in men's superiority and up to now constantly bolstered by the women in men's lives, is now being threatened in a profound way. The loss of man's narcissistic supplies leaves him at the mercy of extreme narcissistic rage.

In describing the reaction of men to feminism, an increase in macho behaviour has been noted above. This is closely related to the suspected increase in impotence amongst men. Machismo is closely related to the underlying fear of impotence. But it is important to stress that the psychological nature of impotence has changed in this century. Respectable men sometimes experienced sexual or psychic impotence (no interest in sexual contact) with women of their own class. They dutifully had sex with their wives, but gained pleasure only by having sex with servants or prostitutes. Freud (1910) saw this as the classic Victorian split between sexual feelings and affection which related to the little boy's Oedipal situation with his mother. During this period of his development the boy has to renounce his urgent and possessive sensual love of his mother. He feels so guilty about these feelings and phantasies that he has to drive them underground. He retains in his consciousness only the purified form of love freed from the forbidden sexual overtones. He loves and respects his mother in an affectionate way. He marries a respectable woman on the unconscious model of his mother. He either has sex with her but cannot enjoy it because it brings up the Oedipal guilt, or there are times when the guilt is so strong he cannot have sex at all. The pent-up sexual energy is only permitted expression with degraded women who are totally unlike the respectable mother, or who represent the phantasies about the pre-Oedipal mother.

This form of impotence represents a clash of culture versus sexuality, where the former wins out. In the present day, cultural taboos and respectable conventions have been swept away, so the nature of male impotence has changed. Men used to complain that women were not sexual enough, but since the famous Masters–Johnson report on female sexuality depicted women as sexually insatiable, with their capacity for multiple orgasms, men feel themselves in the inferior position. Kate Millett (1971) wrote that while the male's sexual potency is limited, the female's appears to be biologically nearly inexhaustible. Now the emphasis is on performance, with biology certainly not in the man's favour. When the conventional woman fell in love, she longed to let herself go but could not conquer her ambivalence towards sex; whereas today's liberated woman exploits her sexuality in an uninhibited and calculating way. Freud's hysterics were emotionally involved yet tortured in their love-life, whereas modern women show a confidence, an independence of any restraint, a determination to get what they want without emotional commitments. This is aggressive sexuality, with hardness, with cold narcissism. Some feminists used the Master's report to attack the 'myth of the vaginal orgasm', thus asserting further women's independence from and superiority over men. Male impotence, now, therefore, is not about excessive guilt over sexual impulses and activity, but has much more to do with the power of woman's sexuality itself. The male fear arises not from the relatively advanced but conflicted derivatives of the Oedipal relationship, but from a far earlier and more primitive relationship with the mother. A terror is mobilised by the unconscious phantasy imago of a vastly potent mother in front of whom all baby boys feel helpless.

Feminism evokes these archaic memories in men, which form perhaps the greatest source of resistance to change towards a more equal society. The resentment of women against men has, as we have seen, a solid foundation in the reality, whereas the hostile attitude of men towards women sharing power seems strangely irrational, until one takes into account the deepest fears in men stirred by the image of the powerful mother. For men, therefore, the stakes are very high indeed.

Images of male impotence are widespread today. Recent recessions in the world economy have dramatically increased male unemployment – known to have a drastic effect on self-regard and self-respect. The loss of authority in home, school, and leadership generally in public life all bear witness to a loss of belief in the father. As Ihab Hassan says: 'The desert grows! God, King, Father, Reason, History, Humanism have all come and gone their way, though their power may still flare up in some circles of faith. We have killed our gods – in spite or lucidity' (1987, p. 203). Their deconstructed power still flares up indeed, in the alarming increase in degraded forms of authority, based on fear and terror – fear of impotence. The growth of paramilitary police forces, death squads, terrorist organisations, secret police and the like – macho authority divested of any moral framework or larger vision.

However, some men have responded to feminism in more or less rational and appropriate ways – appropriate from the feminist viewpoint, not necessarily from an overall viewpoint. They share power, they share child-rearing, domestic chores, money and decision-making and are not too confused about the radical change in role that this entails. They are living in a different way to their fathers.[2]

Jean Baker Miller makes the point that as men are brought up to be masters they have to break the connection with the mother. They are encouraged to become progressively separated from the matrix of life in order to become masters. Women have remained at the heart of the matrix. Men regard certain essential human qualities as weakness. They fear being vulnerable, passive, helpless. They fear homosexuality, which arouses a dread of being anally penetrated, which leaves them in the castrated, weak position. During psychoanalysis the greatest resistance encountered in men is their struggle against their passive or feminine attitude towards other men (Freud, 1937), that is, the ultimate fear of castration. The loss of the organ that symbolises mastery in the patriarchial order is the man's greatest danger. As psychoanalysis built on the work of Freud and came to understand the role the mother plays in the boy's development, a deeper fear emerged which relates to separation from the mother. The feelings that surround the separation from the mother are so conflicted and intense – essentially those of intense neediness and intense rage – that she is never *completely* left. Only the conscious split-off male ego believes he has left his mother. His potency is to an extent illusory; that is why he has to keep demonstrating it. To quote Susan Griffin:

> A man beats another man. And this act reverberates throughout our culture, in the literature of flagellation, in the myth of the hero and the warrior in imagined and real combat, in warfare. Men beating men in prisons, in police rooms, in bar-room brawls, in athletic events. It is always the most 'masculine' of men who involve themselves in these beatings. Because here is the same conflict, the same raging desire for the lost part of the self, the same denial returned as violence. For would a man, in beating another man, be wishing to turn him into a woman? . . . He brings this other man to the verge of tears, to trembling, and he has in this act, also brought himself to vulnerability. (1982, p. 152)

THE SHADOW SIDE OF FEMINISM

Centuries of oppression by men have involved women in a wholesale repression and denial of their aggressive impulses. Instead of the death instincts, as Freud postulated, being turned outwards in the service of self-preservation, too much death has remained within, specifically in women, who therefore have been forced to carry an unassimilable burden of rage that underlies depression, stress symptoms, masochism, hysteria and an often hidden but immense suffering.

But now, with the realisations brought about by feminism, aggression is potentially liberated, and turned outwards against men and patriarchy. It is men who are to blame. Men have created all the problems. A terrifyingly simple paranoid logic comes into play. Woman is idealised for her gentleness, her connectedness, her maternal strength in adversity, her long suffering, her power to create life itself; while man is condemned for his violence, his perversions, his separateness, his weakness, his narcissism, his irresponsibility, his murderous violence and rapacity. This split view is gaining emotional ground quite widely. Men and women are beginning to take seriously this kind of generalisation, which is an example of what Matte-Blanco (1976) refers to as symmetrical logic, the logic of the unconscious, where part stands for the whole (some men rape, therefore all men are bad), and affects reach towards infinity.

Woman finds intolerable and uncontainable her own de-repressed rage, accumulated over centuries. With the collapsing of time (characteristic of the primary process), this rage becomes potentially so intense that it has to be evacuated. This is an example of projective identification, where this raw destructive emotion is forced into the other sex, who then behaves unconsciously in accordance with the foreign body that he has been forced to take in, to introject. So we hear men feeling ashamed to be men, men taking on the image that is projected, men feeling like shit, men confused, men doing the things, acting out the demons that women accuse them of. How much of the increase in reported rape, for instance, is due to better public awareness of the seriousness of the crime, and how much is due to a real increase? There may be some element of men's concurring with the rage that I am suggesting has been projected into them, and indeed becoming *more* violent as a consequence.

Of course the reality of male oppression seems to provide ample justification for these projections and accusations. But the idealisation of woman and her goodness represents a massive denial, a loss of complexity, a loss of asymmetry and the capacity to differentiate, and further represents a totalisation and therefore an ignorance of the unconscious and of truth. So powerful is this denial that Estela Welldon, who works with female perversion (see Welldon, 1991), said that women who openly admitted and wanted help with their perverse behaviour towards their children, for instance, until recently were not taken seriously – another example of women not being taken seriously.

As a point of clarification, it is only the destructive rage that is felt to be unacceptable and split off from consciousness; other more sublimated forms of aggression are welcomed by the women's movement. There has been a growth in the development of courses and training for women in the areas of 'assertiveness' and 'empowering' and a variety of 'How to do . . . ' books that stress not feeling guilty when you say 'No'. But the dividing line between exploitation and assertiveness is a difficult one to draw. Retaliation for all the centuries of slavery, women feel, needs no explanation or justification, especially to men, as Erin Pizzey comments on a radio programme on the family: 'Women are furious, there is no doubt about that. Men who have been quite good fathers and husbands actually find themselves one day in a bed-sit in Fulham with the wife and children in the matrimonial home plus a third of his salary' (BBC Radio 4, 'The Family', introduced by Dr Antony Clare, 1986). She comments further that men of this present generation are having to face all the hostility of centuries of oppression. And frequently the men who are attacked are those who in many respects have accepted and acted upon the wishes of their women to have more equality. She says that the last one or two decades have been cataclysmic for the family and that we are now in a bad state of anarchy in the relations between the sexes. She blames the women's movement. It has achieved contraception, easier divorce, the 'right to choose' on abortion, and social security for women living on their own. This means, she says, that men are made virtually redundant.

The conscious rationale for women's fury against male-dominated society has been outlined above. It is now time to look for the unconscious infantile roots of this rage and to see precisely how unconscious phantasy adds fuel to the flames. Let us look in more detail at the aggression or violence aimed at men, the family and the system of patriarchy.

Freud's celebrated and much-criticised theory of penis envy still holds a central place in psychoanalytic thinking about women's psychology. In his last and arguably his most important article on femininity (1932), he points out that when the little girl notices by direct perception of little boys that she is castrated she has three choices with regard to her future psychosexual development. She can deny the sexual side of her life altogether and live a neurotic and inhibited life. She can turn towards her father in an attempt to get his penis and a baby from him and lead what is regarded as a normal life for a woman, now narcisisstically complete with her husband and her child, and choosing her husband on the model of her father. Or she can acquire a penis for herself by becoming a man and denying her so-called 'female role'.

Penis envy, put like this, does seem rather crazy and too reductive. To an adult mind, the thought that a little girl might worry about whether or not she has or will someday get a penis or grow one of her own seems fanciful. But the truth of these assertions becomes clearer when one considers a number of further points. The penis comes to be regarded not so much as an object in itself but more as a metaphor or symbol, to do with potency, strength and even magical powers. As children we all envy what the other has and we haven't got. It was Karen Horney (1933) who pointed out the little boys envy the mother's capacity to have children and feed them with her breasts – so-called womb envy and breast envy. Because man cannot have children and be creative in this enviable way, he develops technology as a substitute – intellectual creativity becomes his baby.

Furthermore, very small children misperceive the world in magical and frightening ways, so that parts of their bodies become invested with persistent and unaltered unconscious magical ideas, which later become manifest in psychoanalyses of children and adults. So, it is as if the little girl consciously and unconsciously feels, around the age of three to five, that she has been deprived. She gradually gains the impression that she has been made inferior to her little brothers. She feels deeply hurt and wounded and very angry towards her mother, who not only deprived her of the penis; now she remembers the frighteningly angry mother of earlier childhood whom she perceives as having denied her food and love and affection. It was this mother who took control of her body and wanted her to part with its precious contents during the toilet-training period. Perhaps it was this mother who took away her penis as a punishment for all the little girl's aggressive feelings. She feels deeply humiliated and hates her mother for all the wrongs she feels that her mother has visited upon her. In desperation she turns to her father and idealises him, his power and his strength. The possession of his penis will solve all her problems. She idealises his penis and deeply envies its magical powers. If only she had one she would no longer feel inferior, humiliated, hurt, bereft.

Her life can become a denial of this primary humiliation – a desire to get away from this terribly helpless feeling. She wants to get a man and have a child of her own – a demonstration of her own potency and creativity. Or she develops her so-called 'masculine complex' and becomes a man herself, turning her back on femininity and all its reminders of that helpless and wounded state. The significance of the penis and all that it represents in patriarchy is then secondarily reinforced in the growing girl, as it is the possessors of that penis who also have the power in the external world. So, on the one hand, the unconscious phantasies, and on the other, the realities of the external world, work together to intensify hostile adult attitudes which are based on the archaic and now unconscious penis envy.

Research has shown that the external world impinges on the personality of that of the growing girl (and boy) very early on, perhaps even within the first year of life.[3] At this early stage parents may treat little girls and boys differently. But to say, as many do, that it is simply conditioning that makes the little girl feel inferior is to miss a very important part of the equation. The conditioning operates on a rich and developing magical phantasy life, and that this inner world interacts with the outer world in a way that leads to mutual and sometimes destructive reinforcement.[4]

The Kleinians have deepened our understanding of envy as a destructive emotion. In her book *The Psychoanalysis of Children*, Melanie Klein makes this comment in relation to penis envy:

> The oral frustration she has suffered from her mother has stimulated all her other erotogenic zones as well, and has aroused her genital tendencies and desires in regard to her father's penis, the latter becomes the object of her oral, urethral, anal and genital impulses all at the same time. Another factor which serves to intensify her desires in this direction is her unconscious sexual theory that her mother has incorporated her father's penis, and her consequent envy of her mother.
>
> It is the combination of all these factors, I think, which endows her father's penis with such enormous virtue in the eyes of the small girl and makes it the object of her most ardent admiration and desire . . . it can also cause her to have intense feelings of hatred for having been denied the thing which she so passionately adored and longed for; and if she takes up the masculine position it can give rise to all the signs and symptoms of penis envy in her. (1932, p. 272)

The penis envy of which Freud spoke is now understood to be reinforced in its intensity by earlier deprivations by the mother. The all-powerful mother of infancy is perceived as having taken away *everything* from the little girl, including the father's penis. The envy of the penis is greatly reinforced by earlier envies – relating to the withdrawal of the breast at weaning, the taking away of the faeces and the urine during toilet training. Envy in this more primitive form is seen as the most destructive of all emotions. Klein (1957) saw envy as the first direct externalisation of the death instinct. Envy must be distinguished from greed and jealousy. Jealousy is related to rivalry in the Oedipal situation and is based on possessive love and the removal of the rival. Hanna Segal suggests that:

> Greed aims at the possession of all the goodness that can be extracted from the object, regardless of the consequences; this may result in the destruction of the object and the spoiling of its goodness, but the destruction of the object is incidental to the ruthless acquirement. Envy aims at spoiling the goodness of the object to remove the source of envious feelings. It is this spoiling aspect of envy which is so destructive since the very source of goodness the infant depends on is turned bad and good introjections cannot be achieved. (1973, p. 40)

Joseph Berke, in a similar vein, states that the envier uses projection destructively to spoil the object without procuring any advantage or material gain. He speaks of the newborn's 'inherent tendency to get very angry at the very existence of pain in himself and thrust it outside himself with a vengence in order to spoil and devastate a "world" which (from his point of view) caused him to feel so bad in the first place. Vengeful evacuation and malicious projection provide an operational definition of envy' (1985, pp. 171–2).

TURNING THE TABLES

If the above-mentioned psychoanalytic model of envy and penis envy contains truth, what light does it throw on the women's movement, women's place vis-à-vis men and the antagonisms between the sexes? Is there any evidence to suggest the hidden working-out of these unconscious and deeply repressed conflicts in the external world?

Many women internalise good relationships in childhood and the envious tendencies are therefore reduced because the good, helpful parents are already present within the personality. They do not particularly envy men and they are able 'to love and to work', to use Freud's criterion of health. Having children and being creative at work brings a woman deep satisfaction as a woman and as a person. There is no need to be envious because she has incorporated her father's potency and strength. She can use her aggression creatively and constructively in the world. In that world she feels herself to be psychologically equal to the man. And she can use her early close relationship to her mother – the model on which she becomes a woman – to face child-birth and child-rearing confidently. She will not envy her children because she got more or less enough love herself.

But for some women the hostility against men is quite plain to see. These women have turned the tables on men: for so long, they would argue, women have been redundant in the socio-cultural sphere, now the man is unnecessary. There has been a very dramatic rise in one-parent families in recent decades. The overwhelming majority of these are headed by women. Divorce rises by about 10 per cent per year and most divorces are initiated by women. Nine out of ten of those parents who leave the matrimonial home are male. And of all those parents who after separation adopt a visiting rather than a custodial role, half will have lost contact with their children after only two years – most of these will be fathers. The role of the father as one time bread-winner and supporter of the family has been reversed. His bread-winning function can be transferred to the state, making single-parent families more or less viable financially. Removed from the home, his contribution to the family will be taken from him anonymously through the tax system. The father's psychological contribution to the home has become marginalised, as if he himself were some kind of *impediment* to children's welfare, by making his sons too tough and brutal and by ignoring his daughters or sexually abusing them. It is amazing how readily men seem to have accepted this punishment, taking upon themselves the guilt and allowing themselves to be castrated. It is also true that many men absent themselves from the family and experience expulsion as relief.

There can be no doubt that men are being hounded in the media as rapists and sex abusers. There is no doubt that *some* men are rapists and sex abusers, but, as has been indicated above, these men have gross psychopathology. A recent television documentary on child abuse showed an adolescent daughter who had been abused by her father and had emerged through a therapy programme to become angry and confrontational towards her father. The first meeting between the two of them that had taken place for a number of years was now televised so the viewers could see the anger and cold hostility of the abused daughter. She told him that she never wanted to be so much as touched by him again. She had the power to send him to gaol and we were left in no doubt that she would use this power. She would never forgive him for what he had done. He sat there in the chair opposite. He was one of the sex abusers at the 'soft' end of the spectrum of abuse: that is, he had only abused one person and he did feel genuine guilt. He was a pathetic figure, now totally passive, in tears, apologising to his aggressive daughter, saying he did still feel terribly guilty and he didn't expect to be forgiven. The roles were totally reversed: she was the aggressive parent; he was the contrite and meek little boy. One can fully understand the girl's feelings: sex abuse is a crime. But the unstated implication of the painful encounter was that she was right. She must now publicly humiliate her father, as he had in private humiliated her. Like some Nazi guilty of war crimes he must be hounded for evermore.

Another man in the same programme who admitted to abusing his daughter and said he felt terrible remorse at what he had done was attacked by 'incest survivors' in the audience: 'How dare you let a man like this come on the programme and say he's sorry for what he's done . . . does he know what he's done? . . . does he really know the harm he has caused?' It seems as if death would be too good for these people. It makes no difference whether the sex abusers say they are truly sorry and really mean it, or whether they say they are sorry in order to get a lighter sentence or none at all; they are damned by the women whatever they do.

There is little mention and consideration given as to why certain men offend in these ways. The fact is that many of these men were abused as children – both physically and sexually. They suffered gross trauma as infants and have never been able to articulate the hurt. They now repeat with their own children what happened to them, possibly seeking some kind of closeness in the case of incest and revenge in the case of rape. As their own boundaries were invaded and shattered as children, so their own impulses know no bounds in later life. Violence and pornography in public life only serve to exacerbate the problem.

One last point that must be made about the absence or expulsion of the father from the home is the effect that this situation has particularly on the sons in the single-parent family. Far from having less of those violent attributes, they seem to have them in greater abundance. Boys need fathers. Numerous studies, quoted in Anderson and Dawson, suggest that 'there is an association between low paternal participation in child-rearing and aggressive behaviour' (1986, p. 46). And 'boys growing up in conditions of relative father absence are more likely to show violent and hyper-masculine behaviour. Assault and homicide are significantly higher in father-distant cultures' (p. 47). Eva Seligman describes 'the absent father syndrome as encouraging a mutually collusive embrace with the mother, nourishing a shared illusion of oneness, from which the developing child cannot extricate himself, living neither in, nor out of the womb, but wedged, so to speak, half-way, half-alive, half-born' (1985, p. 81). The hypermasculine behaviour of sons without effective fathers can be seen as the urgent attempt at extrication, a fight for life, against an unconscious backdrop of passivity, dependency – the allure and horror of the maternal collusive embrace.

Malan (1979), for example, summarises the experience of many psychotherapists and counsellors working with sons of absent or weak fathers. Without the presence of a real father, the son is left at the mercy of the omnipotent father, exposed to the extreme severity of an internal father imago, or an archetypal father, whose background terror is not mediated by the human presence of a flesh-and-blood father (see also Chapter 6).

We might imagine the son's unconscious thinking:

> The father whom I love and hate, but above all love, has abandoned me. I have driven him away, or I have killed him with my badness, and now there is only a hole, an absence. But I feel a nameless fatherness within me that is terrifying. At times, I feel he is killing me for my softness and my badness. I want to be strong like him. I will kill off all the feminine weakness, suffering and longing in the world . . . [5]

THE TRIUMPH OF 'MALE' VALUES

To explore further the ways in which these unconscious phantasies are expressed in the real world, we must turn our attention to the devaluation of motherhood. In the seventies, women were encouraged to take the class struggle out into the world of work. Laws against sex discrimination were passed and increasing numbers of women entered the professions and public life. The implication was that you were something of a cabbage if you stayed at home and looked after the children, when you should have been out fighting for your rights in the workplace. One of the consequences of this change in attitudes has been the dramatic fall in birth-rates in most advanced countries. There are other reasons for these falls, but one factor must be that having children or many children does hinder one's progress up the career ladder.

To be sure, this was a liberation and gave women a new sense of confidence. The balance was radically shifted away from mothering and towards careers. Women were having children later and having fewer of them, or not having them at all. In the unconscious of women the so-called 'masculine complex' solution to penis envy was favoured at the expense of the traditional route to fulfilment. Women realised that to compete with men they had to become just like them. They emphasised the clitoris in sexual intercourse, they became combative, status-orientated, active in pursuit of their aims – creators of image and power. The irony of this change is that these women were aspiring to just those values which feminism had so cogently exposed as being destructive. Those so-called male values that have been over-emphasised in European culture since the Reformation – the love of science and technical mastery, the one-sided emphasis on reason and logic, the abuse of power, the fear of the irrational and the inner world. And all this is happening at a time in world history when there is an increasingly widespread feeling that the instrumental view of the world has reached its ultimate limit.

The issue of abortion is a complex one beyond the scope of this chapter. But is it somehow symbolic of this shift in attitude? Abortion has always occurred, but never on the scale witnessed since the liberalisation of the abortion laws over twenty years ago. Some abortions will always be necessary, but the 'right to choose' lobby has elevated what was occasionally a tragic human necessity to the status of a political right. Whatever the Society for the Protection of the Unborn Child might say in their self-righteous and grossly idealising propaganda, abortion on demand is symbolic of a denial of the vulnerability and fragility so widespread in modern life.

THE THIRD POSITION

For many, this analysis of sexual division and conflict will seem too reductive – to say that for woman it is the return of the repressed, unconscious, envious strivings that make her attack men, and that for man his continued violent and resistant oppression of woman is in order to maintain some sort of increasingly imperilled potency. But both these strategies of managing strong emotions involve violent repudiations. And the damage that is being done to individuals, to relationships, to trust, to the family, to children is a cause of utmost concern. This is why we have outlined and emphasised so strongly, not only the unconscious causes, but also some of the *effects*, the casualties in this guerrilla war.

The psychoanalytic emphasis is always on the de-centred nature of the human subject. We have underlined this in various ways throughout this book. Psychoanalysis questions identity, and regards as illusory any totalised notion of the human subjectivity which is always present in political and ideological discourse.

With hindsight, we can say that the first-generation feminists, claiming economic, political and professional equality for women, implicated them too much in an incorporation into a phallocentric power structure. The second generation, emphasising separateness and difference, could tend too much towards the sectarianism and violence that the movement expressly opposes. There is a third way, informed by Kristeva's re-reading of Lacan. Lacan emphasised the lack, the division in the human subject, the absolute dominance of language and the division between the sexes. We have to assume a position, some position as man or woman; we must take sexual differentiation into account. This emphasis on the lack caused by castration has been strongly refuted by some of the second-generation feminists, as we have seen.

Kristeva's third way, while acknowledging the cut made by language and the symbolic, has also envisaged a pre-symbolic, an 'outside' to political discourse to paranoid, binary, symmetrical oppositions. This pre-symbolic has to do with the semiotic dimension of poetry and language corresponding to an experience with the mother. Lechte summarises Kristeva's position:

> The pre-symbolic, the semiotic domain came to figure within the very sphere of the Lacanian Name-of-the-Father where it was entirely

unrecognised. 'Chora', 'semiotic', 'negativity', 'heterogeneity' – 'music' ('ultimate position of meaning') – all form part of a vocabulary aimed at speaking what is unnameable and at the same time points to the name as 'legion': a vast plurality of names. The unnameable, heterogeneous element is called 'feminine' . . . To avoid psychosis, the feminine element (in men and women) needs to be inscribed within the symbolic order. (1990, p. 201)

This involves what Kristeva believes to be a necessary stretching and including of a hidden subjective potential, new ways of speaking in spite of the lack, in spite of not knowing, in spite of the necessity of assuming some position in relation to sexual difference.

Kristeva's evocation of the 'happy cosmopolitan' foreign not to others but more importantly to himself or herself, harbouring, not an closed essence, but a 'pulverized origin'; such a person, Kristeva suggests, 'transforms into games what for some is a misfortune and for others an untouchable void' (1988, p. 57). This strangeness to ourselves that psychoanalysis constantly evokes can be seen as a disaster, a catastrophe and an intolerable lack and acted on in violent terroristic ways, as we have illustrated above; or it may be seen as the ground for possibilities of a new transgressive subjectivity, the transcending of difference, involving 'aesthetic practices', confrontation with melancholy and suffering (the abject), and also an abundance of laughter and talk to ourselves and others.

5 CHILDCARE AND THE GROWTH OF APATHY

I: ANCIENT TO MODERN

In the next three chapters, we will be concerned essentially with the structuring and images of childhood during the modern period. If women indeed were 'spoken for', so were children. If children were at one time not seen or heard (they were not portrayed in medieval art until the twelfth century, and not shown on calendars until the sixteenth), now they have taken their place, problematically it will be argued, right in the centre of the picture. From being not depicted at all, or shown only as little adults or little men, they have become the focus of attention in the developed West, while in poorer areas of the world they still have a marginalised existence. Let us begin by reviewing the history of childcare in Europe.[1]

During the Middle Ages, very young children were hired out to other families as servants. They waited at table, made beds, accompanied their masters, essentially as apprentices. All education was carried out through apprenticeship. It was by means of domestic service that the master transmitted to a child – not his child but another man's – all the knowledge, practical skills, experience and human values that the master possessed. Children started their young lives in a different family to learn the good manners of a knight or the practicalities of a trade.

Transmission from one generation to the next was insured by the everyday participation of children in the lives of adults. Wherever adults were, there were children too, in trades, in crafts, in workshops, even in taverns of ill-repute. They learnt about life from intimate contact with adults of all kinds. Children thus escaped their own families. Their parents cared about them insofar as they were to make a contribution to the common task of the larger community – of the village, the farm, the courtyard, or the large house. Education was mediated and practised by means of treatises of etiquette and courtesy which gave detailed instructions on how to behave in every aspect of life, both practical and moral. Children were to be initiated into a life spent in social contacts and conversation all of which were governed by the strictest rules of conduct. Etiquette at mealtimes, where everyone's role was minutely defined, was particularly important. Mealtimes were an important social rite in which everyone had to take special care to behave properly in the interests of everyone else. All anti-social activities were to be curbed; one was to greet people correctly, not talk coarsely, be smart and clean, and not display negative emotions, because one was always in the midst of a large and exacting social network. There was no such concept or notion as 'privacy', as life was to be lived in a social milieu that denied any private space. So the training of the child through apprenticeship during the Middle Ages, and his or her initiation into social interaction, assumed great importance in the absence of schooling and the emphasis on community. The treatises on civility and courtesy were the guardians of the basic values of society and occupied the most central position in education, in complete contrast to today's more or less peripheral acknowledgement of 'good manners'.

During the fifteenth and sixteenth centuries a slow but gradual change was to occur in the type of care extended to children: namely the replacement of the apprenticeship system by the extension of school-based education, in the middle and upper classes at least. Schools were slowly becoming the normal instrument for social initiation. The pedagogues were concerned to isolate youth from what they regarded as the corrupt world of adults, and to give them a more theoretical education to replace the old practical forms of apprenticeship. Schools also facilitated a growing desire on the part of the parents to be in closer contact with their children. A major change was beginning to take place in that the family was beginning to centre itself on the child. No longer satisfied to send their children away for the duration of their childhood to serve some distant family, parents sought closer contact and were more concerned for their children's general well-being.

This radical shift of family sympathies towards their own children and their education occurred first in the middle classes. In the working class the apprenticeship system would continue down to more recent times. Among the aristocracy, the young nobles would do their tours of Italy and Germany and to foreign courts or houses in many countries to learn languages, good manners, noble sports. This was a continuation of the apprenticeship tradition. But by the seventeenth century this custom was beginning to give way to the more theoretical and specialised tuition in the academies.

This gradual extension of schooling applied at first only to boys of the middle classes. Girls at first did not go to school, apart from the few that went to little schools or convents. Most of them were brought up at home or with a neighbour or a relative. They would have to wait until the eighteenth or the early nineteenth century before schooling would be extended to them. There were, however, many criticisms of school-based learning. It was felt that schools were in the hands of pedants or moralists and that discipline was too strict. Children were now separated from their natural social environment and in danger of mixing in evil company or learning 'childish nonsense'. The large number of pupils in each class was considered to be an obstacle both to their studies and their morals. It was widely felt that you could learn more by living in the heterogeneous social environment than by any amount of time spent in studying theoretically from books and masters.

In the seventeenth century, the manuals of etiquette still occupied a central place in terms of social adaptation, but now contained more instruction on how children should behave in school, and how parents should behave towards their children. For instance, parents are told when to punish children, when to start teaching them their letters, and at the end of each day to review what went on in school and consider the nature of any offences committed. If these were bad, such as blasphemy, theft or falsehood, hurling a foul insult at a maidservant or valet, or being stubbornly disobedient, the punishment was to be a birching. Parents were told to adjust themselves to their children's difficulties with learning, to be understanding and to set a good example, to keep an eye on their children's friends and to avoid romances which 'poison the soul'. There was advice on choosing schools and choosing a trade. In short, there was a recognition of the increasingly child-centred nature of the slowly emerging modern family, and a concern for the child's welfare and needs.

This tendency of the early modern family to withdraw into itself was at odds with the overwhelming density of the social network and obligations to the community. Even at the end of the seventeenth century, nobody was ever left alone. Isolation was virtually impossible. The demands of a man's various relationships never left him on his own. This traditional sociability and the development of the modern family as a more isolated unit persisted side by side for a time. The combination was particularly to be found in the houses – big houses – of city notables and others, around whom developed a whole complex social world.

It is important to examine more closely this social matrix by way of comparison with the present day. The houses of the rich were occupied by the family and a whole population of servants, employees, clerics, clerks, protégés, apprentices and so on. There was a constant flow of visitors who came not only on a friendly basis but also on a professional basis. Business was carried on in the same rooms in which people lived their everyday lives. Rooms in these houses had no specialised functions, except for the kitchen. People slept in the rooms where they ate, lived and received visitors. Beds were put up and folded away as necessary. Many people slept in one room and all the rooms on any one floor were intercommunicating. There was a complete social mix, with the sons of the family playing and working with the servants, serving at mealtimes, carving the meat and pouring the wine. They were taught the same rules of etiquette and given the same religious instruction. These houses were intensely social places with a dense network of interdependent relationships which had not yet become compartmentalised. They represented the focal points of life in the community.

Beside these big houses of the rich and important there were tiny houses, comprising only one or two rooms, in which a married couple and only a few of their younger children would live. In the country, one of perhaps the two rooms would be reserved for animals. These houses were hovels in which the very poor could not survive as a family, the children being sent at a very early age to live as apprentices in the houses of the more wealthy.

By the eighteenth century, the family was beginning to hold

society at a distance. Various aspects of life were becoming more separated. The family was becoming more private and more centred on the children. Visitors were not so welcome at any hour of the day or night as they had been previously. One had days when one was 'at home'. New codes of manners emphasised the need to respect the privacy of others. Older customs and ceremonies were shorter and even meals took less time. There was more emphasis on health and hygiene and in particular concern over the health of children. The use of nicknames for children became more common, reflecting a closer bond between parents and children. Parents could no longer seek consolation in the loss of one child by having another; children became more precious and irreplaceable. Health and education became the chief preoccupations of these modern middle- and upper-class parents.[2] The family became more cut-off and opposed to the larger community. With the emergence of the modern family came the more modern type of house with its more specialised rooms. There were no longer beds all over the house, but bedrooms, rooms in which one dined and rooms in which one received visitors. Rooms opened separately onto corridors and it was no longer necessary to go through one room to get to another. Servants were kept at a distance to ensure further privacy.

Naturally these changes towards the modern family occurred at first only in the highest strata of society – the vast majority of people still lived like the medieval families. Since the eighteenth century the modern family ideal has gradually percolated to lower social strata. But many factors, such as late marriage, the difficulties in finding employment, the necessary mobility of journeyman labourers and the traditions of apprenticeship, have been obstacles to the total adoption of the modern family way of life down to quite recent times.

In an attempt to summarise how the related concepts of the family, the child and child-rearing practices have changed from medieval to the beginning of the modern period, it is important to pick out some key themes. Firstly, children have emerged as persons in their own right from their almost complete obscurity during the Middle Ages. Children were seen to have specific needs, the most important of which was to go to school and be educated, frequently in the most strict, moralistic and punitive ways. There was also concern for their general well-being and health and their future careers. Childhood became recognised as a transitional state between infancy and adulthood, in which segregation from the corrupt world of adults was essential. The middle-class modern family separated itself off from the teeming life of the community to devote itself to the children; it became more private, more inward-looking, and it stands accused of destroying the old heterogeneous sociability of medieval society.[3] Increasingly isolationist, it also became more materialistic and class-conscious, wanting separate schooling, separate housing and the freedom to pursue individualistic aims.

II: POPULARISING THEORIES ON CHILD-REARING

THE STATE'S CHILD

It is not until the twentieth century that we begin to see a plethora of popularising psychological theories on child-rearing and an anxious concern to give the best to one's child. By this time agencies outside the family had begun to take over functions formerly fulfilled within the family. Before the First World War, there was already an extensive literature on childcare, much of it medical in tone. Its primary concern was for physical survival, but already there was discussion on the social and emotional needs of children. Women's magazines had already begun to run articles and correspondence on childcare. More consumer goods were being aimed at children. With fewer children per family, homes were less overcrowded and there was more time for individual affection and the giving of presents. In Britain, children were protected by law in the Children Act of 1890 and imprisonment of children was abolished.

The state was becoming much more involved in the socialisation of the young. Organised youth movements grew, encouraged by governments, voluntary societies and the churches. It was around the turn of the century that the concept of 'adolescence' became firmly established and the division made between 'delinquent' and 'disciplined' youth. The felt need to occupy children's free time constructively resulted in the increased popularity of the Scout movement and the Girl Guides among middle-class families in particular. Ill-discipline and 'rowdyism' were already problems between the wars, with numbers of young people who had money and who were without family responsibilities. There was a perceived need to channel their energies: from the Right there was concern about 'national efficiency' and imperial decline; from the Left, humanitarian and social concern led to a network of clubs and organisations aimed at youth.

Children were being seen more and more as an asset of the state and less and less as the property of the parents. Child socialisation was conceived to be far too important to be left to parents. Doctors, psychiatrists, experts in child development, marriage counsellors, leaders of public opinion and others in what we might now call the 'helping professions' all subscribed to the same view: parents were too narrow, too individualistic, too class-bound, to facilitate the optimum development of their offspring into co-operative, hard-working citizens.

Science, and particularly the psychological and social sciences, were becoming important authorities. Considering child-rearing alone, we find that expert opinion evolved through many conflicting stages in its exhortation to parents, each new fashion claiming the scientific high ground.

THE RIGIDLY CONTROLLED CHILD

During the twenties and thirties, behaviourism held sway. In 1928 John B. Watson published his influential book *The Psychological Care of Infant and Child*, in which he strongly argued that parents should take a direct and manipulative control of their children's environments. Counteracting the progressive theories of John Dewey, who advocated letting the hidden possibilities and potentialities unfold within the child, Watson felt that there was no 'within' to develop. He was radically environmentalist in his approach: all that is necessary is to control the child's environment so that its conditioned reflexes develop appropriately. One should try and minimise inappropriate emotional responses: avoiding loud noises which would over-stimulate the fear responses; allowing children to wear loose clothing to minimise rage responses; and, most importantly, not stimulating love responses when the child is trying all the while to become self-reliant. He wanted children to be treated as young adults. Parent–child contacts should be strictly regulated. Perhaps a kiss at bedtime was in order, but he abhorred the coddling of children when they had slipped and hurt themselves. Expressions of parental affection were to be limited to 'shaking hands with them in the morning', or perhaps 'a pat on the head when they have made an extraordinarily good job of a difficult task' (Watson, 1928, p. 82).

Doctors of the time stressed the need for strict feeding schedules and warned against maternal overprotectiveness. The old adage that 'mother knows best' was radically undermined by the belief that science had proven mother love to be inherently dangerous. The young mother's confident belief that she knew 'naturally' what to do for her children was revealed by professionals as ignorance and complacency. Coupled with this, the new understanding was that what the mother did do in relating to her children was profoundly important for their character development and the future psychological health of her children. It is not hard to imagine how deeply insecure these mothers were to become, in awe of the burgeoning medical and psychiatric establishment.

During this early twentieth century, motherhood was attaining the status of a vocation. Being a mother was no longer a blind biological and social inevitability. Developments in contraception meant fewer and fewer unwanted pregnancies, and therefore more time to devote to fewer children. So becoming a mother became a less automatic and much more self-conscious and serious activity.

But the control of children at this time went to something of an extreme in the early decades of this century.[4] The success of the industrial revolution and of science and technology led to a widespread feeling that progress could only go onwards and upwards. Science seemed to hold the key, so child-rearing must be based on sound technical principles. Industrial production demanded regularity, repetition and scheduling; parents must subject their children to the same kind of systematisation as managers demanded of their workers on the production line. It was schedule the child or spoil the child. Parents were advised: 'Never give a child what it cries for, let it cry out and break the crying habit.' Babies under six months were never to be played with, for it was supposed to make them nervous and irritable.

Never, it could be argued, was there more emphasis on control in regard to cleanliness. The use of laxatives and enemas was encouraged to induce regularity of bowel function in children of all ages. Regularity of bowel function attained a moral status in such phrases as 'cleanliness is next to godliness', and constipation was a sign of impurity which would encourage masturbation. Holding onto faeces was seen as a way of spiting mother and withholding and was to be punished with a soapy solution of glycerine as a suppository. Regularity in bowel function bespeaks regularity and cleanliness in the rest of life. But one could go even beyond enemas to irrigation. This was regarded as a valuable treatment for the removal of poisonous wastes from the intestines. The baby is placed on a plastic sheet and six or more inches of tube are passed into the bowel and a flow of soapy water is used to hose out the child. Detailed instructions, together with pictures, appear in Josephine Baker's book *Healthy Babies* (1920).

'Bad habits' also came under strict controls. Nail-biting, masturbation and thumb-sucking were the most frequently targeted and ingenious strategies were devised for stopping them. Circumcision was practised so as to prevent masturbation and some doctors claimed it as a cure for other ailments. To stop thumb-sucking, you could sew up a child's sleeves, use bitter substances on the fingertips, tape the arm to the side, put on an aluminium glove designed for the purpose. But masturbation was seen as the worst habit of all, to be broken at the earliest opportunity. Mechanical restraints were advised for infants, but not regarded as suitable for older children. Masturbation was variously associated with nervousness, lack of self-control, impairment of general health, lowered moral sense, perversions, insanity and so on. There was no scientific basis for these assertions and no effort was made subsequently to establish any such basis, as psychological science in the next decades switched interest to psychometry.

The problem with the so-called bad habits of the young child was not only the perceived harm that they did to the child itself, but more importantly the evidence of a wilful and spiteful spirit that they revealed to the mother. Seeking medical advice was often stressed. The mother was failing in her task of regulating the child and needed help from the experts.

The ideal of the perfectly functioning child in the image of the smoothly running machine which so fascinated the Victorians was given a further boost by Darwin's discoveries, which were becoming popular at the beginning of this century. The young science of genetics was also to become influential. The creation of the perfect child required the bringing together of perfect parents. Some parents should never have children if they carried some serious hereditary taints, and *Mothercraft Manual*, an influential magazine of the time, carried a handy list of 'genetic defects'. Parents were encouraged to go through courses of training to get themselves into the best physical and spiritual condition before having children.[5] Not only society as a whole, but also the individual family unit, which was the functional unit of social and economic Darwinism, would be strengthened and perfected. Each family had to struggle as a unit in a competitive world. Therefore each child was to be pure, unspoiled, moral and wholesome, and would naturally develop into a perfect adult. Society itself would be transformed by its own children.

This essentially behaviourist experiment in social engineering was the first systematic attempt to treat children as objects of study and control. If taken seriously – and such methods were widely disseminated – it meant that children's fundamental human needs were to be deliberately neglected. The insides and outsides of their bodies were to be subjected to rigorous control. Watson's dogma, which ran counter to all received wisdom, was that you 'shouldn't play with your baby'. The dire psychological consequences of such an approach will be discussed later.

THE UNRESTRAINED CHILD

Watson's concepts continued to have influence, but during the thirties and forties the shift in emphasis among some theorists at least was to the opposite extreme. The writing of Freud and the neo-Freudians was popularly misunderstood and misinterpreted as advocating the wholesale lifting of external constraints on behaviour. Liberal and progressive educational methods were becoming known. A.S. Neill's 'Summerhill' school opened in 1921. Dartington Hall was founded in 1926; it was coeducational and pupils lived in rooms instead of dormitories. It too was run on progressive lines. There was Bembridge School (1919) on the Isle of Wight, Rudolf Steiner's Wynstones and Michael Hall, and Bertrand Russell and his wife ran Frensham Heights from 1927 to 1943. While these experiments represented only a tiny fraction of even the private sector of British education, they were very influential in advocating the liberaton of children from pointless discipline, encouraging freedom and choice in all matters, allowing character to develop from within, and permitting openness in sexual matters. Finally, the influence of mass aspirations towards social respectability and conformity which led to a great pressure on working- and middle-class youth to gain badges and symbols of status – the school uniform, the first suit, medals, certificates and so on – inevitably brought a reaction.

Love, which heretofore had been the great danger, was now seen as absolutely essential. Children must be made to feel wanted. Everything was to be geared to the child's needs. All the schedules were given up in favour of 'feeding on demand'. A happy and a free child would become 'self-regulating'. The controlled child was unhappy, alienated, self- and other-hating, unspontaneous, mechanical, uncreative and neurotic. Children must be allowed to find their own way and do things in their own time, free from parental strictures. The central belief was that, given freedom, a child would mature and become a self-confident adult *without* inner conflict and anxiety. To quote A.S. Neill: 'We should allow children freedom to be themselves. In order to do this we have to renounce all discipline, all direction, all suggestion, all moral training, all religious instruction . . . All that is required was what we had, a complete belief in the goodness of the child has never wavered; it rather has become a final faith' (1962, p. 20).

Neill was a close personal friend of Wilhelm Reich, who for many was the prophet of the new liberation. Reich had developed a unique and personal blend of Freud and Marx, according to which modern civilisation is founded upon sexual repression, which begins in infancy with the authoritarian bourgeois family. Repression results in blocking of sexual energies and an inhibition of the capacity to experience orgasm. The resulting defensive psychological structure is manifested psychosomatically in tension in the body and what Reich (1927–33) called 'character armour'. These anti-sexual pressures are maintained in the patriarchal family, which is held together not by love but by the repressive use of power by the father. Patriarchal societies use this power to produce a submissive population capable of rebelling and revolution.

Reich had developed a whole world view which clearly implied that the lifting of sexual repression would end suffering and misery. Allow self-regulation and abolish sexual frustration and mental health will follow on naturally: duty will be replaced by enjoyment of work; alienation replaced by a unity of nature and culture, love and work, sexuality and morality.

Few parents went so far as the Reichians in giving freedom, but permissiveness was here to stay. During the sixties, the popularisation of Reich and anti-authoritarian sentiments generally by such people as diverse as Alexander Lowen, Ronald Laing and Herbert Marcuse further underpinned a radically child-centred approach to parenting.

THE REACTION – PARENTS MUST SET LIMITS

But permissiveness soon produced a reaction, for a number of reasons. First, it was unrealistic to expect parents to give all freedom to the child and reserve none for themselves. Second, parents began to worry that they were not passing on traditions and values which they themselves had been taught as children. Some of these values they felt needed to be inculcated. Third, some children of permissive parents grew up to be overly demanding, tyrannical and self-centred. Other parents felt they had failed their children, but did not know why they had failed or what to do about it.

In 1946, Benjamin Spock published his book *Baby and Child Care*, which went on to sell over twenty million copies. Mistakenly understood as an advocate of permissiveness, Spock is one of its critics. In a letter to the reader of his book he stresses the need for children to be taught to be involved in the community. Harking back to a much earlier tradition, he says, 'trust your own instincts . . . what mothers and fathers instinctively feel like doing for their babies is usually best after all . . . better to make a few mistakes from being natural than to do everything letter perfect out of a feeling of worry' (1946, p. 17). He speaks of 'moderate strictness' and says parents should require good manners, prompt obedience and orderliness. He speaks of acquiring convictions and seeking fulfilment in the service of others. He is aware too of the needs of parents, particularly in the face of the exaggerated emphasis on the need of the child. There is a danger in being too conscientious and giving all to the child; it leads to resentment of the role and of the child itself, who after all didn't ask for so much love. A balance of needs is required. And parents should expect something from their children: 'not spoken thanks for being born or cared for – that's too much – but consideration, affection and willingness to accept the parent's standards and ideals' (p. 31).

There was an awareness at this time of just how much parents' confidence in their ability to raise children had been demolished and some experts had noted how much hostility there was from parents towards family experts and counsellors. Anxious and confused parents with little authority left to impart to their children became an easy prey for a huge growth industry of advertising and consumer goods aimed at persuading young mothers to 'do right' by their children. Being a good mother became closely identified with the clean, bright, sparkling house, the right kinds of food, vitamin supplements, toothpastes, mouthwashes, not to mention the right toys and educational accessories and encyclopaedias.

Although there was a belated recognition by psychologists and paediatricians of the confusion they had wrought and an acknowledgement that the notion 'the child can do no wrong' had gone too far, and that parents must be able to say 'No', there was still a large question mark placed beside the competence of parents. They were now being exhorted to be more prohibitive and to set limits, while at the same time being given dire warnings of the irreparable harm done to children who are not brought up in love and security. Parents' 'uninformed impulses' have to be 'examined critically' for their hidden motives for being a parent. It was clear, abundantly clear, that it was the parents who needed educating. A half-baked attempt by the psychiatric establishment to bolster parental confidence had gone full circle to the perennial theme of parental inadequacy and ignorance. This was after all *The Century of the Child* (the title of a book published in 1909 by Ellen Key, on social improvement), so the parents had better learn how to adapt to the child.

'UP-FRONT' PARENTS AND CHILDREN

Since the critique of permissiveness had failed to restore parental confidence, it soon developed into a new fashion which claimed to bridge the generation gap and to be neither permissive nor authoritarian, but *effective*. The new method, which is derived from principles of 'non-directive counselling', is called Parent Effectiveness Training (PET), and was first introduced in the United States back in the fifties. It is about clarifying communications between parents and children – communications of feelings. Feelings are all-important. The permissive parent felt he or she had to hide negative feelings lest they damage the child psychologically, while the authoritarian parent hid both positive and negative feelings under a cloak of hectoring and criticism. The suppression of the full range of feelings was what was limiting effective communication. Parents are now required to be 'authentic' and 'spontaneous', no longer hiding behind a role. 'Being up-front' and 'getting in touch with your feelings' are part of the sloganising and the attempt to popularise the new vogue. This is essentially a self-help therapy on the side of the client against the medical experts. It is practice much more than it is theory. It is fundamentally democratic – the family has become a democracy – we are all equal.

Thomas Gordon's book, *How to be an Effective Parent* (1970), was an outgrowth of PET schools for parents. In it he analyses how we encode our messages to each other rendering real communication unlikely. If a child does something which annoys the parent, the parent should express annoyance instead of lecturing the child about its bad behaviour. Similarly, if a child expresses feelings about school for instance, the parent should not try to assess his or her accuracy in judging the school, but merely indicate to the child that he or she understands the child's feelings. Gordon encourages parents to use the simple and effective methods used by professional counsellors to elicit feelings. Send 'I-messages' instead of 'You-messages'. For instance, unacceptable behaviour by the child usually ends in the parent's sending a 'You-message', like: You stop that; You are acting like a baby; You are a pest, and so on. But when a parent tells a child how his behaviour is making her *feel*, the message turns out to be an 'I-message', like: I can't rest when I have someone crawling over my lap; I get angry when I see my kitchen dirty again, and so on. The 'You-message' does not communicate the parent's real feeling of tiredness or annoyance. Consider another example given by Gordon. The family is going on a long journey and the children in the back of the car are fighting and crying and making the journey very difficult. Eventually the father pulls off the road and stops the car. Instead of sending a 'You-message' to the effect that they should have more consideration, or that they could cause an accident, or that they should grow up and behave, he sends an 'I-message': 'I just can't stand all this noise and jumping around. I want to enjoy my holiday, but damn it, when there is noise back there, I become nervous and hate driving' (Gordon, 1970, p. 140). The children are startled and say so. They thought he could take it! The mother later reports that the children were much more considerate and cut down their horseplay. With the 'I-message' and the direct expression of feeling, the father had got across his communication very effectively.

In another example, the mother of an adolescent girl was up until 1.30 a.m. waiting for her daughter to arrive back from a party. They had originally agreed she would be back at midnight. When the daughter did finally arrive home, her mother, who was trying to communicate in the PET way, said: 'I'm angry with you; I'm really upset with you for keeping me awake . . . you had me worried sick.' Her instructor in PET was quite pleased, but asked her what was her *initial* feeling on seeing her daughter arrive back. This, they agreed, could have been communicated: 'Oh, Linda, thank God you're home safe. I was so afraid you'd been in an accident.' And Linda might have replied: 'Gosh, mum, you *are* glad to see me, aren't you?' Here Gordon makes the very valid point that parents often miss opportunities for being honest with children about their positive and loving feelings. Feelings such as anxiety, worry and hurt can quickly convert to anger. We prefer to feel angry than remain in the relatively vulnerable position of feeling hurt. He says: 'Eager to teach our kids a lesson, we miss golden opportunities to teach them far more fundamental lessons. For instance, that we love them so much, that it would hurt us terribly if they were injured or killed' (p. 135).

Gordon goes into the whole question of parental power, authority and influence. These only work when the parent is bigger than the child or when the parent can use effective sanctions. As soon as the child becomes less dependent on parental security the parental power-base is undermined. Gordon is critical of parents who feel they must influence their children in ways considered desirable by 'society' and feel that this is in the child's best interests. He poses the question: 'Who is to decide what is in the best interests of society? The child? The parent? Who knows best? . . . there are dangers in leaving the determination of "best interest" to the parent' (p. 195). Furthermore he regards the home as one of the last bastions of power, and urges parents to 'search for creative new non-power methods', because ultimately power doesn't work. He then goes on to talk about the 'No-Lose' method for resolving conflict, which is about negotiating with the children over important mutual decisions. The parent–child relationship is now to be modelled, not on the old power structure, but on the consultant–client relationship. The parent-cum-consultant *shares* his or her knowledge and experience with the client, who has the responsibility for accepting or rejecting the information presented. Normally consultants offer the information only once: they don't nag the clients until they accept it: And Gordon warns: 'Today's youth are discharging their parents – informing them that their services are no longer wanted because few parents are effective consultants to their children . . . parents are guilty of the "hard-sell". No wonder that in most families children are desperately saying to their parents, "Leave me alone. Stop nagging me". . . ' (p. 274).

It is clear that in PET, parents are being asked to abdicate authority over their children for two reasons. First, because authority in the sense of power, force, coercion, is immoral, and, second, because it doesn't work. If you cannot persuade your children to stop smoking, taking drugs, mixing with undesirable friends and so on, if they continue in spite of your advice, then 'you have no feasible alternative but to give up – to accept what you cannot change'. Parents are reduced to informative (and only sometimes!) by-standers, who are encouraged to express their impotent rage at what their children sometimes do, but have little other function than to supply information, express opinions and in other ways treat their children as equals. Gone is the common sense view that children need to be protected from the emotional cul-de-sacs in which they can get trapped – the preoccupation with one single activity to the exclusion of others. Gone also is the duty that parents have felt to pass on the cultural heritage in such a way that children want to become involved with the community and give service. Yes, the parent can pass on this *information*, but if the child on an emotional whim decides not to be interested, there is nothing the parent can do. This means the collapse of parental guidance on the understanding that the child is autonomous. No longer, it seems, are parents to take care of children, as this would be seen as at best a use of benevolent power to enforce parental wishes. No longer can parents and presumably grandparents instruct the child in the ways of the world, or in ethical values which transcend both parent and child. Parents are left helpless and if they persist they are warned that they might be made redundant.

It cannot be claimed, as some PET advocates do, that PET is neither authoritarian nor permissive, for this method of child-rearing (although that term does not mean much in this context) is permissive of children *and* their parents. Both are free to do their own thing, for neither is responsible for the other. Parents are for the first time let off the hook. If their children's rights involve free choice and equality, how can parents be expected to be held accountable in any realistic way for what they do? Of course PET trainers will tell you that the greatest resistance they encounter in 're-educating' parents involves their clinging onto power and responsibility. They will tell you that it is amazing how these old habits die hard.[6] Everyone is liberated from guilt and obligation. We are autonomous, we are individuals. We do things if we want to do them and if we choose to do them, not because someone tells us to do them. This holds true for the children and the parents. Parents, some parents perhaps, may have a slight edge on knowledge, experience, reality, but it is only marginal. In fact in many cases the parent can learn more from the children. So now perhaps we have come to the ultimate confusion: we have legitimised in a theory what in an earlier time and age might have been appropriate to a rebellious adolescent – overthrow the parents and what they stand for; help yourself; choose yourself; be free and live in the here and now . . .

III: THE PSYCHOLOGICAL REPERCUSSIONS DISCUSSED

By the eighteenth century we are beginning to see the break-up of the old complex heterogeneous social network of the community and the emergence of the 'modern family'. We see the separation of children from the world of adults, partly as a matter of policy and partly because many work processes were being taken out of the home. The industrial system was beginning to monopolise production. The net result of these changes was that work – in the widest sense of the word – was becoming less and less visible to the child. When children were apprentices they were surrounded by adults and adult activities the whole day round; when they later went to school and work became done more and more outside the home, their contact with adults became more restricted. Consequently it became more difficult for children to form strong psychological identifications with their parents and other significant adults.

It is by means of various identifications that we grow and develop normally. When a child identifies with an adult, he or she takes on, mainly unconsciously, the qualities and strengths of that person. Furthermore, the presence of these figures now *within* his or her psyche make for confidence and stability and enable the initiation of the child quite naturally into the social matrix. Of course there are bad identifications as well as good ones, but where there is a variety of adults some good figures can be internalised.

As an apprentice (from about the age of seven) the child, now regarded as an adult, would never have been separated from the world of adults. But as the old social world began to break up, work began to be separated from the rest of life. Fathers could no longer work at home and teach their children the skills of their trade. Less and less would children be automatically in the presence of adults working, unconsciously and naturally absorbing the adult world.

As the modern family developed and life became more private, children were more cared for and worried over. Identification with *parents* would have become much more important. One might postulate that psychologically life was becoming more claustrophobic. Any mental pathology on the part of the parents would be transmitted to the children, with less chance of dilution from the close proximity of other adult figures. School classes were very large and the teachers were often excessively moralistic and pedantic, making further bad identifications a real possibility.

As the status of children changed and their basic human needs for health, nutrition and parental attention and concern were at last recognised, there may have been a corresponding increase in the harshness of the super-ego. The super-ego is that part of the personality that attacks and condemns and brings about feelings of guilt and remorse. It is formed partly as a result of bad identifications. So the emergence of the modern family may have coincided paradoxically with *more* division within the personality. The price of increasing individuality and privacy was a bad conscience.[7]

It was just this division within the personality that Freud explored at the end of the last century. He discovered while working with hysterics that there was a split within their personalities. Some forbidden but sexually exciting idea was held in repression and out of consciousness because it was totally unacceptable to the adult personality. The energy associated with the repressed idea was 'converted' into a physical symptom. Once the forbidden ideas could be brought into consciousness the conversion symptoms disappeared. Freud was making sense of the conflicted and guilt-ridden personality of the wealthy Viennese at the turn of the century.

The repression of sexual and other bodily functions we can now see resulted from the excessive regulation and control of babies and children, and led to the neurotically disturbed personality of the early part of this century and the last. As we have seen, the need for regulation and domination of the human personality was regarded as an essential part of nineteenth-century capitalism. The psychological implications of the unholy alliance of science, technology and capitalism and the subjugation of human needs to the overwhelming demands of industrial production were very significant.

Freud (1908) and Abraham (1921) describe the 'anal character' (see also Brown, 1959). This is a complex formation which crystallises around the toilet-training period in infancy. The demands of the mother for cleanliness and regularity in bowel function lead to a battle for control of the child's body, which the mother must win on the outside at least. The child becomes obedient, clean, submissive, well mannered, gentle and to all appearances a little adult. On the shadow side of this personality are more sinister traits which are always in danger of breaking through. The hidden defiance against the mother issues in a stubbornness and refusal to co-operate. The child was taught to deliver the faeces, but retains a secret desire to withhold them. This leads in later development to a tendency to hoard property. The accumulation of money and property and the reluctance to let it go were hallmarks of the capitalist mentality. The child can make a virtue out of necessity and decide that it is good to be clean and orderly. He becomes proud of himself. But this love of regularity and routine can degenerate into pedantry. He develops a bureaucratic attitude, a desire to control others, to do things in *his* own time, and a love of rules and orderliness for its own sake. The obsessional-compulsive personality with its mechanical orderliness on the outside and its repressed anal proclivities within was the result of the interplay of Victorian capitalism and the stringent child training required, so it was believed, for the production line. This is another example of the personality deeply divided within itself, investigated and explained by the early psychoanalysis.

By the early twentieth century, the refining of methods of child and infant training along the lines of the new science of behaviourism made for a quantum leap in our desire for the 'perfect' child. The essential change was that now children were to be treated as *objects* of scientific study, and therefore parents should view them, in effect, as if they had no inner world. The psychological consequences of this new approach resulted in the 'alienated' self. While seemingly perfectly adjusted on the outside, the real humanity of a person was lost in a world of quantities and abstractions. As Erich Fromm pointed out: 'All these people become so many pieces in a gigantic machine which must be controlled, whose effects must be calculated; each man eventually can be expressed as an abstract entity, as a figure . . . ' (1956, p. 112). An alienated person 'does not experience himself as the active bearer of his own powers and richness, but as an impoverished "thing", dependent on powers outside himself, unto whom he has projected his living substance' (p. 124). Karen Horney speaks of neurotic development in individuals arising from feelings of alienation, hostility, fear and diminished self-confidence. It is the combination of these feelings that create 'a basic feeling of helplessness . . . rigid pursuit of strivings for safety and satisfaction . . . emotional isolation . . . feelings of individual powerlessness' (1939, p. 173).

The mechanical, unspontaneous approach to child-rearing demanded by the early behaviourists intimidated mothers into not responding to their babies' critically fundamental needs. Such babies will grow up deeply impoverished, out of touch, with feelings of emptiness and estrangement. Laing states that 'what we call "normal" is a product of repression, denial, splitting, projection, introjection and other forms of destructive action on experience. It is radically estranged from the structure of being'

(1967, p. 24). He goes on to suggest that 'If our experience is destroyed, our behaviour will be destructive . . . we have lost our own selves.' To put it another way: if we are treated like objects then we will behave in a depersonalised way. Our actions will be those of an object devoid of human feeling.

More permissive styles of parenting first appeared in the thirties and forties and were given a boost in the sixties with the Vietnam war and the calls for a cultural revolution in which children (and others) would be free and there would be no more war. It was claimed that repressive child-rearing, coupled with the exposure to what was called the 'military industrial complex', developed life-hating attitudes which created violence within the culture and a lust for war.

One effect of this change to more open parenting was that parents and children were able to communicate more freely with each other. There were fewer and in some cases no taboo subjects. There was more ease and spontaneity. Children were to be enjoyed and the parents were on their side. If psychiatry had been on the side of society stressing the parental need to repress and control children, now 'anti-psychiatry' was on the side of the children against society and old-fashioned bourgeois parents. In fact the anti-psychiatrists' criticism of the nuclear family was only the latest version of an old tradition of exposing so-called parental ignorance and incompetence which goes back to the earliest social reformers. Paradoxically, permissive parenting, far from bringing about a revolution in attitudes to authority and control, was just what capitalism needed – all those liberated needs had to be gratified and gratified quickly. For the first time in history children could have exactly what they wanted!

Herbert Marcuse (1964) speaks of 'repressive de-sublimation'. Sublimation is a mature defence mechanism in which the biological drives (of a sexual and aggressive nature) are diverted in accordance with the reality principle into socially valuable activities. All creative activities in the widest sense involve sublimation. Gratification is delayed and the energy is used to fulfil longer-term objectives. The point is that capitalism works against this tendency in that it offers and creates false needs and desires, diverting energy from sublimation. Children who have been brought up to be free and to have what they want are the perfect consumers, demanding more and more commodities. The instant gratification of these needs leads to de-sublimation. It is repressive because a gratified person is a tranquillised person. Capitalism delivers the goods and therefore any opposition is effectively neutralised.

Anna Freud, speaking of progressive education, was making a similar point:

> In the theory of education the importance of infantile ego's determination to avoid unpleasure has not been sufficiently appreciated, and this has contributed to the failure of a number of educational experiments in recent years. The modern method is to give the growing ego a greater liberty of action, above all to allow it freely to choose its activities and interests. The idea is that the ego will develop better and sublimation in various forms will be achieved. But children in the latency period (6–11 years) may attach much more importance to the avoidance of anxiety and unpleasure than to direct or indirect gratification of instinct. In many cases if they lack external guidance, their choice of occupation is determined not by their particular gifts or capacities for sublimation but by the hope of securing themselves as quickly as maybe from anxiety and unpleasure. To the surprise of the educator (and parent) the result of this freedom of choice, in such cases, is not the blossoming of personality but the impoverishment of the ego. (1936, p. 103)

That freedom has been on the agenda in both education and parenting since the war is not in dispute. What is a cause for concern is the *degree* of freedom and the economic environment in which that freedom operates. The fact that many former parental functions have been taken over by the state, leaving parents feeling inadequate and inept, has meant that the worst idealist excesses have been able to be propagated without checks. By placing the child right in the centre of the stage for the first time and ignoring parents, we have lost that balanced overview that was the hallmark of child-rearing in earlier centuries. No one would doubt that *some* freedom of choice is essential for the developing child. No one should deny that a child requires *some* power within the family and needs to develop self-esteem. But to regard children as adults, to let them have 'equal voting power' within the family, to regard them as 'clients' who are free to choose whatever goods and services they may require, and to glorify this as self-regulation, carries grave psychological dangers, namely a loss in a certain fundamental sense of human subjectivity.

I commenced this overview of childhood by noting that the medieval child, with its non-representation or its representation as a little adult, did not exist. The concept or notion of 'child' or 'childhood' was absolutely marginal until the modern period. Ironically, I am ending this chapter by saying almost the same thing. With the loss of the generational difference implied by modern, democratic, negotiational strategies between what were called parents and children, we have deleted again the notion of child, as child.

The term 'child' means nothing except in relation to the term 'parent'. To be a child means to be of a different generation to a parent. In the last chapter, we highlighted the importance of *sexual* differentiation, and the necessity of assuming some position and some identity as man or woman. Here again, as a consequence of Oedipus, we must emphasise a *generational* differentiation. A father is radically different from a son; a mother is different from a daughter. Each has to assume a position vis-à-vis the other of the different generation. There is of course an infinitely varied number of ways of doing this. There need be nothing overly restrictive about it, as long as a son acknowledges, in some fundamental sense, his father as father, and the father acknowledges his son as son. Without taking on this task – the encounter with Oedipus – we will have no place, no position, or we will be all over the place, a somebody and a nobody, full and empty – not Oedipus, but Narcissus.

Finally, we might add, that this intergenerational confusion and equality could be seen, at an extreme, as legitimating sexual relations between the generations. If there is no generational difference between fathers and daughters, why should they not have sex together? Our revulsion at this underlines our realisation, in this respect at least, that there is a line to be drawn, an Oedipal taboo to be maintained between the generations. The daughter is then protected in her status as 'daughter', *and* as 'child'. Without this line a plague indeed descends.

6   THE EMPTY SELF

I: NARCISSISM EXPLAINED

As we noted in the last chapter, permissive trends in child-rearing became much more widespread in the 1960s, coincident with the popularisation of neo-Reichian views,[1] part of a countercultural avant-garde which rejected the 'high' and 'elitist' pretensions of scientific modernity and arguably instituted or initiated, around this time, the change to what we now call postmodernism.

Reich rejected Oedipus, as did, for instance, Deleuze and Guattari (1972). According to these writers, human misery is caused by the patriarchal nature of the authoritarian state, which is responsible for the instigation of sexual repression and therefore the development of neurosis and unhappiness. Beneath the 'character armour', human nature is good. Reich writes: 'If one penetrates . . . deeper into the biologic substratum of the human animal one always discovers the deepest layer which we call the biologic core. In this core under favourable conditions, man is essentially an honest, industrious, loving and if motivated, rationally hating human being' (1933, p. xi).

Such conclusions are non-psychoanalytic. However, Reich has been far more influential than Freud, and around this time came the great flowering of the new liberation ideologies which linked personal freedom and happiness with the removal of all constraint (Perry, 1970). Personal freedom became linked with the struggles of oppressed peoples in the Third World. One was to throw off oppression in all its forms. As far as child-rearing was concerned the implications of this analysis were obvious: children must be given complete freedom to develop naturally.

What has been described as that naive idealism of the sixties, which was regarded as revolutionary and dangerous at the time, has long since collapsed into the mainstream and hype of late capitalism, where all political ideology tends to be levelled out or marketed as 'lifestyle options'. The permissive parents of today have little in common with those who chanted 'make love, not war' and who put flowers down the barrels of the rifles of the Kent state police.

In the sixties there was still a division between what might have been called 'serious culture' and 'pop culture'.[2] Education and traditional parenting were about the former. They were about things that were difficult, which had to be striven for, appreciated and understood. Like Latin and Greek in schools, or classical studies, or modernist works, they were part of that threatened culture. The idealism of the sixties spoke out of that high culture while at the same time tending to undermine it. It was intensely optimistic and hopeful of creating a better world. The decision to bring up one's kids in freedom was regarded as a revolutionary act and involved great risk of ostracism. One knew that one was going against the whole tradition of that serious culture, and yet one was somehow acting out of the best that there was in that tradition – a concern for truth, for justice, for human dignity and freedom. Of course, many have said with hindsight that it was simply narcissism to believe that one had found the solution. But it is important to emphasise the essential seriousness of those times, the discussions, the intensity of the search, the excitement, the deeply held beliefs. People were thinking for themselves, acting for themselves, but largely out of a tradition which they had absorbed and were now rejecting. The backdrop of the 'high culture' was still in place. There was indeed something substantial to kick against.

In the subsequent years, popular culture has gained ground. Cultural value is now defined by the market. Popular culture is no longer marginal; for most people it is all there is. It is about having reality defined for one in advance, by increasingly sophisticated marketing techniques. Our social identities are defined by what we consume. Questions of depth and meaning seem strangely irrelevant. Even a word like permissiveness no longer has meaning unless one has some notion of restraint. Yet recent developments in consumer capitalism make opposites like permissiveness versus restraint seem quaint and old-fashioned. For now there is only the 'discipline' imposed by the market. It is all down to expediency, there are no longer any absolutes. So when one talks of permissiveness now, one is talking about a way of life that is adjusted to a free-market economy and therefore is essential for survival. One simply doesn't want to be troubled with notions of morality or meaning, depth or height, convictions or beliefs, except insofar as these may make one more marketable. What one observer (Baudrillard, quoted in Hebdige (1988)) has called the 'depthlessness' of modern culture tends to preclude any idealism. A 'sell-by' date is imposed on all meanings and values.

In psychoanalytic terms we have all but removed the old paternal super-ego from the cultural scene. The parental authority which for generations was internalised by children at home, at school and at church has largely collapsed. The super-ego brought order and coherence into individual lives and regulated human relationships. It was a cultural inheritance of the greatest importance for civilisation. Freud was aware of the importance of the super-ego:

> It is in keeping with the course of human development that external coercion gradually becomes internalized; for a special mental agency, man's super-ego, takes it over and includes it among its commandments. Every child presents this process of transformation to us; only by that means does it become a moral and social being. Such a strengthening of the super-ego is a most precious cultural asset in the psychological field. Those in whom it has taken place are turned from being opponents of civilization into being its vehicles. The greater their number is in a cultural unit the more secure is the culture and the more it can dispense with external measures of coercion. (1927, p. 11)

The hope was, say proponents of the sexual revolution, that the super-ego would be overthrown and that society would be brought more into line with the id – that part of the personality kept tightly in check by the demands of reality and internal prohibition. Now many observers would suggest that this has already happened. The reasons for this are various. We have noted the collapse of parental authority and authority generally and the emergence of the 'democratic family'. Many of the functions formerly carried out by the family have been taken over by agencies of the state. The dominating influence of the commercially manipulated youth culture begins to exert its influence on younger and younger ages. Also the presence within the host culture of ethnic groups with value-systems divergent from the host culture has led to an ethical relativism which justifies more or less any behaviour from some standpoint or other. Parents have been more and more absent from the family since the beginning of the industrial revolution. First the father's work, and more recently that of the mother, took parents out of the home, and the work of child-rearing has been left to a new, mostly young and poorly paid, servant class which comprises nannies, au pairs and childminders. And clearly, and perhaps most importantly of all, highly sophisticated marketing techniques are providing us more and more with what we want, which makes a mockery of self-restraint and self-control. Clearly, the super-ego is well and truly redundant.

But the sexual paradise dreamt of by the Reichians has clearly not come about. The shift in psychological emphasis from the super-ego to the id has not increased the sum of human happiness; in fact, some of the social indices of stress point in the opposite direction. The reason is clear: Reich fundamentally misunderstood the nature and origin of the super-ego. He was correct in saying it is coercive and prohibitive, but incorrect in attributing its cruelty to the outside world.

The Freudian position is clearly at odds with the Reichian. For Freud the super-ego arises *endogenously*, in response to the id-drives. It derives its cruelty from the aggressive drives in the id, not so much from the aggression which it may meet with in the outside world. For Freud, the super-ego formed as a result of the Oedipus complex when the child had the urgent need to control its desires: for Klein it develops earlier in response to very early innate destructive drives. But for psychoanalysis generally, the super-ego arises as a counterforce opposing the id; it arises from *within* the psyche, albeit modelled in part on parents and others in the outside world. It therefore cannot be done away with; it is always present. So even if external constraints are removed, the internal ones will persist and may paradoxically grow stronger.

Reich's belief in the essential goodness of human nature is contradicted by psychoanalytic findings. Whether or not one takes on board Freud's speculative ideas on the 'death instinct', frustration is part of human life from the beginning outside the womb. Frustration leads to aggression. Aggression is present from the earliest days and is unavoidable. It therefore arises not only from external sources as a result of being exposed to a cruel society. Aggression arises primarily from the insatiability of desire and the only limited possibilities for fulfilment. The belief that people are good and that it is only the world that corrupts them is illusory.

Psychoanalysis recognises the human condition as being inevitably conflicted. Growth and integration are possible only within limits (see Chapter 2). Janine Chasseguet-Smirgel and Bela Grunberger (1976), in their book comparing Reich with Freud, argue very clearly that Reich was essentially pre-Freudian in his outlook and based his thinking on his own paranoia, whereby he located all badness outside and all goodness within. In so doing, he mobilises within us the regressive desire to be re-fused with the mother in the original perfect conflict-free paradise, before the split between subject and object, ego and non-ego, inner and outer. Such thinking, they point out, is based on wish-fulfilling phantasy or illusion. It is compelling because we all long for that blissful reunion. It is the stuff of political ideology and abandons truth, science and reality.

Let us return to the fate of the super-ego in our time. Clearly, as we have said, the collapse of parental authority has led to the collapse of the old paternal super-ego. The super-ego as a psychical agency persists, but without the modifying influence of parental control, the child or the adolescent can sometimes feel overwhelmed by feelings and impulses that threaten to destroy the self. In order to control such feelings, in the absence of external support, the ego is thrown back onto more primitive control mechanisms in which more archaic and aggressive elements predominate.

In the past one could speak of the parental internalisations which occurred during adolescence as acting as a modifying influence on the more primitive and ruthless super-ego of early childhood. The provision of external support and control removed the need for the harsh countermeasures adopted by the ego when it was in a relatively helpless state. Contact with parents and other adults whose normal discipline and authority was looked up to and identified with had the effect of mitigating strong and irrational unconscious and conscious guilt feelings. The child or adolescent's sense of right and wrong was brought more into line with reality and the super-ego functioned as a conscience. The warfare between the super-ego and the id became modified and reduced and the person was left relatively free to pursue a productive life. Of course there were always bad identifications, where parental pathology was internalised. In general, as mentioned in the previous chapter, the more adult figures a child had to identify with, the better for his or her mental health. So, in this respect, the break-up of the extended family, and more recently the nuclear family, has been detrimental.

The imbalance created by the shift in values from self-restraint in favour of self-indulgence has led to the abandoning of the old super-ego and the uncovering of its infantile prototype. The loss of external support brought about by the collapse of parental authority has left children exposed and threatened from within. The old inhibiting super-ego has been replaced by a tyrannical new one. Increasing external freedom increases internal guilt and self-punishment, making it more difficult than ever for instinctual desires to find acceptable outlets.

Let us briefly look more closely at what is meant by the 'archaic super-ego', which is the forerunner of the mature adult super-ego. First, it must not be understood as a moral agency. It does oppose instinct but in an entirely irrational way. It operates on the principle of talion, using aggression to oppose aggression. The ruthlessness of the infant in procuring its needs is matched by the ruthlessness of the super-ego response. Freud saw this severity in his work on melancholia and obsessional neurosis.

> How is it that the super-ego . . . develops such extraordinary harshness and severity towards the ego? If we turn to melancholia first, we find that the excessively strong super-ego which has obtained a hold upon consciousness rages against the ego with merciless violence, as if it had taken possession of the whole of the sadism available in the person concerned. Following our view of sadism we should say that the destructive component had entrenched itself in the super-ego and turned against the ego. What is now holding sway in the super-ego is a pure culture of the death instinct . . .
> In obsessional neurosis . . . the instinct of destruction has been set free and it seeks to destroy the object . . . The super-ego behaves as if the ego were responsible . . . by the seriousness with which it chastises these destructive intentions . . . (1923, p. 53)

Melanie Klein, in her work with young children, greatly increased our understanding of the early formation of the super-ego. She points out that the early super-ego is 'immeasurably harsher and more cruel than that of the older child or adult and that it literally crushed down the feeble Ego of the small child . . . In the small child we come across a super-ego of the most incredible and phantastic proportions . . . ' (1933, pp. 248, 249). The younger the child the more severe is the super-ego. 'We get to look upon the child's fear of being devoured, or cut up, or torn to pieces, or its terror of being surrounded and pursued by menacing figures . . . ' (p. 249).

Klein's analyses of children pointed up the importance of aggression in early development, When aggression is at its height they never tire of 'tearing and cutting up, breaking and wetting and burning all sorts of things like paper, matches, boxes, small toys, all of which represent (unconsciously) parents, brothers, sisters and bodies and breasts, and this rage for destruction alternates with attacks of anxiety and guilt' (p. 255). These frustrated and destructive rages within the child cause him great anxiety, 'for he perceives his anxiety arising from his aggressive instincts as fear of an *external* object [person], both because he had made that object their outward goal, and because he has projected them onto it, so that they seem to be *initiated against* himself from that quarter' (p. 250). He cannot own up to his rage; instead he will create terrifying images of his parents, who are now felt to rage against him. This is a desperate attempt at control by turning sadism against the self.

In the archaic super-ego, we clearly do not have a conscience. Instead we have a brutal instrument of self-punishment which is as impulsive and dangerous as the drives of the id that it is trying to control. This is part of our early development. It remains mostly unconscious and we only become aware of it during nightmares, certain drug states, horror movies and certain paranoid states as well as depressive ones. But with the loss of the more mature and benign super-ego and suitable identification figures, children are increasingly exposed to this frightening internal world.

It is not just the loss of the old paternal super-ego which is at issue, but the simultaneous systematic exploitation of id-cravings[3] targeted at younger and younger age groups in the face of increasingly helpless and demoralised parents who use a mixture of threats and bribery to get by from day to day. The question now is: what effect are these changes having or what effect will they have on children and adults?

Psychoanalysts, therapists and psychiatrists speak of an increase in the number of people seeking help who show narcissistic disturbances or borderline conditions (see Lasch, 1979). These people experience themselves as fragmented. They have very profound swings in levels of self-esteem, from a grandiosity which seems to triumph over everything to a sense of inferiority which feels like a void or empty space. Kohut speaks of 'the depleted self (and the empty depression, i.e. the world of unmirrored ambitions, the world devoid of ideals)' (1977, p. 243). It is as if the narcissistic person is trying to love against a background of emptiness – a void within, where there is no overall sustaining other. Consequently he tries outwardly to get others to love him, he yearns for this, but experiences his needs as too great and too dangerous. His apparent self-love is only a gesture against a self-hate, which corresponds to the ferocity of his archaic super-ego. He seeks perfection and peace, but is constantly bored, unable to concentrate, and is therefore shallow and superficial. Kernberg (1970) points out that narcissistic pathology represents a defence against a fundamental rage that is felt to be so destructive, so full of impotent anger at being frustrated, that it threatens completely to destroy the self and other.

In Winnicott's terms, a *false* self is invested as a cover against the enraged and enfeebled true self. In Kleinian terms, the subject is unable to reach the depressive position in any lasting way. This is the central element in narcissistic pathology, namely the subject's inability to feel, and to feel real and spontaneous. Feelings there are, intense feelings, but these are uncontained and too extreme to be thought about. Instead they are acted out. The archaic super-ego continuously persecutes and tyrannises, destroying any incipient capacity for privacy, reverie, intimacy or sadness.

There is still some disagreement concerning the relationship between narcissistic, borderline, schizoid and psychotic states. Generally speaking, narcissistic disorders are regarded as the least severe of the disorders of the self, but severe nevertheless.

Frosh has considered whether or not contemporary culture is best represented by the diagnosis of narcissism or schizophrenia. He favours the former:

> If psychotic fragmentation is so pervasive, how is the ordinary interaction of individuals (no selves to call their own), sustained? If we are all narcissists, it is imaginable: we just use others as mirrors of ourselves, empty vessels threatened by envy and rage. But what kind of social intercourse is possible if we are all mad? (1991, p. 133)

Let us now turn to look briefly at just two social outcomes in the light of the above formulation of narcissistic pathological processes.

II: THE SOCIAL PATHOLOGY OF NARCISSISM

Perhaps the most dramatic indicator in the recent decades of self-pathology has been the massive increase in addictive behaviours. I will take the example of drug abuse, realising that this is only one aspect of a larger problem of addictive disorders.

Clearly there has been an explosion worldwide in drug abuse since the experimental days of the 1960s. Most concern has centred around the abuse by young people of amphetamines, cannabis, heroin, cocaine and other more recent and exotic substances. However, alcohol abuse has always been out in front, in a league of its own. According to a recent report, we have more than doubled our consumption of alcohol since the fifties, and more young people are drinking, and drinking excessively, at younger and younger ages. The heaviest drinkers today are young males in the 18–24 age bracket, and heavy drinking is also found increasingly in the younger teenage groups. Alcohol-related deaths (under 24) exceed deaths of young people from abuse of illicit drugs by an astounding ratio of 14 to 1.

How can we account for these alarming figures, these steep rises in consumption? Health professionals will cite a number of factors: greater availability, the growth of delinquent subcultures, the break-up of the family, abuse by other family members, recession and unemployment, inner-city urban decay, the specific pharmacological effects of the substances themselves, social class, ethnic group and so on. Unconscious factors are not considered, although a genetic predisposition is sometimes noted as an innate factor.

Clearly the position is very complex, but our interest here is to look specifically at unconscious factors. And from the point of view being advanced here we are bound to stress the link between the loss of a certain essential stability in the family and community, which has corroded *internal* prohibitions leading to a return to a primitive pleasure ego away from reality, a retreat from the external world into unconscious phantasy.

Addicts have what Kohut calls 'a structural void in the Self'.

Everyone will need to take drugs at certain times for specific medical or recreational purposes, but for the addict the drug holds a powerful, subtle and pervasive significance. According to Fenichel, addicts use the effect of the drug to 'satisfy the archaic oral longing which is sexual longing, need for security and a need for the maintenance of self-esteem simultaneously. Thus the origin and nature of the addiction are not determined by the chemical effects of the drug but by the psychological structure of the patient' (1946, p. 376). He goes on to describe how addicts regress from interest in genital sexuality to more primitive forms in which the libido (life-energy) becomes pure craving. Addicts are ready to give up relating to others, although characteristically relationships were for them never secure, which is the origin of their problems. During the 'high' of intoxication, the experience of pure pleasure and extreme elation involves feelings of deep, abiding security and satisfaction of all cravings. Feelings of being 'at one' with everything are common. This has been described as 'artificial mania', and it is followed by depression and a profound sense of emptiness and bleakness. As tolerance for the substance increases, the 'lows' become longer and the 'highs' become shorter, necessitating an increase in dosage and causing a spiralling down into depression and apathy. The intense longing, which is the need of the infant to be mirrored, which the addict unconsciously sought to assuage by abuse of the drug, has not been resolved. He is at the mercy of unbearable tension and oscillations in mood and self-esteem.

In considering the abuse of alcohol, it is frequently noted that alcoholics have experienced their mothers as dominating and frustrating. Fenichel comments that:

> The chronic alcoholic's difficult family constellations created specific oral frustrations in childhood. These frustrations gave rise to oral fixations, with all the consequences of such fixations for the structure of the personality. In boys the frustrations resulted also in a turning away from the frustrating mother to the father, that is to - more or less repressed - homosexual tendencies. The unconscious impulses in alcoholics typically are not only oral but also homosexual in nature. (1946, pp. 379-80)

The fact that alcohol banishes cares and removes inhibitions points to the truth about the old joke that the super-ego is defined as that part of the personality which is soluble in alcohol. Its particular attraction for young people may well be its power temporarily to remove the archaic super-ego and allow the emergence of an uninhibited, grandiose and pseudo-potent self with the power to wreak havoc in society. But the levels of alcohol abuse already referred to, among younger and younger age groups, may be evidence of the severity of this super-ego and the urgent need to escape it.

Many on the Left would argue that it is the harshness and unpredictability of the external world that drives young people in ever-increasing numbers into the illusory world of drug addiction.[4] Some still argue that illicit drugs should be decriminalised, especially as few of them are as harmful as alcohol. The argument being expounded here is that the drug abuse is part of an increased permissiveness in a culture in which more or less anything goes. Paradoxically, the laxity in the external world requires of each self that it redoubles its efforts at control *internally*. This excessive internal control is felt as oppressive and drugs offer temporary relief. There is gratification of archaic impulses and the simultaneous relief from the archaic super-ego.

However, the self-destructive consequences of drug abuse must be seen as gratification for the archaic super-ego. So the symptom of drug abuse is clearly a complex and condensed phenomenon gratifying id and super-ego simultaneously or in a bi-phasic way. As I have implied, the gratification of the oral craving is immediate and intense, thereby totally subverting more conventional routes to fulfilment based on modulation of drives and sublimation. But for the addict, the drives represent an unbearable and unassuageable craving that cannot be delayed. The deeper we get into the unconscious, the more time, in the ordinary linear secondary process sense, contracts. The demand in addictive states reduces time to close to zero.

Modern capitalism also narrows the gap between desire and satisfaction, finding more and more new commodities with which to gratify desire. Drug addiction can been seen as an inevitable result of that process – the ultimate, the extreme in gratification, the perfect commodity for which there is always a spiralling demand, for which people are prepared to kill or die. Indeed, for those vast numbers in the world who by virtue of their position in an underclass, or marginalised group, or geographical region, have little stake in external reality, or who are damaged and alienated within, drug abuse offers an immediate but temporary way out. It proposes itself as an immediate solution to an unbearable lack. As ·capitalism proceeds apace, with its renewed confidence, more and more people, we might safely conclude, will seek this solution.

One criticism of drugs education programmes is that they largely ignore these unconscious factors. To teach children about the effects of different substances, and to teach them behavioural skills in selecting, using or avoiding certain substances (particularly when under peer pressure to experiment) is all very well, but it ignores the fact that a small proportion of children or young adults unconsciously seek self-destructive activities.[5] Drugs for these individuals can be seen as welcome relief from punishment for the pain of survival in a world that is perceived as brutalised and empty.

It may be stretching a point to include addictive behaviours under the rubric of narcissism, but the same may be said of the next topic, violence. However, narcissistic disorders of the self often barely conceal their underlying violent propensities, as we shall see in the following discussion.

For instance, Lacan has very productively linked narcissism and aggression, by the very way in which the ego of the subject comes into being. 'Aggressivity is the co-relative tendency of a mode of identification that we call narcissistic, and which determines the formal structure of man's ego and the register of entities characteristic of his world' (1948, p. 16). This is the 'mirror stage', in which the child identifies himself with an image of himself. The self is then forever divided, torn and in turmoil in relation to this double, whom it loves and hates, whom it envies and despises. The stage is inexorably set for a fight to the death between the self and its double. We might add that, in the language we have been using here, this self-image, the image of perfection in the mirror, when it becomes persecutory is the archaic super-ego.

Grunberger (1980) links narcissistic shame and humiliation with violence. The child is faced, as he develops, with two narcissistic setbacks: his own underlying sense of biological immaturity and weakness; and his defeat by his father in the Oedipal struggle. Grunberger gives a telling example of a drunkard in a pub who behaved badly. The publican asked him to leave, and apparently he was 'treated like dirt'. Shortly afterwards, the man came back and blew up the place with a Molotov cocktail. There were no survivors. Grunberger comments that this action 'can be explained as his desire to make null and void his narcissistic injury by causing all those who were witnesses to disappear' (1980, p. 617). The narcissistic humiliation had been witnessed, and the witness can be dealt with in many ways, including elimination. One tries to cloud the mirror by preventing the image being reflected. But as Grunberger points out, this reflection can go very far indeed and the whole world can take on the aspect of a mirror to be eliminated.

I have made reference earlier to crime (see Chapter 3) and our pervasive need to protect ourselves from each other in the conditions of modern culture. But violent crime is also on the increase in a most dramatic way. There has been a sevenfold increase in violent crime within a generation, and a massive 40 per cent increase during the 1980s. Again many factors can be invoked to explain these increases. Perhaps this illustrates clearly the ugly excesses that can rise to the surface in the absence of a generally internalised moral framework.

The removal of the external super-ego structures has not led to a diminution of violence as progressives predicted. Instead the increase has exceeded society's capacity to cope, with prisons full, and understandable calls for harsher punishments. Although there is a clear link between crime, poverty, unemployment and urban deprivation, these rising crime figures have coincided with great increases in the overall living standards generally, and even the Left no longer cites only poverty as the cause of crime.

All public representatives now talk about a 'breakdown' in law and order, about greed, about selfishness. There are increasing pressures to crack down harder on criminals, making it easier to justify paramilitary-style and covert activities – useful practice, as far as Britain has been concerned, being gained in Northern Ireland. Law enforcement of the kind advocated by the New Right has little in common with the old paternalistic authority. Sergeant Dixon[6] has given way to the cop in riot gear. We can anticipate that outright coercion will be necessary with those in the population who have for many reasons no moderating inner controls, only brutalising ones. Limits will have to be set externally through sheer force, in the 'public interest'.

It is arguable that the loss of authority has simply facilitated the more open expression of aggressive impulses. This may be true, but it ignores the repetitive and self-destructive nature of criminal activity. Just as with the other social pathology we have been discussing, permissiveness has increased self-indulgent behaviour, but with paradoxical consequences: a rise in the number of people who get locked into a vicious circle of impulse and punishment.

It would be wrong and facile to caricature the criminal (as some on the Right do) as a person who is enjoying his new-found freedom to act on his aggressive impulses in the absence of effective authority and at the expense of the law-abiding citizens. The jibe has always been he has been getting off scot-free. If the levels of unsolved crime are anything to go by, this has been and will continue to be true. Victims will go on suffering so-called 'motiveless attacks' without adequate punishment being meted out. But the criminal is clearly not acting rationally or out of any sense of freedom. He is very much a loser rather than a winner in psychological terms. This does not help the victim of the rape, the mugging, the burglary, who justifiably feels deeply traumatised, aggrieved and vengeful. But it is necessary to understand the internal world of criminals, their general psychology and how it presents as a symptom of a wider social breakdown. Without some sort of analysis, we are in danger of siding with those wanting to scapegoat criminals, deprive them of human rights and – most importantly – to deny the psychological reality of a culture in chaos.

Much criminal and delinquent behaviour arises out of an unbearable unconscious sense of guilt. Guilt actually *precedes* the crime. Freud comments, 'such deeds were done principally *because* they were forbidden, and because their execution was accompanied by mental relief for their doer. He was suffering from an oppressive feeling of guilt, of which he did not know the origin, and after he had committed a misdeed the oppression was mitigated. His sense of guilt was at last attached to something.' (1915b, p. 332).

But one might reasonably ask, where does this sense of guilt come from in the absence of the actual crime? The guilt arises from 'crimes' carried out *in phantasy* in early childhood which are punishable by the archaic super-ego. Melanie Klein noted the 'criminal tendencies' at work in normal children and found that they would

> act them out (of course in their childish way) over and over again, the more they were dreading a cruel retaliation from their parents as a punishment for their aggressive phantasies directed against those

parents. Children who were unconsciously expecting to be cut to pieces, beheaded, devoured and so on, would feel compelled to be naughty and get punished, because the real punishment, however severe, was reassuring in comparison with the murderous attacks which they were continuously expecting from phantastically cruel parents. I came to the conclusion . . . that it is not (as is usually supposed) the *weakness or lack of super-ego, it is not in other words the lack of conscience, but the overpowering strictness of the super-ego*, which is responsible for the characteristic behaviour of asocial and criminal persons. (1934, p. 258; my italics)

Winnicott agrees:

Repeatedly we find these acts [petty crimes] are done in an unconscious attempt to make sense of guilt feeling. The child or adult cannot reach the source of a sense of guilt that is intolerable, and the fact that the guilt feeling cannot be explained makes for a feeling of madness. The antisocial person gets relief by devising a limited crime. (1958a, p. 27)

He goes on to make a further point: 'At first the substitute crime or delinquency is unsatisfactory to the delinquent, but when compulsively repeated it acquires the characteristics of secondary gain and thus becomes acceptable to the self' (p. 27).

As has been stressed in this chapter, the modifying effect of the old paternal super-ego would have been more likely in days gone by to have prevented 'secondary gain' from taking a hold over the personality. Ways would have been found by which the potential adolescent criminal could contribute to the community and build up his self-esteem in socially acceptable ways. But today the picture is different, with a whole variety of subcultures which would esteem delinquent acts, reinforcing the initial anti-social trends and making a virtue out of an aberration. More and more, children of younger and younger ages spend time with each other, unsupervised, without any responsible adult presence. On their own, young people cannot face their extreme feelings of tension and lack, so unless there is some receptive adult available to intervene and help them confront their problems rather than act on them, they will be drawn into their peer groups, where their deviance will confer on them a pseudo-potency. As Guntrip says: 'Human beings prefer to feel "bad somebodies" rather than "weak non-entities". Much crime and delinquency must be motivated by a quest for power, and for notoriety for destructive behaviour, to cover the felt inability to achieve true value by constructive work' (1968, p. 137).

Much post-Kleinian work throws light on this sense of power, the pleasurable power in badness. In 1950, Bion wrote about 'the imaginary twin' self whose psychical function was 'to deny a reality different from himself' (1950, p. 19). In 1962, Bion has the earliest origins of this development of total power in mind when he talks of 'the establishment internally of a projective-identification-rejecting-object [which] means that instead of an understanding object the infant has a wilfully misunderstanding object – with which it is identified' (1962b, p. 117). This object is a very bad object, an object suffused with envy, that has the power to destroy emotional thinking and feeling.

Rosenfeld's work describes moves that the self can make to protect and hide an excessively fragile self, by turning environmental failure into triumph, via the valuing of omnipotent destructiveness. If you can't beat them (the death instincts), join them. Rosenfeld spoke of a 'destructive narcissism' – essentially, being loved, not for one's goodness, but for one's powerful badness. He is considering narcissism in its negative and violent aspects, and he says that 'self-idealization plays a central role, but now it is the idealization of the omnipotent destructive parts of the self. They are directed both against any positive libidinal object relationship and any libidinal part of the self which experiences need for an object and the desire to depend on it' (1971, p. 173). Further on, he says that 'the destructive narcissism of these patients appears often highly organized, as if one were dealing with a powerful gang' (p. 174). There exists absolute domination 'by an omnipotent or omniscient, extremely ruthless part of the self, which creates the notion that within the delusional object there is complete painlessness and also the freedom to indulge in any sadistic activity' (1987, p. 112).

Rosenfeld also speaks of the self being trapped in a 'psychotic infantile narcissistic omnipotent character structure', which remains all powerful and 'which not only pulls him away towards death, but infantilizes him and prevents him from growing up, by keeping him away from objects who could help him to achieve growth and development' (1987, p. 113). Furthermore, this structural configuration 'poses as an ideal friend and helper' (p. 122). Imprisoned in this way, damaged personalities believe that they will at least be free from pain and anxiety, but at the price of being terrified of change, clinging to the persecutory imago (the archaic super-ego) rather than facing the extreme anxiety that would be induced by any sort of breaking away. That is why these narcissistic, borderline or schizoid personalities are so difficult to treat therapeutically.

In a similar vein, speaking this time of perversion, Meltzer suggests that, 'an illusion of safety is promulgated by the omniscience of the destructive part and perpetuated by the sense of omnipotence generated by the perversion or the addictive activity involved. The tyrannical, addictive bad part is dreaded . . . [because] . . . the essential hold over the submissive part of the self is by way of the dread of loss of protection against terror' (1968, pp. 105–6).

Insofar as these analyses of negative narcissistic personalities are correct, they point the way as to how these patients should be managed, helped or rehabilitated. By supporting the vulnerable damaged self (the self that retains some traces of the capacity to feel hurt and pain), the psychotic defence – the tyrant protector within – can be confronted, challenged, dethroned, so that the person can come more into life and begin to think about his or her feelings instead of repeatedly acting upon them in destructive ways. All the various ways that this difficult therapeutic work can be done depend on the need for a strong, reliable, truthful human environment that can be very confronting without being rejecting. Merely to be confronting and attack the psychotic defence is only to repeat countertransferentially the subject's history; while simply to be supportive is to have this help endlessly destroyed. Something of Winnicott's approach is required: 'A main task of the analysis of any patient is to maintain objectivity in regard to all that the patient brings, and a special case of this is the analyst's need to be able to hate the patient objectively' (1947, p. 196).

But the ubiquity of these psychotic defences indeed should serve to emphasise and underline for us the absolute necessity of providing for the infant's *inaugural* protection by what Winnicott (1971a) termed 'primary illusion', against an otherwise inevitable violent fragmentation and emptying of the self. And beyond this primary moment in infancy, a reliable mature adult presence, to keep the child in life, in feeling, in hate and in reality. Otherwise, as we have tried to illustrate, there is escape into omnipotent unfeeling.

I have emphasised throughout that the various losses – of the community, the church, the family, the social bondedness – have led to a loss of cohesiveness within the self. All psychoanalytic theorists agree that the self is a *construct*. The self's existence is not primordially given and is in no way guaranteed. Psychoanalysis is well placed to make this point very clearly. The self is created in the shadow of an object, in the mirroring of an other. As Winnicott says, 'There is no such thing as a baby . . . [always] a baby and someone' (1964, p. 88) – a baby/mother unit.

Therefore, it may be no coincidence that, for instance, when Klein was conceptualising the depressive position (1935, 1940), when Bion (1959) was formulating his notion of the container, when Winnicott (1951) was introducing us to the transitional space, when Bowlby (1953) was talking about the child's real and intense feeling of loss in separation anxiety, and when Balint (1952) was talking about primary love or *Arglos*, there was concomitantly an accelerating process of fragmentation of human social bonds in the wider culture. Perhaps all these theorists subliminally recognised that the necessary conditions for the creation of a self could no longer be taken for granted. So there was an implicit and increasingly urgent desire to describe the optimal conditions for self-formation before it was too late. There was, as a consequence, a definite privileging and idealisation of the mother–infant, analyst–analysand dyads, as if to underline and dramatise the absolute necessity and privacy of this founding and fateful relation. We live now, increasingly, in my estimation, with the mass, public and pathological consequences of our failure to heed these implicit warnings.

It took a Lacan to come and cut into this blest and imaginary reciprocal mirroring, its exclusivity and reliability, with his notion of the Symbolic and the 'Name-of-the-Father', lest we lost touch completely with Otherness, with difference, with discontinuity and with the fragmentary omnipotence of language. A self so cosseted, so carefully managed by the mother or the analyst, was destined to live in a make-believe world, tyrannised into health by a good-enough mother and the empathic interventions of the analyst to be internalised as the ideal of human functioning.

Lacan, following Freud, revivified the concept of castration, paradoxically re-creating a tension which was in danger of being lost by our staying with and protecting what he saw as an imaginary ego/self-as-construct and missing the essential and impossible task of eliciting the subject through speech. Lacan does not do away with the subject, but points us to the radical impossibility of ever resting in a confident subjecthood. He was thereby safeguarding analysis from acquiescing in a kind of self-serving falsity completely out of touch with the harshness of modernity.

Lacan therefore applies a necessary corrective against a belief that we might construct a self that is proof against adversity. Lacan does not answer narcissistic demands, but instead requires the subject to speak, not for himself or herself, because there is no stability in this, but more to speak and *be* spoken. There is no haven to run to, there is less and less of a family to turn to, and the analytical process has to reflect this absence (through the short sessions, for instance), rather than try to fill it in with illusory supports.

This is a long argument, but here, in this chapter, we have noted the *social* effects of some crucial absence, a disconnectedness and loss of primary emotional safety. And all we can say is that more and more people cannot bear it. More and more adolescents and young people are retreating into narcissistic illusory worlds, turning desire inwards where they can feel satiated temporarily, or they can unfeel and act violently, by siding with the death instinct, with totalitarianism, in fear and dread of life and creativity.

This was to be the 'Century of the Child'. It has seen enormous advances in our understanding of childhood and the creation of facilities for health, education, recreation and leisure. It has also seen a radical undermining of parental authority and security, and therefore the creation by default of new and more ugly forms of tyranny and compulsion.

7   THE CRISIS IN AUTHORITY

I: THE CULTURAL REVOLUTION

In many chapters of this book we have had cause to mention the cultural revolution of the sixties which marked a break, perhaps a final break, with what was left of tradition and convention, and heralded (when viewed in the best light) a new openness, a democratisation of relationships and institutions. And, arguably, nowhere has this change become more apparent than in schools. It is difficult to generalise, and the changes have been uneven, but everywhere has been affected.

Children no longer fear going to school. Much of the severity, and sometimes cruelty, of former years or decades has gone from the classroom. Corporal punishment has been abolished. Pupils can talk to teachers much more frankly and openly, and in some cases can call them by their first names. Teachers are more human, more understanding, more prepared to listen than they were just a generation ago. Gone is that arbitrary and institutionalised authoritarianism which made schools for so many children a gruesome experience. The whole atmosphere in the school is different, with the classrooms being brighter and the teachers using materials that are more interesting, where you are encouraged to find out for yourself. At best, you are encouraged to be yourself, to learn, to enjoy learning, not just when at school but also later in life, throughout life. If one also takes in the wide variety of materials produced, especially on television and video, in science, history, geography, the environment, literature and drama and so on, then the possibilities for learning and education surely are better than at any other time.

But this all presupposes the right psychological environment for learning: a capacity for learning – something which paradoxically may be less available than before. This something is the capacity to experience. It requires the availability within of a private transitional space, which as Winnicott has noted is the location of all cultural experience. But it is this essential privacy which is in question now, and therefore throws into doubt the value of whole educational process. If education is going to be more than just entertainment, more than just a superficial scanning of the vast quantities of material presented, then some deeper appreciation and motivation are fundamental.

We have noted the increasingly fragmented nature of culture. We must now focus specifically on how this revolution has affected schools and education. We have noted the breakdown of the extended family and more recently the steep rise in single-parent families. Traditional nuclear families with a mummy and a daddy are now in the minority. There are now, in Britain, more than twice as many divorces as there were in 1971. A quarter of all births occur outside marriage. A number of long-term studies have shown how children of divorced parents suffer long-term effects in their emotional and social development. They do less well in school, and are more likely to leave home early and try to live on their own. Later in life they have higher unemployment rates and rates of marriage breakdown than their counterparts whose parents didn't divorce. Single-parent families tend to be a disadvantaged group financially. And for many children generally now, life is much more unpredictable and unstable, with both parents going out to work. Parents tend to be less and less parents, demanding, like their children, to be seen as people with needs, desires and worries of their own. And so there is more stress in the home. Less and less time is spent together as a family, fewer meals are taken together, and there is less time generally to facilitate those essential interactions that provide for identifications – a time and place to mature in.

Children are now coming to school with an increased variety of emotional and behavioural problems. Teachers have become alert to these problems within the communities they serve. This has necessitated a radical change in their role. In the last twenty or more years, and particularly in the last decade, teachers have been required and have been willing to take on more and more

156 CULTURAL COLLAPSE

responsibilities. They have always taught their own subjects, of course, but they have taken on new methods, more practical methods, integration of subjects, new subjects, and new methods of pupil assessment. On top of this there has been a new emphasis on seeing the pupil as a 'whole person' who must be educated in social and personal skills. Teachers are now expected to (and expect themselves to) take account of the pupil's family and social background and intervene where necessary to help. Teachers have stepped in to fill the void left by the cultural changes that have gone on apace since the late sixties. They have seen that there is a need to help children who have been, in effect, the casualties of these changes. Teachers have responded by developing new educational programmes that will address the problems thrown up by these changes, for which we were totally unprepared.

Nobody can easily argue against this greatly extended professional agenda for the modern teacher, but the cumulative effect of all this extra responsibility is now becoming apparent. What has actually happened is that teachers and schools have changed their traditional position from being *in loco parentis, as father*. They are now more and more expected to replace *both* parents, and to be in effect on call, on demand, *as mother*. (I am using the terms 'father' and 'mother' here to denote a set of traditional expectations structured within our culture.)

In the seventies and eighties, we can see the increasing pressure, the increasing need for schools and teachers, in short, for someone to act in the role of mother. The father-type role was seen as too distant, too cerebral, too authoritarian. The emphasis which had been placed on good mothering in healthy child development, by such influential psychoanalytic thinkers as Melanie Klein, John Bowlby and David Winnicott, in the post-war years, radically shifted the focus of attention from the role of the father, emphasised by Freud, to the role of the mother. She was to be supportive, facilitating, permissive, always available, infinitely attentive and tolerant lest her child should fall prey to mental ill-health. The new father had little to do, it seems, but to support the mother in her crucial role. More recently there has been a renewed interest in fathers, but closer inspection reveals that these fathers are required to share the mothering activities, more than to be fathers in their own right.

This emphasis on mothering – and, it is clear, mothering of a rather idealistic kind – has shifted to schools and teachers. The qualities required of the new progressive mothers of the 1950s have now become the qualities required by today's teachers. Let us look in parallel at the mothering function and the teaching function in more detail.

Teachers are now planners, facilitators, enablers. As their workload has increased, their status has diminished. As they no longer set themselves up as anything in particular, they are no longer feared or attacked. Instead they find themselves submerged in the mass of seething and noisy humanity, overloaded with copy-books, paperwork, extra responsibilities, pleading with their charges to co-operate. As mothers they cannot get angry and cannot complain for fear of being thought incompetent or inadequate. Discipline becomes a problem because the gap has been removed. We are all learners together, as the democratic myth goes. Unrestrained children have more needs to be fulfilled, and fulfilled immediately, than their relatively repressed counterparts of a generation ago. So we now have the combination of more needs to be satisfied more quickly, and the removal of the traditional discipline that kept these needs more tightly bound. This creates a specific and ever-present tension during the teacher's day.

Teachers, now designated as primary health carers, have taken over many of the functions traditionally associated with the family. Schools are now containers in Bion's sense, expected to be able to assimilate and detoxify a whole range of social problems. They are expected to teach their subjects, get good results, understand their pupils' problems and be sympathetic, as well as maintain authority. More and more it falls to teachers not only to teach but also to be carers. Teachers have always been expected to produce good citizens. But today they have less and less support from the larger community for this broad educational task. It is perhaps these additional responsibilities, as much as reduced status, low funding and low salaries, that have contributed to stress and low morale in the profession.

It was in response to the broadened role of the teacher as mother, that programmes of social and personal development were devised to try to meet, somewhat belatedly, the needs of the confused pupils who had been taught, it was said, 'too much in the head', and not enough 'in the heart'. Social and personal development, which in earlier generations had been part of a strong family and community, was now to be provided for in schools, in order to attempt to fill the huge emotional gap left by the collapse of the family and other structures of authority.

The New Left, in its most extreme form, saw the family and its surrogates in the community as an 'ideological conditioning device . . . the ultimately perfected form of non-meeting . . . [which] reinforces the effective power of the ruling class in any exploitative society' (Cooper, 1971, pp. 5-6). The calls were for a deinstitutionalisation of society, for instance in *The Radical Therapist* (1974), Illich (1971), Boyers (1971). Mitchell, using Freud, Marx and feminism, argues for a cultural revolution, which will be 'a struggle based on a theory of the social non-necessity at this stage of development of the laws instituted by patriarchy' (1974, p. 414). The Left, which had demanded the new freedoms and had aimed at destructuring family and community values in the first place, now moves in with its antidote – 'Lifeskills education'. Lifeskills education ranges widely over very many different aspects of community health and education, but in some specific areas which will be described in more detail in the next section, it is very radical and a cause for concern. But that there is a need for some action cannot be doubted.

One in fifty fifteen-year-olds becomes pregnant as sexual activity among teenagers is rising steeply. In the mid-eighties, about 25 per cent of sixteen-year-olds were sexually active, while the most recent research (early 1992), done by the Policy Studies Unit in areas in Britain as far apart as Newcastle and Exeter, shows that 40-50 per cent of that age group are sexually active. The moral and psychological dangers of these early involvements have been swept aside because anxiety within the helping professions is bound to centre on the more immediate problems to do with early pregnancies, abortions and AIDS. Less well known are the risks to young girls who are sexually active of cervical cancer and pelvic inflammatory disease, which will lead to infertility in later life.

Experts believe that teenagers, while appearing superficially sophisticated about sexual relationships, are in reality confused and naive. The peer pressures to have sex have acquired a momentum of their own. Adults and parents want young people to be responsible about sexual matters, while they themselves are increasingly confused and irresponsible. We will now turn to examine what is being offered to help these young people.

II: LIFESKILLS[1]

The back cover of Hopson and Scally's *Lifeskills Teaching* (1981) tells us that 'The post-industrial revolution is here and education must change to equip individuals with the competence, flexibility, and personal resilience needed to cope with social and working life in the age of the microprocessor.' The authors detail the flexibility required by someone leaving school today. This person can expect to have three or four different occupations in his or her lifetime; to have six to ten changes of job; to move away from where he or she grew up; to get married twice; to be prepared to be frequently retrained and to be involved in further education; and to spend some time unemployed.

The adaptability required goes quite deep. For instance, in relation to work, Hopson and Scally point out: 'the remnant of the Protestant work ethic, the belief that working at a job, any job is essential and a sign of one's moral integrity, must be eliminated. People must not feel guilty or be made to feel guilty because they do not have a job . . . What are we doing in our schools to help eliminate the Protestant work ethic and to alert our young people to the new facts of economic life . . . ?' (pp. 18–19).

In relation to marriage, they are equally radical. Relationships can no longer be considered lifelong because of the mobility that will be required of people in terms of changing jobs and places of work:

> People are having to learn to create relationships quickly in the knowledge that many of them will be temporary, and need also to learn how to end relationships. Creating, maintaining and ending relationships involves skills that we are only just beginning to identify; skills that were simply not required by the majority who lived in the community they were born into, rarely left the neighbourhood, and relied on blood ties for their security and identity. Ending relationships causes great problems, with guilt left-over from a bygone era. (p. 17)

They pose the question to teachers: 'Are we teaching them the skills of making, maintaining, and ending relationships, or are we reinforcing models of interpersonal relationships that may be less relevant to the new era?' (*ibid.*, p. 17). We can no longer expect permanency in relationships. We must make relationships quickly and be prepared to give them up quickly – not to become too attached or dependent, as this would restrict our freedom of movement and our growth as people.

The pace is hotting up: new jobs; homes moved; fashions adopted and discarded; more and more information gained and outdated. Images, ideas, possessions are taken in and discarded; diversities in lifestyles, subcultures, ethnic groups have to be understood and adapted to: what Alvin Toffler in his book *Future Shock* (1970) described as the era of 'overchoice', in which apathy and violence follow on as a result of being blasted with a bewildering array of demands and choices of nightmare intensity. Christopher Lasch spoke of a 'defensive contraction of the self', and our 'emotional disengagement' that has arisen out of fundamental social transformation: 'the replacement of a reliable world of durable objects, by a world of flickering images that make it harder and harder to distinguish reality from phantasy' (1984, p. 19).

'Lifeskills' attempts to prepare children for the post-industrial world. The skills needed to function well are first identified, and then learning strategies are designed to bring about the acquiring of those skills. These skills include:

(1) communication skills, which include how to deal with relationships, managing conflict, being assertive, working in groups, expressing feelings constructively, influencing and being influenced;

(2) self-skills, which includes basics like the three Rs, finding information and resources, problem-solving, identifying creative potential and developing it, managing time, discovering values and beliefs, developing positive self-esteem, decision-making, coping with transitions, developing a healthy lifestyle, coping with stress, and managing sexual needs;

(3) situational skills, including those needed in education, such as discovering options, and study methods; those needed at work would include job options, finding, keeping and changing jobs, coping without a job; those needed at home would include maintaining a home, living with others, managing leisure, using leisure to increase income;

(4) skills needed in the community, including being a skilled consumer, developing and using political awareness, using community resources.

Hopson and Scally subtitle their Lifeskills programme: 'Taking charge of yourself and your life', and the fundamental theme running through such Lifeskills programmes is the need to feel 'self-empowered', which implies the rather grandiose and omnipotent phantasy of having power *over* one's life. They write: 'the more self-empowered a person is, the more the person will experience fulfilment, achieve his or her potential, and become a more socially responsive caring and committed citizen' (1981, p. 24).

Another theme is the notion of choice. It is suggested that we can choose how we live our lives. One is encouraged to become aware of the fact that one is the 'author' of one's life. We may have been given a script by our parents, school, culture and social background, but we have a chance to rewrite the next chapter or chapters. The implication is that if you are a victim, you have chosen that path at some level. We must suspend judgement on such assertions until the next section.

In discussion with a group of sixth-year students who had been through a fairly intensive Lifeskills programme two years previously, I endeavoured to find out what they had gained from their experiences at that time and how they had been helped. They had had time to reflect and would, I felt, be able to give a reasonably balanced account. They were all in favour of the Lifeskills programmes, saying that they felt more confident, more extroverted and prepared to talk to other members of their class group whom they might otherwise have avoided. They felt they were more tolerant of others' viewpoints and had greater understanding of controversial social issues. They had got to know themselves better and were more aware of their own feelings and those of others. They still slagged each other off, but with less viciousness and less scapegoating.

An important part of their programme was a class trip away from the school setting, where they would spend a period of about four days living together under supervision. The task: to explore some of the issues affecting their lives, in depth, with trained counsellors and their form teacher, in group sessions. It was what they experienced on that trip that affected them the most and would leave a lasting impression, they said. A warmth and closeness was generated within the class group that they said would always stay with them. They spoke by way of contrast of the shock of coming 'back to reality' when the trip was over. When I asked them about confidentiality within the group and the risks that people run in exposing themselves in this way, they all said their confidentiality had been respected. Were any of the more isolated group members left painfully outside the group discussions? They said this was not the case in their groups, although some took longer to participate than others.

Then I asked them what their parents felt about these activities; they all said that their parents were very encouraging and supportive. One person said that her father was angry about her hearing a talk from a member of gay rights, but she was more or less able to talk him round – at least they had had a discussion about this subject.

I asked them what their feelings were about the churches and about authorities in general. They felt that they could speak to teachers more easily and felt less inferior. They felt more equal to their teachers. With the churches, they felt the same as many adolescents: the churches were out of touch, too remote and far too inclined to moralise. We have to work things for ourselves, it is our lives and we have to live them, they insisted. So then I asked them what did they believe in and value. After a pause, they spoke about caring for one another, listening to the other's point of view, not hurting other people.

Such a positive response to Lifeskills education is common. The students have a good time and there is much positive feedback, in stark contrast to the grind of the daily timetable. Parents are pleased as they feel something is being done. To criticise programmes that seem to be so popular and successful, from a superficial point of view, becomes all the harder, while of course it is also all the more necessary.

The whole Lifeskills philosophy has an amazing optimism about it. It is about getting up and doing things for yourself. All you have to do is master the required skills, whether or not these be car maintenance or parenting. Everything is fluid, so you can change your life: 'we can't change the world but we can change our part of it'. 'Tomorrow can be different from today.' 'We are all learners and teachers.' 'We can do too much for people.' 'When you feel you need a cigarette, grab a human being.' 'Good intentions are never enough.' Sloganising is part of the Lifeskills business: it helps positive reinforcement, it sets the mind in the right direction. The positive feedback that one gets from learning the new skill reinforces the behaviour, and so on. It is simple, it is appealing, it meets people's needs, it is popular because it is direct and not hidebound with jargon and academism. It is democratic and egalitarian: we are all learning and we all need to continue updating our skills. Above all, Lifeskills has developed the skill of selling itself. Similar human relations training techniques and skills training are used in the professions, in industry and even the church. But there are problems and concerns with both the philosophy and practice of Lifeskills and related progressive methods of education which began to grow during the eighties.

For instance, Peter Scott writes in the *Listener* (6.2.86) of the backlash uniting both Left and Right against the new liberal methods of education pioneered during the sixties and seventies, creating 'a rising tide of mediocrity in education'. There was concern fundamentally about the loss of traditional values and academic standards. This was a multinational phenomenon. In America the new conservatism stemmed from a perceived need 'to recover national pride after the dark Vietnam years'; whereas in France, a 'left-wing patriotism informed educational policy . . . trying to revive the more rigorous traditions of nineteenth-century education'. In Britain, it was Labour's leader Jim Callaghan in 1976 who first called for the implementation of the National Curriculum. In Ireland, concern was expressed about the loss of traditional Catholic values.

There is more to these concerns than the normal historical swing of the pendulum from tradition to liberalism and back to tradition again. Perhaps the apparent or real demands of the post-industrial revolution involve a deeper break with the past than has ever occurred before. There is a feeling of panic which stems from the ever-increasing pace of technological change, from the fear of new and deeper recessions, from the constant revelations of abuses of power in both the political and the personal spheres.

There is concern too about the weakened state of the family. It has taken rising crime rates, juvenile delinquency, increases in mental illness and escalating costs of socialised welfare for us to realise that state agencies are a poor substitute for the strong family.

The progressive Lifeskills philosophy seems so frighteningly superficial in its belief that relationships and the important commitments of life can be sustained through hardship and despair as well as fulfilment and success by rationally setting goals and learning communication skills. We can learn new skills in communicating only on the secure foundation based on the lived experience of being held in a more or less reliable family which has endured. It is true that families do cause their children problems, and gross psychopathology in one or the other parent causes deep disturbance. But one hundred years of psychoanalytic research has convincingly pointed up the profound need that children have of sustained contact with and encouragement from reasonable, normal (not perfect) parents and relatives.

The prospect of more frequent changes in important relationships which involve children, and of teaching students that this is a necessary adaptation to the new society and that we should be able to end relationships 'without guilt', raises the spectre of even more social and personal pathology in the future. Many experts believe that the dominant pathology at the present time does not involve guilt about sexual impulses or unruly drives, as was common earlier this century, but now centres around the existence or non-existence of a self (Kohut 1977, Guntrip, 1964). The formation of the person and the security or lack of it in that self-structure is the dominant issue. To put it another way and to quote Martin Amis (1986, p. 208), 'We are reminded that "being human" isn't the automatic condition of every human being.' Perhaps children are going to pay an increasingly high price for the newly found (and learned) freedoms of their parents.

There is one other worry at least: that is the elimination of the work ethic. Of course if it hadn't been for some kind of work ethic – Protestant or otherwise – we wouldn't have had the industrial revolution, let alone the post-industrial revolution. Productive work (whether or not it is paid employment) requires concentration, discipline, creativity, toleration of tedium, frustration and disappointment, and what Freud called an adaptation to the 'reality principle' over the 'pleasure principle'. This training takes many years (often without self-motivation) and does not immediately yield pleasure or satisfaction. The belief that new work skills can be acquired almost effortlessly and that one might be able to turn one's hand to anything seems dangerously naive, especially if it rests upon a poor work record in school. Of course students need more choices, vocational guidance and training, but these can only be valuable when they emerge out of an exposure to the richness of the cultural heritage.

Are Lifeskills education and the related 'Psycho-business' (Hinds, 1988) a form of American cultural imperialism which has the power to sweep all traditions before it? Or is this the new paradigm for modern education, which must fit its students for the realities of the post-industrial age and the horrendous pace of change? Or is it a subversive ideology in the guise of an educational programme?

III: CRITIQUE OF LIFESKILLS EDUCATION

I have traced the origins of Lifeskills educational programmes to the cultural revolution of the sixties and have noted the influence of the New Left. I have briefly outlined the theory and practice of Lifeskills education and discussed its popularity among many pupils and parents. But it is appropriate now to look in more detail at some of the criticisms levelled at these and related trends in education, some of which were alluded to in the last section.

Under the influence of the Left in Britain, education has been used for the purposes of social engineering in recent decades.[2] The purpose of teaching was above all else to produce equality of class, race and gender. Academic standards are elitist – part of a white literary culture which was imposed totally inappropriately on the masses both in Britain and her colonies. Efforts to uphold intellectual standards were seen as a way of keeping the masses in their place. Consequently, when standards began to fall, the Left justified this as liberation. The wave of immigrants from the New Commonwealth during the fifties and sixties gave a new impetus to egalitarianism. Concern began to be expressed that Afro-Caribbean children performed badly in school, especially those from low-paid and socially deprived backgrounds. Asian children had little or no English and a cultural heritage totally distinct from the white British secular culture. Initially, the immigrants, as they were then called, were encouraged to become part of mainstream British culture. But as children from ethnic minorities became concentrated in various inner-city areas in, for example, London and the Midlands, there was an increasing demand for 'multicultural' education for blacks as well as whites. But, for those on the far Left, multiculturalism was a palliative to deceive the minority ethnic communities, to hide from them the real racist nature of British society. So an 'anti-racist' policy was focused on in some schools.

A Lifeskills programme would include not only those personal skills referred to in the last section dealing with relationships, work, leisure and so on, but also an awareness of ethnic difference and racism. With so much effort being put into teaching children the skills of living in a classless and multiracial society, it was not surprising that educational standards suffered in quite such a dramatic way. A number of reports at the end of the last decade showed just how far the rot had set in. The Adult Literacy Unit was indicating that nearly six million adults in Britain now experience 'literacy problems'. English teachers no longer know enough about English grammar to teach their own language effectively. Britain has fewer students in full-time education up to eighteen than any other major industrialised nation. Only 40 per cent of sixteen-year-olds study French for examinations, compared to 80 per cent of French sixteen-year-olds who study English. The science journal *Nature* reported that an astounding two-thirds of the British population did not know that the earth goes round the sun once a year.

Furthermore, an important academic report by the Policy Studies Unit in June 1989, entitled *The School Effect: a Study in Multiracial Comprehensives*, confirmed what Rightist critics of egalitarian education have asserted all along, that both black and white children have suffered from their ideologically based curriculum. This was a very thorough study involving following more than 3,000 children from the ages of eleven to sixteen in twenty urban comprehensive schools. It concluded that levels of educational achievement are 'radically higher in some schools than in others'. The school was found to be a more important factor than the child's ethnic group as far as educational attainment was concerned. Or, to put it another way, 'schools that are good for white people tend to be equally good for black people'. Also, the report found little evidence of racism in multiethnic schools or of parental complaints about racial prejudice. The quality of the school, and in particular the calibre of the head teacher, was indeed the decisive factor in pupil performance.

We might note in passing that poor schools and poor education are not recent phenomena in England. As Jenkins (1987) makes plain, education was not seen historically as a priority. Early industrialisation led to complacency and the 'cult of the gentleman' and the 'cult of the practical man'. This was part of the British national economic decline which has been a long-term trend since the First World War.

But let us return to the present. The pendulum has swung more to the Right with the advent of the National Curriculum, the regular testing of students and the overall 'return to basics'. But the situation is still fluid. The Left has been partially discredited and the 'new realism' has spread to education. But the cultural revolution has happened, and the return cannot ever be a simple moving back. So much has changed. However, we must leave these complex issues here and return to the psychological needs of the young people who are at the heart of this ideological confusion.

Psychoanalytic theory identifies the primary school age as roughly the stage of *latency*. During this time psychosexual maturation marks time. It is a time of relative emotional tranquillity. It is the fourth stage of Erikson's (1950) eight stages of human development, 'industry versus inferiority', which is the time when a child can turn its attention to the world of work and begin acquiring the skills of work. Puberty and adolescence, by contrast, is a time of emotional turmoil, characterised by Erikson as 'identity versus role confusion'. According to Erikson:

> The integration now taking place in the form of ego identity is more than the sum of the childhood identifications. It is the accrued experience of the ego's ability to integrate all identifications with the vicissitudes of the libido, with the aptitudes developed out of endowment, and with the opportunities offered in social roles. (1950, p. 253)

But there is the danger of role confusion, which includes doubt about one's sexual identity. The fear of this confusion may lead to an over-identification with heroes, gangs, cliques and crowds to the point of apparent complete loss of individuality. What Erikson has to say next is especially relevant to this chapter:

> The adolescent mind is essentially the mind of the *moratorium*, a psychosocial stage between childhood and adulthood, and between the morality learned by the child, and the ethics to be developed by the

adult. It is an *ideological* [my italics] mind – and, indeed, it is the *ideological* outlook of a society that speaks most clearly to the adolescent . . . (p. 254)

It is indeed a time of idealism, of extremes and of danger. Anna Freud speaks in a similar vein: 'Adolescents are excessively egoistic, regarding themselves as the centre of the universe and the sole object of interest, and yet at no time in later life are they capable of so much self sacrifice and devotion' (1936, p. 137). It is a time when a relatively strong id confronts a relatively weak ego. The sheer quantity of sexual and aggressive energy can be threatening and can be acted upon or strongly defended against. Anna Freud notes the extremes that can occur: between instinctual excess and asceticism; between instinctual conflict and abstract thinking and intellectualisation; between self-isolation and passionate and sometimes quickly alternating relationships.

Melanie Klein notes the recrudescence of the early anxiety situations in the adolescence – the anxieties of the paranoid-schizoid and the depressive positions. She notes the increase in aggression during adolescence and links it with idealism: 'When hatred reaches such strength, the necessity to preserve goodness within and without becomes all the more urgent. The aggressive youth is therefore driven to find people whom he can look up to and idealize' (1937, p. 329).

For Winnicott, growing up and separation from the parents unconsciously is regarded as a life-and-death struggle. Growing up means taking the parent's place. 'In the total unconscious phantasy belonging to growth at puberty and in adolescence, there is *the death of someone*' (1971a, p. 145). And as a corollary, Winnicott says that 'it seems that the latent sense of guilt of the adolescent is terrific, and it takes years for the development in an individual of a capacity to discover in the self the balance of the good and the bad, the hate and the destruction that go with love, within the self' (p. 148).

Let us say that, viewed from the vantage point of the unconscious, adolescence is an intensely dramatic and disturbing time where anything from the point of view of phantasy is possible. Fortunately there is an ego which comes between that unconscious and the outside world, but that ego is in a relatively immature state.

How does Lifeskills education impinge upon that cauldron of

unconscious phantasy that we have briefly outlined above? Firstly, we can assert that the sorts of interventions that are likely to occur in the Lifeskills classes do not take sufficient cognisance of the potential *depth* and *power* of those unconscious forces. For instance, let us take the widely held belief that adolescents are adult, free to choose, and are able to take charge of their own lives if only their parents and teachers would leave them alone, that is, not try to exert authority and guidance over them. The idea is that given the right environment they will become 'self-empowered'. This is quite clearly not the case. It is not demeaning but merely realistic to say that adolescence is a time of immaturity. Adolescents are experiencing new and strong impulses for the first time since the infantile prototypes of the Oedipal and pre-Oedipal period were laid down. Now, in contrast to the infantile situation, they have the physical capacity to *act* on those impulses. The weakness of the ego in the face of these impulses makes for very little freedom.[3] The adolescent is often pushed, pulled and driven by impulse and defence which frequently must be contained and *not* acted upon. The notion of self-empowerment then plays into the hands of a grandiose defence which is a denial of weakness and immaturity. It inflates and narcissistically gratifies an ego which is in reality beleaguered by intimidating internal and external forces. It conjures up infantile phantasies of omnipotence and triumph and fosters and nurtures these tendencies, which can make real education, which requires some acceptance of one's limitations, almost impossible.[4]

A closely related idea is that children will learn better if they are given more freedom to choose activities that interest them, if they can experiment and find out in their own way, work at their own pace. Often work-cards are provided which will lead the student through a particular topic while the teacher tends to be only an intermittent guide or a 'facilitator'. Such methods are part and parcel of the child-centred approach to learning. Again the assumption is that children are adults and will be highly motivated and inquisitive, given the freedom to do it themselves. The reality is that new learning, particularly learning that is not immediately rewarding or appealing, creates anxiety, and this can be of sufficient quantity to deter a child from embarking on a course of study that might ultimately yield pleasure and a sense of ego-mastery. But instead the ego takes the line of least resistance and the anxiety is avoided. The presence of the teacher is essential to the extent that he or she lends ego-support to the child enabling him or her to overcome the initial worries.

Together with a belief in freedom for the adolescent, the Lifeskills philosophy also implies an antagonism to authority, which is clearly subversive. Parental values in relation to work and sexuality come under scrutiny. One hears some teachers openly sharing their own views about a wide range of experiences, with drugs, with alternative lifestyles, their views on the 'pointlessness' of the exam system, and so on. And one has seen hard-working pupils with potential dramatically change into 'laid-back', 'cool' individuals who give up their studies and take up radical issues which they wear as a kind of badge. Of course there is nothing new in this. During the fifties and sixties one was encouraged to 'drop out' for a while and see the world. This was to be a temporary experience and essentially prophylactic in the otherwise ongoing career of a very middle-class child. Working-class school leavers had no such options. But today, the situation is quite different: what was rare and interesting in the fifties has now become an alternative lifestyle option which means many years of life wasted in relatively unproductive work or indeed no work at all. One is reminded of the high notions of the characters in Doris Lessing's novel *The Good Terrorist*. The reason why the situation now is considerably more dangerous is because a *normal* tendency of adolescence, namely to overthrow (kill off in phantasy) authority, has become part of an educational philosophy of liberation. The rebelliousness of adolescence, if left to its own devices, in healthy individuals works itself out in giving teachers and others a hard time, but ends in deepening the personality and establishing individuality. But when the rebellion is also advocated by a small number of teachers there is a danger of fundamental destabilisation of the personality, particularly in those individuals more vulnerable to identity confusion. For some people this means a more or less permanent impairment of ego functioning. One cannot lay all the blame for these casualties on any aspect of a modern curriculum, but an educational programme that lends its weight to such a powerful unconscious phantasy is a factor in the breakdown of those personalities.[5]

Another result of the general overthrow of authority is the loss to adolescence of the collected wisdom of the past. The loss of the old paternal super-ego, which was noted in the last chapter, means the loss not only of valuable ego-support but also of the collected knowledge of generations. This is why modern education is criticised for being so shallow and it is the reason why there is a demand to bring back the classical languages and the teaching of content-based history, to take just two examples.[6]

The absence of real external authorities tends to create a craving for substitute super-ego structures in the outside world which perhaps will assuage the anxiety generated by rebellious impulses. We witness the growth in recent years of religious cults which answer the adolescent's need for self-sacrifice, but unfortunately in a way that abandons reason. At the end of a class on evolution a sixth-year female student approached the teacher with the suggestion that he should join the particular religious group that both she and her parents belonged to. During the class itself the teacher had alluded to the so-called gaps in the fossil record. The student had taken this to mean that the teacher was uncertain about the whole theory of evolution. Her group believed in 'creation theory', and she went on to point out how much evil and destructiveness there was in the world and that Christianity was able to save her from this. When the teacher pointed out that perhaps she had sacrificed her critical faculties for the sake of peace of mind, the student left without replying.[7]

Another cause for concern is the intrusion into the essential privacy of the young person. Some of the methods used in Lifeskills classes derive in part from the Human Potential movement. Implied here is the need to 'get in touch with your feelings', to become less defensive and inhibited, to 'get the anger out', to beat the cushion (standing for your mother or your teacher). Reason and thought tend to be devalued as probably being defensive. The discussions are democratic and the teacher – now designated facilitator – remains 'neutral', not imposing his or her point of view. The facilitator is just another member of the group. There may be talks given by a woman from the rape crisis centre, or someone from gay rights, or a reformed drug addict, or someone who has been sexually abused as a child, and so on. There can be a highly evocative atmosphere and hype which involves exhibitionistic and voyeuristic gratification and a feeling of being exposed too directly to the most pornographic elements in the adult world. One sixteen-year-old boy emerged from a talk given by a prominent and articulate member of the women's movement feeling guilty for being male. She was speaking from a highly committed position and with much experience of life (she was in her mid-thirties) and he, on the other hand, was slowly emerging into an awareness of sexuality and what it means to be male. The intrusive and castrating nature of her talk had clearly unnerved him.

Similarly, adolescent girls are likely to hear about rape and sexual abuse sometimes before they have had any sexual experience themselves. One wonders about the hidden sadism of those who arrange for such 'frank and open' discussions. There is a story told of a priest who used to go to Catholic girls' schools to give their only sex education classes. In order to deter them from sexual experimentation he used to produce his jar containing a foetus suspended in formalin. However, I should add that he was not part of a Lifeskills programme. In another class the students were asked to write down all the common terms in current usage on the street for the sexual parts of the body. A number of children were reluctant or inhibited, but they were told it was to free them from just those inhibitions that the exercise was carried out.

The danger of these more intrusive aspects of Lifeskills programmes is not so much the methods (although some are questionable even for the adults for whom they were first designed) but the *timing*. Adolescence is a time of *privacy*, a time of beginning to possess one's own world, gradually separating off from the parental world. To do this one needs space. It does not mean that one has to be alone, but it does mean relative freedom from intrusion. The very close friendships of adolescence are part of that process of natural sharing which is in sharp contrast to exercises in group discussions. There is a natural reticence, a natural tentativeness that must be respected.

The greatest intrusion into privacy for the adolescent is likely to be in the area of human sexuality. The radical approach to sex education is that all forms of sexual activity must be freed from anxiety and control. And surely the removal of anxiety must be a good thing. First, children can be told about sexual practices that they didn't know existed, which can be disturbing on the conscious level and even more disturbing when these link up with unconscious infantile phantasies. For instance, all children are reassured about masturbation, that is a normal part of adolescence and doesn't affect you physically or mentally. Yet masturbation still causes anxiety, because it is linked unconsciously to incestuous phantasies. And anxiety about sexuality, up to a point, is necessary and correct. Unconsciously sexuality is linked to death and creativity and is therefore profoundly disturbing and exciting. Attempts to sanitise sexuality and *Make it Happy* – the title of a book for teenagers by Jane Cousins (1979) – are at best a diversion and at worst intrusively remove the adolescent from an essential psychical conflict for the enriching of his or her personality.

One point should be made here about the gay rights movement. Adolescent boys at male schools are likely in some cases to form strong homosexual attachments for a time. Left alone, most will eventually form a heterosexual orientation albeit with a strong repressed homosexuality. But with the publicity given to gay rights, there is a danger that the adolescent boy, possibly filled with anxiety, may have these elements within his total personality accentuated to the possible exclusion of an emerging hetero-sexuality. Left alone – this is the important point – the homosexual and the heterosexual potentialities will not be prematurely foreclosed and therefore both can contribute to the enrichment of the personality.

It will be clear from the foregoing that adolescents need privacy to allow the *internal* evolution of the various psychical elements each of which strives at different times to take command of the personality. Ideologically motivated adults upset this delicate balance: those on the Left favouring impulse at the expense of defence; those on the Right favouring defence and cutting off impulse. Both approaches impoverish psychical development, because they tend to foreclose development *through* conflict and anxiety. As we have seen, conflict and anxiety are inherent in life in general, but reach an extreme during adolescent development. It is important that the adolescent's environment can understand and to some extent limit and contain these stresses. The adolescent ego needs support and restriction at times by adults and teachers. He or she needs figures with whom to identify and to idealise in order to elaborate a personal idiom.

Adolescents need adult figures with whom to interact and conflict, adults who are available to receive projections, contain them and return them in a less dangerous form. Let us take for example the student who becomes extremely anxious about examinations. The other members of the family receive the anxiety and begin to feel depressed and anxious themselves. With difficulty they tolerate these feelings, talk about them, remember their own exams, think of ways to deal with the anxiety and so on, and the student in many cases will be better able to tolerate the distress, because it no longer assumes such overwhelming proportions.

But of course such containing is not always possible. Consider the much more serious difficulty posed by the adolescent who abuses and attacks the family and the parents. Here it is important for the parents to survive intact so that the adolescent's worst fears – namely that his or her attacks *in reality* destroy people – will not be realised. The parents' opposition to the adolescent's behaviour and their survival of it will perhaps enable the adolescent to better tolerate and *use* his or her own aggression instead of having to act it out. By surviving it they have detoxified it and made it safe. However, this is not always the case and outside help may be needed, in a minority of more disturbed individuals. As has been pointed out in earlier chapters and in this one, the cultural conditions now prevalent tend to foster destructive acting-out.

Sublimation is the process that sponsors psychical evolution. It involves the displacement of sexual (mostly pregenital, component instincts) from their original forbidden aims onto 'higher' or more civilised aims, retaining 'the main purpose of Eros – that of uniting and binding – insofar as it helps towards establishing unity, or a tendency to unity, which is particularly characteristic of the ego' (Freud, 1923, p. 45). Melanie Klein's concept of reparation is closely linked to sublimation in that the child seeks ways to repair the damage it has done in phantasy by later creative efforts. Clearly, education is essentially about sublimation – a leading-out from phantasies of omnipotence and grandiosity towards creativity and the search for wisdom and truth. This is facilitated by adults who themselves embody those same qualities.

Lifeskills education – and let us broaden things slightly to include the general propaganda in the media aimed at youth outside the school – makes of the adolescent psyche a marketplace to be colonised by powerful ideological forces. These invade and pollute the space required for psychical maturation, disrupting or reversing sublimatory processes in favour of the pleasure principle over the reality principle. All these trends we have been discussing are popular, because they side with the impulses against the restraints of the ego and super-ego. They imply that struggle, conflict, guilt and anxiety are pathological, rather than being essential, in some measure at least, for the attainment of depth and vitality.

George Steiner (1989) invokes those Renaissance and Enlightenment manuals on courtesy concerned with children, with which I introduced these three chapters, as a metaphor which completely reverses the current cultural idiom. These manuals of decorum detail the nuances of gesture and a necessary openness, which define varying degrees and intensities of reception of the world in terms of welcome.

> The issue is that of civility towards the inward savour of things. What means have we to integrate that savour into the fabric of our own identity? We need a terminology which plainly articulates the intuition that an experience of communicated forms of meaning demands, fundamentally, a courtesy or a tact of heart, a tact of sensibility and an intellection. (1989, pp. 148-9)

But we can only speak of reception and welcome if on the one hand we have an approach, a method, a training, and on the other a reserve that is a space and a place into which the other can be greeted in freedom. It was education that used to be about the former, but the irony is that while we have greater and greater availability of cultural products from the past and the present to be welcomed, we have less and less the means of savouring and accommodating them. And the question of a place – an internal space – that will be respected is the crucial question for adolescence and later. It was Winnicott, amongst psychoanalysts, who was most keenly aware of the need to provide this space, free from impingement, which leads to falseness. He was clear that this space has to be fought for, ruthlessly and anti-socially if necessary, against an environment which always threatens.

As Bellow says:

> None of this would matter if there were no such thing as human nature. That is to say, if there was not some unexplained inner primordial disagreement with what is happening . . . And what a writer like me is apt to feel . . . is some loss of power to experience life. That people are in a sense deprived of it now, to experience it on their own terms . . . to be able to interpret what happens to you independently. And now it's all jargon, it's all nonsense, it's all slogans. It's all false descriptions and fabrication. And of course, one resists that. (Quoted in Bourne *et al.*, 1987, pp. 24-5)

But this kind of creative resistance, this pushing back of the welter of consumerism, propaganda, entertainment, pornography of the public space, this capacity to retreat into a private core, is a psychological achievement. It is not to be confused with a schizoid retreat into isolation. Instead it has much to do with the capacity to be alone in the presence of the other. It is not based on hatred of the world, but is instead a holding onto a personal centre from which to experience the world in all its diversity. Without some sense of this centre, the private space is overwhelmed, apathy and violence ensue.

Education has been the battleground, and it is no wonder that standards have fallen so low. The attempt to liberate children from the so-called white, middle-class, sexist, racist, elitist, inhibited and repressive past has led to confusion and crisis. The question now is whether or not the New Right in its counteroffensive will come closer to respecting the needs of young people for reticence, privacy, security, unforced intimacy and the search for ideals.

A CONCLUSION

Psychoanalysis, since Freud, has become an exciting, complex and sometimes contradictory set of ideas about the human condition, as different workers and theorists have exploited various themes in Freud's pioneering work.

In the early part of this century psychoanalysis was seen as a radical critical theory. During the thirties, the influential Frankfurt school of critical theorists developed a strong interest in psychoanalysis, elaborating a radical critique of modern technological society with its positivist philosophy of science, its 'culture industry', and its domination of the individual. Exiled during the Nazi period to North America, the school became a prominent influence throughout much of Europe and America on the return to Germany of at least some of its members in 1950.

With the rise of the radical student movement in the sixties, it was Herbert Marcuse, rather than such significant figures as Adorno and Horkheimer, who was to be the leading representative of the new form of critical thought. Marcuse (1956) had developed a reinterpretation of Freud. He criticised Fromm, an important figure in the movement in earlier years, for his so-called neo-Freudian revisionism. Fromm had indeed shifted the emphasis from the psychoanalytic to the cultural, which was part of a trend that included Karen Horney, Harry Stack Sullivan, Alfred Adler and Clara Thomson.

Indeed many on the Left were to abandon Freud and his conception of the basic unchangeability of human nature. The notion of happiness and liberation, forever unattainable within civilisation, was rejected as reactionary. The quest for happiness was to pass, as we have seen, to the new groups who believed in human potential.

But central to this book is the argument that the escape from psychoanalysis is also the escape from the prohibition on desire instigated by the father.[1] The essential helplessness of the human infant, combined with the precocity of its sexuality, makes for a deeply humiliating experience as formative of the first months of postnatal existence.[2] The substance of psychoanalytic theory is not just the discovery and description of the unconscious, but also those instinctual vicissitudes which make conflict, ambivalence and unhappiness the bedrock of human existence. And paradoxically, it is just this impossibility of fulfilling desire that is essential for human *activity*. Desire requires a lack or an obstacle in order to be created. Complete fulfilment of desire is death. The gulf between desire and satisfaction is the transitional space described by Winnicott as the location of cultural experience. That space contains a promise. It contains a hope for the future emanating from the ego-ideal, because it contains an interdict from the father. He is the barrier that will keep us forever alienated from a *total* pleasure, and will place us within reality and the law.

Therefore, what is the nature of this promise, or this hope? It implies the *sublimation* of desire at the behest of the father, in accordance with the reality principle. We must leave the exciting, terrifying, incestuous fusion with the mother of infancy, and situate ourselves within the world of the father. We must leave the privileged dyadic relationship, which is a perfect unity and a perfect satisfaction, and allow the entry of a third term – namely the Symbolic dimension, which is an acceptance of Otherness, of differentiation, of separation, which constitutes the birth of desire.

Norman O. Brown, however, is dismissive of sublimation, as it 'perpetuates the incapacity of the infantile ego to bear the full reality of living and dying and continues the infantile mechanism for diluting (desexualising) experience to the point where we can bear it' (1959, p. 155). Instead, he favours what he calls 'the Dionysian Ego', following Nietzsche, against Apollo, who is the god of form, of sublimation and the rational. He acknowledges that there are dangers in following Dionysus – namely, the excesses of de Sade and the politics of Hitler. His Dionysian ego is a psychoanalytic consciousness, 'which is not the Apollonian scholasticism of orthodox psychoanalysis, but a consciousness

embracing and affirming instinctual reality – Dionysian consciousness' (p. 159).

Marcuse is likewise critical of sublimation. 'Freedom in
civilization is essentially antagonistic to happiness: it involves the
repressive modification (sublimation) of happiness. Conversely,
the unconscious . . . is the drive for integral gratification which is
the absence of want and repression' (1955, p. 33). Psychoanalysis
is far more than a therapeutic device. It involves 'the liberation of
memory . . . [and] as cognition gives way to re-cognition, the
forbidden images and impulses of childhood begin to tell the truth
that reason denies. Regression assumes a progressive function'
(p. 34).

Badcock regards psychoanalysis as 'the ultimate stage in man's
emancipation from the past and from the neurosis of religion'
(1980, p. 248). He argues that 'there exists a deep and significant
analogy between the history of the individual and that of the entire
human race as reflected in religion' (p. 251). With the advent of
psychoanalysis, he believes, humankind has recovered from a long
illness and finally achieved the 'exorcism of God'. This means that
for the mature individual, 'the ego has become master in its own
house and has established the reality principle as the main arbiter
of its own action' (p. 231). He goes on:

> The process of the replacement of blind repression by conscious and
> reasonable renunciation is the outcome of the tremendous advance in
> rationality, represented by psychoanalysis, over all previous moral and
> psychological progress. It is the ultimate embodiment of the reality
> principle in morality; it marks the final achievement of realism, reason
> and truth in the assessment of human conduct. For the culture as a
> whole, it represents the state of ideal, rational maturity which
> psychoanalysis aims to provide for the successfully analysed individual.
> (1980, p. 232)

However, he does also acknowledge that there are problems in
Western civilisation: 'the mass-psychopathology of Christianity is
still strongly present, masquerading under the name of Socialism'
(p. 232).

Badcock's over-valuation both of psychoanalysis and what it can
achieve, and this highly rational ego, is as excessive as the view of
those on the Left who would seek the full embracing of instinctual

reality for the sake of happiness.[3] Freud is more modest. In speaking of avoiding suffering, he says:

> The task here is that of shifting the instinctual aims in such a way that they cannot come up against frustration from the external world. In this, sublimation of the instincts lends its assistance. One gains the most if one can sufficiently heighten the yield of pleasure from the sources of psychical and intellectual work. When that is so, fate can do little against one. A satisfaction of this kind, such as an artist's joy in creating, in giving his phantasies body, or a scientist's in solving problems or discovering truths, has a special quality . . . (1929, p. 79)

Freud acknowledges that the 'intensity is mild as compared to that derived from the sating of crude and primary instinctual impulses', and that this method is 'accessible only to a few people'. But he also points out the value of everyday work in this context, in 'the possibility it offers of displacing a large amount of libidinal components, whether narcissistic, aggressive or even erotic' (p. 80).

But let us attempt here to situate this debate, which has been going on within psychoanalysis, more precisely within our late twentieth-century culture. Here is Milan Kundera in his book *Immortality*:

> Suddenly frightened by her hatred she said to herself: the world is at some sort of border; if it is crossed everything will turn to madness: people will walk the streets holding forget-me-nots or kill one another on sight. And it will take very little for the glass to overflow, perhaps just one drop: perhaps just one car too many, or one person, or one decibel. There is a certain quantitative border that must not be crossed, yet no one stands guard over it and perhaps no one even realises that it exists. (1991, p. 23)

Such a fragility is expressed through the character of Agnes in this book. Such a potentiality for madness: is this just the phantasy of a borderline patient, or some registration of the effects, or some representation of postmodernism? If a patient spoke like this in a psychoanalytic or psychiatric interview, we would think in terms of borderline pathology. We would think in a restricted way like this, which is appropriate for the consulting room. But we might also note her permeability and sensitivity to cultural impingements, her lack of protection, her closeness to and acute sense of danger.

Recently, I was stopped in the street by a woman I had once taught, and after our mutual greeting she launched into an attack on the dangers of radioactive pollution in the Irish Sea from Sellafield. She was pointing and shaking her hand towards the sea, which was less than a mile away. We were all in great danger from this nuclear reprocessing plant, which lies only a few dozen miles to the east. Of course, she is right. There are dangers, and there have been leaks, from this plant. But many of us can go on with our daily lives without undue worry, in a state of alienation. But of course, she, like Agnes, is closer to the truth. They are less separated off or barred from the unconscious, they are less alienated, but in fact they find it harder to live and get on with a particular life in a particular place, because they have got caught up in a greater totality of Being. They are constantly in danger of losing their specific identity, which is limiting and allows for a proper separate otherness of the Other.

But the question is, who or what, under contemporary conditions, protects us from this inner world, who keeps consciousness separated off sufficiently from the unconscious? We can no longer count on this. We can no longer count on a certain essential privacy, a certain inner reserve involving the capacity to sublimate, to which Freud was alluding. In our time, privacy and reserve are regarded as almost pathological. We have lost a certain fixity of personal boundaries. Ours is a culture of expression, of telling all, of sharing intimacies, preferably to a mass readership or to television and radio audiences. Such intimate revelations are valued as courageous, honest, open and so on. Privacy and a certain reticence are now seen to be connected with inhibition, something to be slightly ashamed of.

It is therefore small wonder that we have so many people who appear to have lost or are close to losing a certain boundedness, a circumscription which guards an essential privacy and therefore an essential sanity. We can be without boundaries, and therefore things can flow out of us and into us without restriction; or, in terror of this possibility, we can erect boundaries of such intensity that nothing can get in or out. This is perhaps most dramatically represented by the incidence of rape and child abuse. From this perspective, these crimes involve a break into the most primitive and therefore most essential defences which stand guard over a fundamental autonomy and unknownness. We correctly regard these crimes very seriously, because we are aware of these fundamental breaches. It is sexuality that symbolises our privacy (the genitals are the private parts), and it is around sexuality therefore that invasions – both psychical and physical – will occur in a culture of total openness.

Critics of psychoanalysis would argue that it is precisely psychoanalysis that initiated and has been formative in a certain undoing of the personality. It is psychoanalysis that sponsored our excessive openness with each other and an emptying of ourselves. In earlier times, there were the great disciplines of silence, of diary-writing and letter-writing, as a means of preservation and self-reflection. Freud himself was a most private man. He made it a point twice in his life to destroy all his private papers. He wanted his private papers to be destroyed after his death. In the dream book, he analyses his own dreams, but only to a certain point.

But Reiff points to the post-Freudian belief that nothing is sacred. He suggests that, after Freud, 'everyman must become something of a genius about himself. But the imagination boggles at a culture made up mainly of virtuosi of the self' (1966, p. 28). He asserts that psychoanalysis, with its focus on the self, undermines values and brings about 'deconversion' and 'moral disarmament'. There is no escaping the assertion that psychoanalysis, coming as it did just as the old values of high bourgeois culture were collapsing, was catalytic in an historical process of 'liberation' from all constraint, which has been enthusiastically taken up by post-Freudian therapists. These, as we have seen, reverse much analytic theory and practice.

But it is at least arguable, and has been argued throughout this book, that psychoanalysis stops short of the wholesale overthrow of the super-ego, inscribed in the self during the Oedipus complex. Grunberger makes this clear. 'Where narcissism was, there Oedipus will be' (1989, p. 34). And 'psychoanalysis lives or dies by Oedipus' (p. 176). Psychoanalysis understands the absolute necessity of constraint and the impossibility of living a life of unbridled desire. It reserves the right to explore meanings and motives, but it cannot undermine the existence of meaning itself. To attempt deconstruct all meaning is an omnipotent act, and removes that core of privacy, of unfathomableness, which is at the heart of all creative and cultural action. This is the reason why an analysis never comes to an end and never finds out everything, because it always rests on the unknowable and the unfindable – the void, the silence from which we, as castrated and limited, must act.

The modern and postmodern exploration of nothingness, of an absolute zero, of nihilism, which is the implicit centre around which we revolve, cannot, however, be discounted. We live now with a total ephemerality, an instability, an illegitimacy, an endless recycling of texts, with no ultimate point of reference, no authorisation, and no longer any appeal to Logos. We have subjected ourselves to a rigorous disillusionment about which there can be no trivial consolation and no appeal.

However, it could be argued (but not by the deconstructionists themselves, of course) that such a radical denaturing of the modern self, such a pursuit of the last vestiges of meaning, is in itself an intensely ethical project, which owes a debt to the traditions which it is at the same time annihilating. It calls forth a movement, a radical concern, a desire to find meaning beyond an apparent meaninglessness. But any appeal to ultimacy on our part, or any other appeal to common sense, to the obvious meanings in life, the traditional interpretive consensus, and so on, cannot refute the deconstructionist argument. It cannot be refuted on its own terms.

Clearly this book does not hold with such a position. We live with the disastrous effects, the results on a huge scale of the annihilation of meanings and values. By suffering the massive incongruities and insanities that proceed from such a radical absence, we are asserting here the need for the essential privacy of the self, a place of resistance, the absolute necessity of it and the absolute unknownness of it – the place from which the subject, still with some centre of gravity, addresses the Other. Is this a place of absolute nothingness, or is it a place of potential plenitude? There must be no early closure of this question. Preoccupied as we always are with preliminary concerns, we block off this question. Psychoanalysis presses beyond these preliminary stories, these defensive screens, towards what has not yet been symbolised – always, as Freud pointed out, in the face of resistance. The resistance is analysed, but there is always a further point of absolute resistance which protects the essential muteness of what is unsymbolisable, of what is unspeakable (see Winnicott, 1963b). This is the area of primary illusion upon which the patient's essential experience of his or her own aliveness and reality depend.

It is this area which is threatened in our times both personally and globally. It is the solidity of this core subjectivity that resists psychosis – the implosion and loss of everything. Psychoanalysis drives us towards this point, towards the point of our own death, it circles around it, but never traverses it. Psychoanalysis loosens the secondary repressions, makes the conscious more permeable to the unconscious significations, but the primary repression, which establishes the subject as a distinct entity, isolated from the totality of Being, must remain in place.

It is just this in-placeness, this groundedness which is in question for the individual and for the culture as a whole. We have noted the omnipotent tendency to annihilate the past, to question and uproot cultural meanings. We have noted also the terrible crimes that have been enacted in the absence of those meanings. We witness the loss of social cohesion and supports and the massive release of instinctual energy which had formerly been held in repression by the individual and civilisation. This has led, on the one hand, to a pervasive primitivism which sweeps all before it, and on the other, to our reliance on the ego which, in the absence of any transcendental world view, has become inflated in the erroneous belief in its own self-mastery, technology and freedom. Our ignorance, denial and loss of respect for the unconscious, for this big Other, has involved us in an overwhelming by those forces.

Lacan, when questioned about why he was predicting the rise of racism worldwide, commented:

> It is foreseeable and the symptoms are everywhere. It is necessary, because as I am trying to explain, our enjoyment [*jouissance*] is going off the track. Only, the Other, the Absolute Other, is able to mark the position of this enjoyment, but only insofar as we are *separated* from this Other. As soon as we begin to mingle in this way, certain fantasies arise which have never been heard of before and they wouldn't have otherwise appeared . . . [Now] there is only the Other of another race.
>
> The precariousness of our own mode of enjoyment takes its bearings from a position which I designate as a surplus of enjoyment, and takes its bearings also from the ideal of overcoming (*plus-de-jouir*: both 'end-of-coming'/'excess of coming'/'overthrowing') . . . [This] is what we find today. This is what surplus value is. It is this base which locates us in relation to enjoyment; I refer to it as our mode. How can we hope

that the empty forms of our humanhysterianism [*humanitairerie*], disguising our extortions, can continue to last?[4]

It is indeed as if the assassinated father, who has no resting place, returns to fill the emptiness left by his humiliating departure, with new and daemonic images.

NOTES

PREFACE

1. The case histories or vignettes presented throughout this book have all of necessity been radically altered and fictionalised so as to guard confidentiality. Therefore any apparent likeness to any individual is purely coincidental.

CHAPTER 1

1. Psychoanalysis is expensive, but perhaps not as elitist as some of its critics might allege. Some analysts make allowances for patients on lower incomes, adjusting fees or reducing the frequency of visits. A distinction should perhaps be made between psychoanalytic psychotherapy and psychoanalysis in its 'purist' form. The latter normally requires five sessions per week and is clearly expensive. The former is more flexible and therefore is less of a financial burden.
2. Extracts taken from Malan (1979); see pp. 46–50 for a full description of the case.
3. Clearly the best way to a full understanding of psychoanalysis is through being analysed oneself and reading the psychoanalytic literature, while leading a full life. However, we should be reminded that our resistances are always present. The danger of a purely academic approach to analysis without going through the experience of therapy is of over-intellectualisation. It is for these reasons that all analysts must undergo the experience of therapy themselves during their training.

CHAPTER 2

1. The Religious Experience Unit in Oxford has investigated the occurrence of such experiences, and Sir Alistair Hardy, who founded the unit, maintains that as many as half the adult population of Britain have had such experiences, even though they may not belong to an institutional church.
2. Jonathan Hanaghan, encouraged by Ernest Jones, pioneered psychoanalysis in Ireland, following his own analysis with Douglas Bryan (first secretary of the British Psychoanalytic Society and translator of Karl Abraham) during the First World War. Hanaghan brought analysis to Ireland in 1917 and founded the Irish Psychoanalytical Association in 1942. He expounded a highly original synthesis of Freudian psychoanalysis and New Testament readings. He felt that if psychoanalysis was about truth, then ultimately it was about the truth of God within us.

His thinking would have something in common with others who wanted to situate psychoanalysis within a religious or existential framework. One thinks of Fromm (1957, 1976), Williams (1965), Lee (1948) and Macmurray (1954), who would all think in broadly similar terms. Suttie's view of religion as a psychosocial therapy of love has something in common with Hanaghan's approach, and we have already noted the influence of Buber and Tillich. Guntrip also had in mind the importance of religion when he pointed out that love was the fundamental therapeutic factor in psychotherapy. Religion in his view always stood for the good object relationship. But Hanaghan argues his case with more force, intensity and conviction than these writers.

After his death in 1967, Anna Freud wrote, in a private communication to his wife, that 'Hanaghan was a man who lived up to his ideas and ideals, and fulfilled his mission in life. That explains his strength and his happiness . . . I know it grieved him that we others could not share his union between analysis and religion. But I think it did not make him bitter, nor did it shake him.'

Hanaghan was clearly a leader, a teacher and an analyst of considerable inspirational power. He affected many people deeply. People came from many parts of the world to be analysed by him. However, he was not an *orthodox* analyst. He had an ecstatic vision of what people could become, which raises all kinds of problems from a psychoanalytic point of view, connected, broadly speaking, with our desire to be saved. This issue is taken up in the following pages.

3. Hanaghan's concept of the ego-ideal departs considerably from the classical view as expressed by Freud in his paper, 'On narcissism: an introduction' (1914b), and in *Group Psychology and the Analysis of the Ego* (1921). For Hanaghan, the ego-ideal is that structure which perceives truth, beauty and ultimate values. It perceives a transcendental reality beyond the ordinary everyday reality, which Hanaghan called 'actuality'. It is the ego's function to attend to the actuality-principle (Freud's reality principle), while it is the function of the ego-ideal to act as an inner guide to the ultimate reality and the realisation of our truest nature.

I shall refer to the ego-ideal again later in the next chapter.

4. Lacan, seminar given 16.4.58,

CHAPTER 3

1. For a fuller account of Klein's statements on the paranoid-schizoid position, see Klein, 1946. Hanna Segal (1973) makes explicit Klein's views, particularly in Chapters 3, 4 and 5. See also Segal, 1979,

Chapter 9. For a very good introduction and situating of Klein's work in relation to Freud, see Mitchell (1986).

2. Klein formulated her ideas on the depressive position before working out her hypothesis of the paranoid-schizoid position. The paper in 1935, and its more clearly formulated sequel in 1940, are central to the whole of Kleinian theory. See also Segal, 1973, Chapter 6, and 1979, Chapter 7, for further clarification.

3. At the beginning of this paper Winnicott makes clear his indebtedness to Klein, who had made real for him the *internal* world.

4. The notion of projective identification has become fundamental to Kleinian psychoanalysis since Melanie Klein introduced the term in 1946. Put simply, in its pathological form, it means the splitting of the self, and the forcing of the bad parts of the self and objects into another object. The other is then violently forced to comply, and carry the projection in a way of which he or she is often unaware. The cap is made to fit.

CHAPTER 4

1. The women's movement has a long history. The sixties and seventies saw a great resurgence of interest in feminism. Some of the leading writers include de Beauvoir (1952), Friedan (1963), Millett (1971), Greer (1970), Morgan (1970), Mitchell (1971), Oakley (1972, 1974), Rowbotham (1973), Brownmiller (1975), Sharpe (1976), Baker Miller (1976). Psychoanalysis has gone more or less silent on the subject since the so-called Freud–Jones debate during the thirties. However, more recently, the Lacanian re-reading of Freud helped to clarify and develop Freud's position by stressing the essential *symbolic* nature of the penis/phallus. Mitchell (1974) and Mitchell and Rose (1982) offer helpful elucidations here. The phallus is radically different from the penis as organ, and as such is *not* possessed by either sex. Of course, Freud was aware that boys do not actually lose their penis, and girls cannot actually have one, and therefore an accurate reading of Freud demands that the penis and castration must be considered in a symbolic sense. Lacan's thesis, which cannot be developed here, is that post-Oedipally both sexes are confronted with this fundamental 'lack', and that men and women have to assume this lack as they enter the 'Symbolic order'. Much of this chapter is concerned with the effects of the fight, by both men and women, against the realisation of this central issue, namely castration.

2. The men are still very much in a minority. Women who work outside the home still do most of the housework as well. A recent survey showed that these women prepare 77% of the meals, do 72% of the cleaning and 88% of the washing and ironing.

3. Stoller (1986) has shown that by the age of eighteen months a child can recognise itself as either male or female.
4. See, for instance, Eichenbaum and Orbach, 1982. They describe their approach as feminist and psychoanalytic, yet they seem to align themselves with the culture pattern school of Karen Horney, Clara Thompson, Harry Stack Sullivan and Erich Fromm. They emphasis the socialising impact of patriarchy, and implicitly reject the dynamically repressed unconscious. 'We do not believe that instinctual drives of libido and aggression are what shapes human psychology' (p. 109). And, appreciating Klein, they also deny her fundamental insights: 'What Klein saw in practice was in fact much richer than her explanation claims, for her observations are continually short-circuited by the insistence on the inner psychic life as instinctual rather than social' (p. 110). They stress that they diverge from the object relations theorists. Commenting on the work of Fairbairn, Guntrip and Winnicott, they stress that they

> acknowledge that the mother is not an object, mother is a person, a social and psychological being. What becomes internalised from this perspective then is not the object, but the different aspects of the mother. What the object relations theorists have failed to take into account is the psychology of the mother and the effects of the social position of women on the mother's psychology. (p. 113)

Therefore, by emphasising the realistic aspect of the mother and by playing down the magical, phantastic, mother-as-an-instinctual-object, side they are ignoring one-half of the truth. Of course the mother is a person, but she is also an object of desire and aggression and counteraggression. Avoidance of these psychical realities enables the 'badness' within to be exported and located in the patriarchal system. The infantile helplessness (of boys and girls) at the hands of a phantastically powerful mother is denied, split off and projected into a world that becomes, by virtue of the projection, victimising and destructive.

5. A brief example will illustrate how this phantasy can sometimes be acted out in the community. A boy in his teens began picking fights with the older boys in his school. Whenever he was requested to obey even a minor rule, he would react with violence. This boy had had a violent relationship with an impulsive father who had left the family when the boy was much younger. On occasion the boy would attack his teachers, particularly the young male teachers, many of whom were trying to help him. His school work deteriorated and eventually the school felt unable to contain his violent outbursts. He left in a triumphant mood to join a delinquent subculture.

This phantasy of revenge is not always acted out in the community. Sometimes the aggression is turned inwards against the self. In another case, a boy whose father was a chronic alcoholic and effectively absent from the family became accident-prone. Every year he would have a serious accident. On one occasion he jumped from a great height and broke his pelvis. On another he was playing with blank cartridges and one went off, cutting his arm badly.

CHAPTER 5

1. It is necessary to examine the history of childhood in some detail, in order to make clear the radical contrast between the old and the modern environment of children (see Aries, 1960).
2. Davidoff and Hall (1987) deal in more detail with the middle-class family of the time.
3. There is no intention here of idealising the 'old heterogeneous sociability'. It took place in the midst of degrading poverty and hardship, but it did have an important psychological function, which will be taken up in section III.
4. Of course this kind of extreme control was also prevalent during the nineteenth century. Let me cite one important and illustrative example. Freud's analysis of Schreber's *Memoirs* (Freud, 1911), for instance, directed researchers to correlate Schreber's paranoia with his father's very influential writing on the necessity for extreme strictness in child-rearing. Niederland (1984) returns to Schreber's father's writings, including editions of *Arztliche Zimmergymnastik* (Medical Indoor Gymnastics), as well as published and unpublished biographical material.

   The father's methods were not untypical of the time, the mid-nineteenth century. He was a doctor, lecturer, writer, educator and clinical instructor in the medical school of the University of Leipzig. He specialised in orthopaedics, and wrote about twenty books on the subject and guidelines for rearing children. He was a reformer, fanatically dedicated to his goals in the field of physical culture and health. He was a personality of great and lasting influence. He founded a cultist movement which has lasted until the present time. According to Niederland, Dr Schreber's biographer, Ritter, expressing his admiration of both Dr Schreber and Hitler, saw in the former a sort of spiritual precursor of Nazism.

   Dr Schreber's advice to parents was to use maximum pressure and coercion during the earliest years of a child's life. The child was to be subjected to vigorous physical and emotional training to promote health. Postural training was emphasised, and Dr Schreber developed various contraptions for the enforced maintenance of straight postures, even when sleeping. There were very strict rules governing behaviour orderliness, cleanliness, with no deviation allowed from the procedure, once established. Bad speaking habits were to be combated, as were 'the beginnings of passions' which were to be crushed, by frequent corporal punishment, 'because the ignoble parts of the child's crude nature must be countered through great strictness' (Niederland, p. 56). When the child had been punished, he had to shake hands with the punisher to avoid spite and bitterness. Dr Schreber advocated hanging a blackboard in the child's room on which the child's bad behaviour could be recorded. Monthly family sessions were to be held, he advised, for the purpose of sitting in judgement on the child's violations and misbehaviour, which had been meticulously recorded on the blackboard. He told parents that these methods would ensure docility and submissiveness, and would be so effective that they would not need to be continued after the fifth or sixth year of life.

Dr Schreber used these methods on his own children, driving his two sons – but not, it seems, his three daughters – into complete submission and passivity. One son, Gustav, committed suicide by shooting himself, and the other became paranoiac.

Around the turn of the century the expanding sciences of medicine, anthropology, criminology, biology and psychology were providing a persuasive rationale for this kind of extreme manipulation of infants and children (see Beekman, 1979).

5. Lamarck's notion of the inheritance of acquired characteristics, which underpinned ideas on heredity during the nineteenth century, was still influential and remained unchallenged until the beginning of the twentieth (Donnelly, 1983). Therefore, to be in good physical, psychological and moral condition at the time of conceiving a child, meant that these good qualities would be transmitted to the offspring. To be degenerate in any way spelt trouble for one's children, for one's line of descent, and for the nation.

6. The trainers regard these 'old habits' as defences to be got rid of, instead of seeing them as part of a received wisdom that guaranteed ongoing support and care of children.

7. This bad conscience might arise from a number of sources: the harshness of the moral teaching, which was evangelical across all religious groupings (Thomson, 1950); the severity of child-rearing practices; the loss of the wide range of adult contacts exposing children to more specific adult pathology, as indicated earlier; and the new temptations offered to some by material progress.

Chapter 6

1. I am thinking specifically of Neill (1962), Marcuse (1964) and Lowen (1967), but also other influential figures such as Laing (1967), Cooper (1968) and Fromm (1956, 1957).
2. 'Pop culture' includes that wide range of cultural forms that are easily available and accessible to everyone, anywhere in the world. It spans all class and ethnic divisions. It is not a uniform culture as the term implies, but contains great ethnic diversity and richness. It includes commercials and 'soaps'. The central question is: does the very availability of these cultural products twenty-four hours a day in every escalator, supermarket and shopping mall reduce them all to a homogeneous background noise? How can we any longer discriminate, or even pause to understand that which is trying to shock, inspire or evoke something in us?
3. The id-cravings that are targeted are (a) oral – to do with drinking, smoking and eating, (b) sexual in the widest sense, having in particular to do with narcissistic needs – for instance, the need to look well for others and oneself, to be a sexually exciting object that will be adored and loved for ever.
4. At this point it will be essential to stress the relationship between severe *external* hardship and drug abuse. Marginalised groups, such as the long-term unemployed and the poor of the Third World, are more likely to seek relief from appalling outer conditions by the use of drugs. Here the overwhelming need is to escape from the outer world, and the consideration of internal factors is probably irrelevant.
5. Bollas has some interesting comments: 'Some drug addicts may have sided with the death instinct and have withdrawn from the parents, nullifying parental ability, . . . deadening themselves as an attack on the parents. A child may never forgive a parent, say, for introducing a rival. Sibling hate may be sufficient cause for a child to remove himself from parenting and to impose a deadening isolation on himself' (1989, p. 147).
6. Sergeant Dixon was a fair-minded and reasonable, if somewhat paternalistic, policeman in the BBC series *Dixon of Dock Green*, which was popular in the fifties and sixties.

Chapter 7

1. The 'Lifeskills' programmes were chosen as being representative of progressive education strategies in general. I will focus my discussion on this one controversial area.

2. We noted in Chapters 5 and 6 that the advent of mass education involved social engineering. Whether from the Left or the Right, there has always been an ideological input into education.

3. The immaturity and lack of freedom referred to here are relative. Some adolescents are more mature than others. A degree of freedom is essential for testing reality and learning from experience, but it must be kept within bounds.

4. This process of narcissistic inflation is a general one, which becomes particularly intensified during adolescence. The central theme throughout this book is that our culture intensifies that split between outer performance and inner emptiness.

5. What is being suggested here is that the Lifeskills approach (at its most extreme) has something in common with anti-social subcultures, and that Lifeskills teachers, without necessarily being aware of it, create the same confusion in values. In the one school, there will be traditional teachers of history, mathematics, etc., who will be wanting good work, dedication, co-operation with authority and a willingness to learn. At the same time you will have some teachers implying something quite the opposite – a negative attitude to authority, a critical attitude to 'the system', a desire to expose the world as corrupt, racist, sexist and so on. These teachers seem to be saying, in effect: 'Look! We're on your side in the overthrow of authority. Forget repression, sublimation and restraint. Be free!'

6. But there is a real danger here of a right-wing authoritarianism, which would perhaps favour, for instance, teaching 'creation theory' instead of evolutionary theory, banning controversial texts, and limiting genuine critical thinking. The point at issue is that education becomes shallow to the extent that it is hijacked by the more extreme ideologies and propaganda. Education can only attain depth and power when it is relatively free from bias and control and allowed to approach its subject matter in a spirit of humility – the self in search of the truth.

7. Psychoanalytically speaking, we might say that the teacher, in this instance, became the focus for the student's projection of her own uncertainty. She perceived him to be the one full of *her* doubts. When he refused to contain the projection, and in effect sent it back, she had to leave.

A Conclusion

1. 'Father' here is not necessarily the actual father, but what Lacan refers to as 'the paternal metaphor', or 'the name of the father', or 'the no of the father' – *le nom du père/non du père*. This is the 'symbolic father' that institutes the cutting of the symbiotic relationship with the

mother. It is this function that sets limits, sets boundaries, and establishes subjectivity.

2. The memory traces of these formative humiliations and the affects associated with them remain mostly unconscious. They can, however, return and form the basis of hysterical symptoms, of masochistic suffering, of extreme anxiety states and panic attacks, of psychosomatic symptoms, and indeed of psychosis.

3. These psychoanalytic cultural debates are part of the history of the psychoanalytic movement, and from time to time have been summarised (see Jacoby, 1975). However, it is Freud's position, in the end, which is still relevant and informs the critical position of this book.

4. Lacan's comment on racism is in fact taken from a Channel 4 programme, *Lacan*. The televised translation differs somewhat from the printed version, which can be found in Lacan (1987), p. 36.

BIBLIOGRAPHY

Place of publication is London unless otherwise indicated.

Abraham, K. (1921) 'Contributions to the theory of anal character', in *Selected Papers*. Hogarth, pp. 370–92.

Adair, G. (1989) *Hollywood's Vietnam*. Heinemann.

Alexander, F. (1956) *Psychoanalysis and Psychotherapy*. New York: Norton.

Amis, M. (1986) *The Moronic Inferno*. Jonathan Cape.

Anderson, D. and Dawson, G., eds (1986) *Family Portraits*. Social Affairs Unit.

Anzieu, D. (1971) 'L'illusion groupale', *Nouvelle Revue de Psychoanalyse* 4: 73–93.

Aries, P. (1960) *Centuries of Childhood*. Paris: Librairie Plon. Peregrine, 1979.

Badcock, C. (1980) *The Psychoanalysis of Culture*. Oxford: Blackwell.

Baker, J. (1920) *Healthy Babies*.

Baker Miller, J. (1976) *Towards a New Psychology of Women*. Harmondsworth: Penguin.

Baudrillard, J. (1983) *Fatal Strategies*. Paris: Edition Crasset. Trans. P. Beitchman and W.G.L. Niesluchowski, Pluto Press, 1990.

Bauman, Z. (1988) 'Britain's exit from politics', *New Statesman and Society* 1(7), 28 July 1988: 34–8.

Balint, M. (1952) *Primary Love and Psychoanalytic Technique*. Hogarth.

Beekman, D. (1979) *The Mechanical Baby*. Dobson.

Bettelheim, B. (1967) *The Empty Fortress*. New York: The Free Press.

—— (1976) *The Uses of Enchantment*. Thames & Hudson; Peregrine, 1978.

Bion, W.R. (1950) 'The imaginary twin', in Bion (1967), pp. 3–22.

—— (1959) 'Attacks on linking', in Bion (1967), pp. 93–109.

—— (1962a) *Learning from Experience*. Heinemann; Maresfield, 1984.

—— (1962b) 'A theory of thinking', in Bion (1967), pp. 110–19.

—— (1963) *Elements of Psychoanalysis*. Heinemann; Maresfield, 1984.

—— (1967) *Second Thoughts: Selected Papers on Psychoanalysis*. Heinemann; Maresfield, 1984.

Boadella, D. (1976) *In the Wake of Reich*. Coventure.

Bollas, C. (1989) *Forces of Destiny: Psychoanalysis and the Human Idiom*. Free Association Books.

Booker, C. (1980) *The Seventies*. Penguin.

Bourne, B., Eichler, U. and Herman, D. (1987) *Modernity and its Discontents*. Nottingham: Spokesman.

Bowlby, J. (1953) *Child Care and the Growth of Love*. Harmondsworth: Penguin.

—— (1980) *Attachment and Loss*, vol. 3. Hogarth; Penguin, 1981.

Boyers, R. (ed.) (1971) *Laing and Anti-Psychiatry*. Salmagundi; Penguin, 1972.

Brown, N. (1959) *Life Against Death, The Psychoanalytic Meaning of History*. Sphere.

Brownmiller, S. (1975) *Against our Will: Men, Women and Rape*. Martin Secker & Warburg; Harmondsworth: Penguin, 1976.

Buber, M. (1947) *Between Man and Man*. Kegan Paul, Trench,Trubner & Co. Fontana, 1961.

—— (1950) *The Way of Man*. Vincent Stuart.

—— (1958) *I and Thou*. Charles Scribner's Sons.

Berke, J. (1975) 'Envy loveth not', *Br. J. Psychother.* 1(3): 171–86.

Chasseguet-Smirgel, J. (1984) *Creativity and Perversion*. New York: Norton. London: Free Association Books.

Chasseguet-Smirgel, J. and Grunberger, B. (1976) *Freud or Reich? Psychoanalysis and Illusion*. Paris: Collection Les Abysses, Tchou. Trans. C. Pajaczkowska, Free Association Books, 1986.

Chomsky, N. (1991) *Deterring Democracy*. Verso. Vintage, 1992.

Cixous, H. (1976) 'The laugh of Medusa', in E. Maks and I. de Courtivon, eds, *New French Feminisms*. Harvester.

Cooper, D., ed. (1968) *The Dialectics of Liberation*. Penguin.

Cooper, D. (1971) *The Death of the Family*. Allen Lane The Penguin Press.

Cousins, J. (1979) *Make It Happy*. Virago.

Davidoff, I. and Hall, C. (1987) *Family Fortunes: Men and Women of the English Middle Classes 1780–1850*. Unwin Hyman. Routledge, 1992.

de Beauvoir, S. (1952) *The Second Sex*. Penguin.

Deleuze, G. and Guattari, F. (1972) *Anti-Oedipus: Capitalism and Schizophrenia*. New York: Viking.

Donnelly, M. (1983) *Managing the Mind*. Tavistock.

Eichenbaum, L. and Orbach, S. (1982) *Outside In and Inside Out*. Harmondsworth: Penguin.

Eliade, M. (1957) *Myths, Dreams and Mysteries*. Trans. P. Mairet, Harvill Press, 1960. Fontana, 1968.

Erikson, E. (1950) *Childhood and Society*. New York: Norton. Penguin, 1965.

Fenichel, O. (1946) *The Psychoanalytic Theory of Neurosis*. Routledge & Kegan Paul.

Ferenczi, S. (1929) 'The unwelcome child and his death instinct', in S. Ferenczi, *Final Contributions to the Problems and Methods of Psychoanalysis*. Hogarth, 1955.

Fisk, R. (1990) *Pity the Nation, Lebanon at War*. Oxford University Press.

Fitzgerald, M. (1987) 'The effectiveness of psychotherapy', *Journal of the Irish Forum for Psychoanalytic Psychotherapy* 1(1): 29–35.

Frankl, V. (1946) *Man's Search for Meaning*. Hodder & Stoughton.

Freud, A. (1936) *The Ego and the Mechanisms of Defence*. Hogarth.

Freud, S. (1895/1950) 'A project for a scientific psychology', in James Strachey, ed., *The Standard Edition of the Complete Psychological Works of Sigmund Freud*, 24 vols Hogarth, 1953-73; vol. 1, pp. 281-392.

—— (1908) 'Character and anal erotism'. *S.E.* 9: 167-76.

—— (1910) 'Contributions to the psychology of love. A special type of object choice made by men'. *S.E.* 11: 165-75.

—— (1911) 'Psycho-analytic notes on an autobiographical account of a case of paranoia (Dementia paranoides)'. *S.E.* 12: 1-82.

—— (1912a) 'Recommendations for physicians on the psychoanalytic method of treatment'. *S.E.* 12: 109-20.

—— (1912b) 'The dynamics of transference'. *S.E.* 12: 97-108.

—— (1912-13) *Totem and Taboo*. *S.E.* 13: 1-162.

—— (1914a) 'Further recommendations in the technique of psycho-analysis: recollection, repetition and working through'. *S.E.* 12: 145-56.

—— (1914b) 'On narcissism: an introduction'. *S.E.* 14: 67-104.

—— (1915a) 'Instincts and their vicissitudes'. *S.E.* 14: 109-40.

—— (1915b) 'Some character types met with in psychoanalytic work'; section 3 'Criminality from a sense of guilt'. *S.E.* 14: 332-6.

—— (1921) *Group Psychology and the Analysis of the Ego*. *S.E.* 18: 65-144.

—— (1923) *The Ego and The Id*. *S.E.* 19: 1-66.

—— (1926) *Inhibitions, Symptoms and Anxiety*. *S.E.* 20: 77-175.

—— (1927) *The Future of an Illusion*. *S.E.* 21: 1-56.

—— (1929) *Civilization and its Discontents*. *S.E.* 21: 57-146.

—— (1932) 'Femininity', in *New Introductory Lectures on Psycho-Analysis*. *S.E.* 22: 112-35.

—— (1933) 'The psychical dissection of the personality', in *New Introductory Lectures on Psycho-Analysis*. *S.E.* 22: 57-80.

—— (1937) 'Analysis terminable and interminable'. *S.E.* 23: 144-208.

—— (1939) *Moses and Monotheism*. *S.E.* 23: 1-138.

Friedan, B. (1963) *The Feminine Mystique*. Penguin, 1965.

Fromm, E. (1942) *Fear of Freedom*. Routledge & Kegan Paul; paperback, 1960.

—— (1956) *The Sane Society*. Routledge & Kegan Paul; paperback, 1963.

—— (1957) *The Art of Loving*. Unwin paperbacks.

—— (1976) *To Have or To Be*. Jonathan Cape, 1978; Abacus, 1979.

Frosh, S. (1991) *Identity Crisis: Modernity, Psychoanalysis and the Self*. Macmillan Educational.

Gordon, T. (1970) *How to be an Effective Parent*. Collins.

Greenson, R. (1967) *The Technique and Practice of Psychoanalysis.* Hogarth, 1981.

Greer, G. (1970) *The Female Eunuch.* Penguin, 1971.

Griffin, S. (1982) *Pornography and Silence.* The Women's Press.

Grunberger, B. (1980) 'The Oedipal conflicts of the analyst', *Psychoanal. Q.* 49: 606–30.

—— (1989) *New Essays on Narcissism.* Free Association Books.

Guntrip, H. (1961) *Personality Structure and Human Interaction.* Hogarth.

—— (1964) *Healing the Sick Mind.* George Allen & Unwin.

—— (1968) *Schizoid Phenomena, Object Relations and the Self.* Hogarth.

Hanaghan, J. (1957) *Society, Evolution and Revelation.* Dublin: The Runa Press.

—— (1962) 'An evolutional weakness in the ego-defence apparatus', in J. Hanaghan, *Lectures in Psychoanalysis.* Dublin: The Runa Press.

—— (1966) *Freud and Jesus.* Dublin: The Runa Press.

—— (1973) *The Courage to be Married.* Cork: The Mercier Press.

Harrison, C. (1984) *Freud.* Penguin.

Hassan, I. (1987) 'Pluralism in postmodern perspective', in ed. C. Jencks, *The Postmodern Reader.* Academy Editions, 1992, pp. 196–207.

Hebdige, D. (1988) 'Banalarama: Can Popular Culture Save Us?', *New Statesman and Society* 1(27), (9.12.88): 29–32.

Hillman, J. (1975) *Re-visioning Psychology.* Colophon Books. New York: Harper & Row, 1977.

Hinshelwood, R. (1985) 'The patient's defensive analyst', *Brit. J. Psychother.* 1(2): 30–41.

Hinds, A. (1988) 'Psycho-business', *The Listener* 119(3045), 14.1.88: 8–9.

Hopson, B. and Scally, M. (1981) *Lifeskills Teaching.* McGraw-Hill.

Horney, K. (1933) 'The denial of the vagina', *Int. J. Psycho-Anal.* 14: 57–70.

—— (1939) *New Ways in Psychoanalysis.* Kegan Paul.

Hughes, R. (1980) *The Shock of the New.* BBC Books.

Horne, H. (1966) 'The concept of the mind', *Int. J. Psycho-Anal.* 47: 42–9.

Ignatieff, M. (1986) 'Time to take new political bearings', *The Listener* 115(2958), 1.5.86: 16–17.

Illich, I. (1971) *Deschooling Society.* New York: Harper & Row; London: Calder & Boyars, 1972.

Jacoby, R. (1975) *Social Amnesia.* Harvester.

Jameson, F. (1991) *Postmodernism or the Cultural Logic of Late Capitalism.* Verso.

Janov, A. (1970) *The Primal Scream.* Abacus.

Jencks, C. (1991) *The Post-Modern Reader.* New York: St Martin's Press; London: Academy Editions, 1992.

Jenkins, P. (1987) *Mrs Thatcher's Revolution.* Jonathan Cape.

Khan, M. (1988) *When Spring Comes, Awakening in Clinical Psycho-analysis*. Chatto & Windus.

Klein, M. (1932) *The Psychoanalysis of Children*. Hogarth.

—— (1933) 'The early development of conscience in the child', in Klein (1975a), pp. 248–57.

—— (1934) 'On criminality', in Klein (1975a), pp. 258–61.

—— (1935) 'A contribution to the psychogenesis of manic-depressive states', in Klein (1975a), pp. 262–89.

—— (1937) 'Love, guilt and reparation', in Klein (1975a), pp. 306–43.

—— (1940) 'Mourning and its relation to manic-depressive states', in Klein (1975a), pp. 344–69.

—— (1946) 'Notes on some schizoid mechanisms', in Klein (1975b), pp. 1–24.

—— (1952) 'Some theoretical conclusions regarding the emotional life of the infant', in Klein (1975b), pp. 61–93.

—— (1957) 'Envy and gratitude', in Klein (1975b), pp. 176–235.

—— (1975a) *Love, Guilt and Reparation and Other Works 1921–45. The Writings of Melanie Klein*, vol. 1. Hogarth/Institute of Psycho-Analysis.

—— (1975b) *Envy and Gratitude and Other Works 1946–63. The Writings of Melanie Klein*, vol. 3. Hogarth/Institute of Psycho-Analysis.

Kohut, H. (1977) *The Restoration of the Self*. International Universities Press.

Kolakowski, L. (1986) 'The ghosts of religion', *The Listener* 115(2956), 17.4.86: 18–20.

Kristeva, J. (1988) *Étrangers à nous-mêmes*. Paris: Feyard.

Kernberg, O. (1970) 'Factors in the psychoanalytic treatment of narcissistic personalities', in A. Morrison, ed., *Essential Papers in Narcissism*. New York: New York University Press.

Kundera, M. (1991) *Immortality*. Faber & Faber.

Lacan, J. (1932) *De la Psychose paranoïaque dans ses rapports avec la personnalité*. Paris: Le Seuil, 1975.

—— (1938) 'La famille: le complexe, facteur concret de la pathologie familiale et les complexes familiaux en pathologie', in *Encyclopédie Française*, vol. 8, pp. 3–16. Paris: Larousse. This article, translated by Cormac Gallagher, School of Psychotherapy, St Vincent's Hospital, Dublin, is available by private circulation only.

—— (1949) 'The mirror stage as formative of the function of the I', in Lacan (1977), pp. 1–7.

—— (1964) *The Four Fundamental Concepts of Psychoanalysis*. A. Sheridan, trans. Penguin, 1977.

—— (1977) *Écrits. A Selection*. Alan Sheridan. trans. Tavistock.

—— (1987) *Television*. Trans. D. Hollier, R. Krauss, A. Michelson. MIT Press.

Laing, R. (1967) *The Politics of Experience and the Bird of Paradise*. Penguin.

Laing, R. and Esterson, A. (1964) *Sanity, Madness and the Family*. Harmondsworth: Penguin.

Laplanche, J. and Pontalis, J.-B. (1973) *The Language of Psychoanalysis*. Hogarth.

Lasch, C. (1979) *The Culture of Narcissism*. New York: Norton; London: Abacus, 1980.

—— (1984) *The Minimal Self*. New York: Norton; London: Picador, 1985.

Lechte, J. (1990) *Julia Kristeva*. Routledge.

Lee, R. (1948) *Freud and Christianity*. James Clarke; Harmondsworth: Penguin, 1967.

Lowen, A. (1967) *The Betrayal of the Body*. New York: Collier; London: Macmillian.

Lyotard, J.-F. (1979) *The Postmodern Condition*. Manchester: Manchester University Press, 1984.

Macmurray, J. (1954) *Persons in Relation*. Faber.

Malan, D. (1979) *Individual Psychotherapy and the Science of Psychodynamics*. Butterworth.

Malcolm, J. (1982) *Psychoanalysis: the Impossible Profession*. Picador.

Marcuse, H. (1955) *Eros and Civilisation*. New York: Beacon Press; London: Sphere, 1969.

—— (1964) *One-Dimensional Man*. Routledge & Kegan Paul; Sphere, 1968.

Marwick, A. (1982) *The Pelican Social History of Britain. British Society since 1945*. Penguin.

Maslow, A. (1971) *The Farther Reaches of Human Nature*. Penguin.

Matte-Blanco, I. (1976) *The Unconscious as Infinite Sets*. Hogarth.

May, R. (1969) *Love and Will*. New York: Norton; London: Fontana, 1972.

—— (1974) *Paulus*. Collins.

—— (1975) *The Courage to Create*. Collins.

Meltzer, D. (1967) 'Terror, persecution and dread', in D. Meltzer, *Sexual States of Mind*. Clunie Press, 1973, pp. 99–106.

Meltzer, D. (1978) *The Kleinian Development*. Clunie Press.

Millett, K. (1971) *Sexual Politics*. Rupert Hart-Davis; Abacus, 1972.

Mitchell, J. (1971) *Women's Estate*. Harmondsworth: Penguin.

—— (1974) *Psychoanalysis and Feminism*. Harmondsworth: Penguin.

—— (1986) *The Selected Melanie Klein*. Harmondsworth: Penguin.

—— (1987) 'Psychoanalysis: What do women want?', in B. Bourne, U. Eichler and D. Herman, eds, *Voices: Psychoanalysis*. Nottingham: Spokesman, pp. 58–72.

Mitchell, J. and Rose, J. (1982) *Feminine Sexuality: Jacques Lacan and the École Freudienne*. Macmillan.

Morgan, R. (1970) *Sisterhood is Powerful*. New York: Vintage.

Neill, A.S. (1962) *Summerhill*. Victor Gollancz; Harmondsworth: Penguin, 1968.

Niederland, W. (1984) *The Schreber Case*. The Analytic Press.

Oakley, A. (1972) *Sex, Gender and Society*. Temple Smith.

—— (1974) *Housewife*. Allen Lane.

Owens, C. (1983) 'The discourse of others: feminists and postmodernism', in Jencks (1991), pp. 333–48.

Oz, A. (1987) *The Slopes of Lebanon*. Maurie Goldburg-Batura, trans. Vintage, 1991.

Paz, O. (1986) 'The ghosts of religion', *The Listener* 115(2956), 17.4.86: 18–20.

Perls, F. (1973) *The Gestalt Approach and Eye Witness to Therapy*. Bantam.

Perry, H. (1970) *The Human Be-in*. New York: Basic; London: Allen Lane The Penguin Press.

Rama, S., Ballentine, R. and Ajaya, S. (1976) *Yoga and Psychotherapy*. Glenview, Illinois: Himalayan Institute.

Reich, W. (1927–33) *Character Analysis*. 3rd edn, New York: Orgone Institute Press, 1949.

—— (1933) *The Mass Psychology of Fascism*. New York: Simon & Schuster.

Reiff, P. (1966) *The Triumph of the Therapeutic*. Chatto & Windus; Harmondsworth: Penguin University Books, 1973.

Rogers, C. (1961) *On Becoming a Person*. Constable.

Rosenfeld, H. (1971) 'A clinical approach to the psychoanalytic theory of the life and death instincts: an investigation into the aggressive aspects of narcissism', *Int. J. Psycho-Anal.* 52: 169–78.

—— (1987) *Impasse and Interpretation*. Routledge.

Rowbotham, S. (1973) *Women's Consciousness, Man's World*. Penguin.

Rubin Suleiman, S. (1990) 'Feminism and postmodernism: a question of politics', in ed. C. Jencks, *The Postmodern Reader*. Academy Editions, 1992, pp. 318–32.

Rycroft, C. (1968) *A Critical Dictionary of Psychoanalysis*. Nelson; Penguin, 1972.

Schaffer, R. (1983) *The Analytic Attitude*. Hogarth.

Segal, H. (1964) *Introduction to the Work of Melanie Klein*. Hogarth.

—— (1979) *Klein*. Fontana Modern Masters.

Seligman, E. (1985) 'The half-alive ones', in Andrew Samuels, ed., *The Father – Contemporary Jungian Perspectives*. Free Association Books, pp. 69–94.

Sharpe, S. (1976) *Just Like a Girl. How Girls learn to be Women.* Harmondsworth: Penguin.

Shukman, D. (1988) 'A guided tour of Vietnam', *The Listener* 119(3050), 18.2.88: 20.

Spock, B. (1946) *Baby and Child Care.* New English Library.

Steiner, G. (1989) *Real Presences.* Faber, 1991.

Stevenson, J. (1984) *The Pelican Social History of Britain. British Society 1914-45.* Penguin.

Stoller, R. (1968) *Sex and Gender: On the Development of Masculinity and Femininity.* Harmondsworth: Penguin.

Stone, L. (1961) *The Psychoanalytic Situation.* International Universities Press.

Sturrock, J. (1979) 'Jacques Lacan', in ed. J. Sturrock, *Structuralism and Since.* Oxford University Press, pp. 1-18.

Tart, C. (1975) *States of Consciousness.* New York: E.P. Datton.

Thomas, D. (1952) *Dylan Thomas Collected Poems 1934-1952.* Everyman, 1966.

Thomson, D. (1950) *England in the Nineteenth Century.* Harmondsworth: Penguin.

Tillich, P. (1949) 'You are Accepted', in P. Tillich, *The Shaking of the Foundations.* SCM Press; Harmondsworth: Penguin, 1962.

—— (1956) 'On healing: part 1', in P. Tillich, *The Boundaries of Our Being.* Fontana, 1973.

—— (1959) *The Theology of Culture.* Oxford University Press.

Toffler, A. (1970) *Future Shock.* Pan.

Watson, J. (1928) *The Psychological Care of Infant and Child.* New York: Norton.

Watts, A. (1961) *Psychotherapy East and West.* Pantheon Books; Penguin, 1973.

Weiss, J. (1967) 'The integration of defences', *Int. J. Psycho-Anal.* 48: 520-4.

Welldon, E. (1991) *Mother, Madonna, Whore: The Idealization and Denigration of Motherhood.* Free Association Books.

Williams, H. (1965) *The True Wilderness.* Constable; Harmondsworth: Penguin, 1968.

Winnicott, D. (1935) 'The manic defence', in Winnicott (1958b), pp. 129-44.

—— (1941) 'The observation of infants in a set situation', in Winnicott (1958b), pp. 55-69.

—— (1947) 'Hate in the counter-transference', in Winnicott (1958b), pp. 194-203.

—— (1951) 'Transitional objects and transitional phenomena', in Winnicott (1958b), pp. 229-42.

—— (1958a) 'Psychoanalysis and the sense of guilt', in Winnicott (1965), pp. 15–28.

—— (1958b) *Through Paediatrics to Psychoanalysis*. Hogarth.

—— (1963a) 'The development of the capacity for concern', in Winnicott (1965), pp. 73–82.

—— (1963b) 'Communicating and not communicating leading to a study of certain opposites', in Winnicott (1965), pp. 179–92.

—— (1964a) *The Child, the Family and the Outside World*. Harmondsworth: Penguin.

—— (1964b) *The Family and Individual Development*. Tavistock.

—— (1965) *The Maturational Processes and the Facilitating Environment*. Hogarth.

—— (1968) 'Contemporary concepts of adolescent development and their implications for higher education', in Winnicott (1971a), pp. 138–50.

—— (1969) 'The use of an object and relating through identifications', in Winnicott (1971a), pp. 86–94.

—— (1971a) *Playing and Reality*. Tavistock.

—— (1971b) *Therapeutic Consultation is Child Psychiatry*. Hogarth.

Wren-Lewis, J. (1966) 'Love's coming of age', in J. Wren-Lewis, *Psychoanalysis Observed*. Constable; Harmondsworth: Penguin, 1968, pp. 83–115.

INDEX

abortion 109
Abraham, K. 130
absent father syndrome 107-8
Adair, G. 72
addictive behaviours 143-6
adolescence 117; Lifeskills education
    in 158, 159-76
agape quality of love 37-43
aggression: childhood 141; female,
    against men 100-5; *see also*
    violence
Ajaya, S. 23
alcohol abuse 143-5
Alexander, F. 38
America: psychoanalysis in 2, 17;
    Vietnam War and 71-3
Amis, Martin 164
anal character 130-1
analyst: *agape* quality of love and
    38-43; as mental healer 25, 28;
    role of 6-9
Anderson, D. 108
Anzieu, Didier 86
apocalyptic mood and return of death
    81-3
apprentices, children as, in history
    112-5, 128-9
archaic super-ego 140-3, 145, 148,
    151
architecture, modern 84
Auden, W.H. 1
authority, crisis in 99; education and
    154-76

Badcock, C. 179
'bad habits' in young children 120
Baker, Josephine *Healthy Babies* 120
Baker Miller, Jean 99
Balint, M. 38, 152
Ballentine, R. 23
Baudrillard, J. 61, 93, 137
Bauman, Zygmunt 65
Beethoven, L. van 31-2
behaviourism and childcare 118-21,
    131
Bellow, Saul 78, 175
Bembridge School 121
Bennett, Alan 'Soldiering On' 77
Berke, Joseph 105

Bettelheim, Bruno 32, 62
Bion, W.R. 38, 56-7, 65, 150;
    container notion 43, 152, 157
Bleuler, E. 49
Bollas, Christopher 45, 79
Booker, Christopher 67
Book of Kells 69
Bowlby, J. 156; on separation anxiety
    53-4, 152
Boyers, R. 158
British Independent tradition,
    presence of analyst in 42
Brown, Norman O.: Dionysian ego
    178-9
Buber, Martin 58; 'I-It' and 'I-Thou'
    relations 29-30

capitalism 57-8; anal character and
    130-1; children as consumers
    132-3; drug abuse and 145-6
case studies 3-5, 12, 14, 81-2; Brian
    46-7, 48-9, 55-6; Jim 47-9,
    55-6; John 65-6
Chasseguet-Smirgel, J. 86, 139
child: on becoming a 35; ideal of
    perfect 120-1, 131
childcare 112-34, 138; ancient to
    modern 112-17; parents must
    set limits 123-4; psychological
    repercussions discussed 128-34;
    rigidly-controlled child 118-21;
    state's child 117-18;
    unrestrained child 121-3;
    'up-front' parents and children
    124-8
Chodorow, Nancy 92
Chomsky, N. 60
Christianity: decline of 58, 89;
    psychoanalysis and 19-21, 25-38;
Christian and patient, wretchedness
    of 30-1
Cixous, Hélène 92, 93
cleanliness and childcare 119-20
concentration camps 32, 74
consciousness raising and feminism
    95-6
container notion 43, 152, 157
Cooper, D. 158
countertransference 7, 8, 9, 27, 28

Cousins, Jane *Make It Happy* 173
crime 67, 147-52
cultural revolution (1960s) and
    education 154-8
culture, modern/post-modern: mainly
    Kleinian perspective 46-89
culture, popular 136
cure and psychoanalysis 15-17

Dartington Hall School 121
Dawson, G. 108
death: denial of 76-81; return of and
    apocalyptic mood 81-3
defence mechanisms 3, 5, 13-14
Deleuze, G. 135
depressive position 52-6, 61-2, 81,
    152, 168
de-sublimation, repressive 132-3
Dewey, John 118
Dionysian ego 178-9
drug abuse 143-6

Eastern mysticism and psychotherapy
    22-4
education: crisis in authority and
    154-76; cultural revolution
    (1960s) and 154-8; early
    progressive 121-2, 133; history
    of 112-14, 116, 121-2; Lifeskills
    programmes 158, 159-76
ego, structuring of in mirror phase
    and paranoia 69-71
ego-ideal 25-30
Eliade, M. 79
Elkins, Michael 75-6
envy 12, 64, 104-5
Erikson, E. 68, 167-8
etiquette manuals 113, 114, 175
Euclidean geometry and paranoia
    68-9
Eysenck, H.J. 16

fairy tales 50-1, 62
family, modern, emergence of
    115-17, 128-9
father: absence/expulsion from home
    106, 107-8; as giant in fairy tales
    50, 51; lack of paternal imago in
    modern period 86-7; role of
    schools and 156; sublimation of
    desire and 88-9, 178

fear, spiral of in modern culture
    66-71
feminism 63, 90-111; consciousness
    raising 95-6; critique of
    patriarchy 92-5; male narcissism
    shattered 96-100; shadow side
    of 100-5; third position 92-3,
    110-11; triumph of 'male' values
    108-9; turning the tables on
    men 105-8
Fenichel, O. 144
Ferenczi, S. 38
Fisk, R. 73-5
Fitzgerald, M. 16
Frankfurt school 177
Frankl, Victor 32
free association and play 35
Freud, Anna 90, 133, 168
Freud, Sigmund 1, 12-13, 15-16, 18,
    20-1, 24, 44, 78, 130, 148, 156,
    164, 180, 182; on ambivalence
    36; on analyst 6; 'The dynamics
    of transference' 7; feminism and
    90, 92, 99-100, 102, 104; *Group
    Psychology and the Analysis of
    the Ego* 85-6; *Inhibitions,
    Symptoms and Anxiety* 41;
    Moses and Monotheism 80;
    'Project for a scientific
    psychology' 9; on resistance 13,
    19, 99, 183; on splitting 49; on
    super-ego 137, 138, 140; theory
    of sexuality 11, 12, 97-8, 174;
    Totem and Taboo 80
Fromm, Erich 131, 177
Frosh, S. 142

gay rights movement and adolescents
    173
generational differentiation,
    importance of 134
Gordon, Thomas *How to be an
    Effective Parent* 125-7
Greenson, R. 7, 43
Greer, Germaine *The Female Eunuch*
    95
Griffin, Susan 100
groups: special interest 60, 63;
    splitting and 70-1; utopian
    illusions and 85-7
Grunberger, Bela 139, 146-7, 182
Guattari, F. 135

Guntrip, H. 149–50, 164

Hanaghan, Jonathan: Christian
    psychoanalytic viwpoint 25–7
Hansel and Gretel 50–1
Hassan, Ihab 99
hate 35–7
health and longevity, concern about
    76
Hillman, James 79
Hinds, A. 165
Hinshelwood, R. 9
Hopson, B. and Scally, M. *Lifeskills
    Teaching* 159–65
Horney, Karen 103, 131, 177
Hughes, R. 84
Human Growth movement 24

id-cravings, exploitation of 141
identification figures and children
    129, 139–41, 155
ideologies and utopian ideas 85–8
Ignatieff, M. 63
Illich, I. 158
image and mass projections 74, 76; of
    America 72; of Israel 75
images, media 58–62
impotence, male fear of 96–100
Irigaray, Luce 92–3
Israelis 73–6

Jack and the Beanstalk 51
Jameson, F. 61, 93
Janov, A. 22
Jenkins, P. 167
Jung, C. 1, 50

Kennedy, Ludovic 27
Kernberg, O. 142
Key, Ellen *The Century of the Child*
    124
Khan, M. 39
Klein, Melanie 156; depressive
    position 52–6, 61, 62, 81, 152,
    168; on envy 12, 64, 104–5;
    feminism and 90, 97, 104–5;
    paranoid-schizoid position
    49–52, 53, 55, 69, 168; on
    presence of analyst 42–3; *The
    Psychoanalysis of Children* 104;
    on reparation 12, 53, 174; on
    super-ego 138, 140–1, 148–9

Kleinian perspective on
    contemporary culture 56–89
Kohut, H. 36, 67, 142, 143, 164
Kolakowski, Leszek 57
Kristeva, Julia 31, 92, 110–11
Kundera, Milan *Immortality* 180

Lacan, Jacques 87, 152–3; feminism
    and 93, 110; on mirror stage 28,
    69–70, 146; on the Other 42, 44,
    184–5; on the Real 78
Laing, Ronald 28, 123, 131–2
Laplanche, J. 13
Lasch, Christopher 65, 68, 141, 160
Lebanon, Israeli invasion of (1982)
    74–6
Lechte, J. 110
Le Corbusier 84
legalism and 'rights', growth of 67–8
Le Gaufey 41
Lessing, Doris *The Good Terrorist* 170
Lifeskills educational programmes
    158, 159–65; critique of 165–76
Little Red Riding Hood 51
love: *agape* quality of 37–43; and
    hate 36
Lowen, Alexander 123
Lyotard, J.-F. 58

macho behaviour 96–9
Mailer, Norman 72–3
Malan, D. 108
Malcolm, Janet 17
male narcissism shattered 96–100
'male' values, feminism and triumph
    of 108–9
manic defence 54–5
Marcuse, Herbert 83, 123, 132, 177,
    179
masculine complex in female 103, 109
Maslow, A. 22
mass projections 71–6
Matte-Blanco, I. 101
May, Rollo 24, 78
Maya concept in Vedantic teaching
    29
media: adolescents and 174–5;
    creation of reality and 58–62;
    feminist issues and 94–5
Melman, Charles 34, 68
Meltzer, D. 151

men, turning the tables on, and
    feminism 105-8
mental healing, psychoanalysis as 25,
    28
Middle Ages: childcare in 112-13;
    crumbling of old order in 57-8
Miller, Alice 84
Millett, Kate 98
mirror stage 28, 69-71, 146
Mitchell, Juliet 91, 158
modernism: origins of schizoid nature
    57-8
mother: separation from 53-4, 88-9,
    99-100; as witch in fairy tales
    50-1
Mothercraft Manual 121
motherhood: devaluation of 108-9;
    as a vocation 119
mothering role of teachers 156-8
multicultural education 165-6

narcissism: explained 135-43; male,
    feminism and shattering of
    96-100; social pathology of
    143-53
Neill, A.S. 122; opens Summerhill
    School 121
New Left 158, 165
New Right 63, 65, 147, 176
New Testament 29, 37; on becoming
    a child 35; on hate 35-6; on sin
    19-20; on suffering 31

object-relating 57
obsessive-compulsive personality
    130-1
Oedipus complex 19, 80
old age and hidden problems of
    modernity 76-7
old order, crumbling of 57-8
Owens, C. 92, 93-4
Oz, Amos 75

Palestinians 73-6
paranoia in modern culture 66-71
paranoid-schizoid position 49-52, 53,
    55, 69, 168
Parent Effectiveness Training (PET)
    124-8
parents, effects of child-rearing
    theories on 117-28
Parker, Charlie 32

part-objects 51-2, 97
Patanjali: Yoga Sutras 23
patient and Christian, wretchedness
    of 30-1
patriarchy: decline of 87; feminist
    critique of 92-5
Paz, Octavio 89
penis envy 102-4, 109
Perls, F. 22
permissiveness 85; in childcare
    121-4, 132; drug abuse and 145;
    market economy and 136-8
Perry, H. 135
Pizzey, Erin 102
play and psychotherapy 35
Policy Studies Unit 158; *The School
    Effect: a Study in Multiracial
    Comprehensives* 166
Pontalis, J.-B. 6, 13
popular culture 136
post-industrial revolution and
    Lifeskills programmes 159-61,
    164
power, pleasurable, in badness
    149-50
privacy 181-2; adolescent need for
    171-3, 175-6; early modern
    family and 115, 116, 117, 129;
    education and 155
private security business 66-7
projective identification: mass
    projections 71-6; women's rage
    and 101
psychoanalysis: common sense of
    1-17; cure and 15-17;
    misunderstandings about 9-15,
    121; process 1-9; religion and
    18-45
psychotherapies as religions 21-4

Radical Therapist, The 158
Rama, S. 23
rape and sex abuse 96, 106-7, 181-2
Real, dimension of, and death 78-9,
    80, 81, 82
reality, versions of 58-62
Reich, Wilhelm 1, 22, 88, 122-3, 135,
    138, 139
Reiff, Philip 96, 182

religion: cults 171; ghosts of in
    modern culture 83-9;
    modernism and decline of 58;
    psychoanalysis and 18-45
reparation concept 12, 53, 174
repression 49, 130; sexual 122-3, 135
resistance 13, 19, 99
Rogers, C. 22, 39
Rosenfeld, H. 150
Russell, Bertrand 121

St John 19-20
St Luke 35-6
St Paul 29
saviours, modern 21-4
Schaffer, Roy 79
schools *see* education
science: psychoanalysis as a 9-10;
    return of death and 83; utopian
    ideas and 84, 85
Scott, Peter 163
Segal, Hanna 2, 8, 105
self: as a construct 44-5, 152; empty
    135-53
Seligman, Eva 108
sex education 172-3
sexuality: adolescent 158, 172-3;
    criticism of psychoanalytic
    theory of 11-12; modern female
    98; obsession with 77-8
Shukman, David 72
sin 30, 34; as separation 19-21
single-parent families 106-8, 155
Smith, Les 71
solidarity, human, loss of 62-6
splitting 46-52, 55-6; modern
    culture and 57-71
Spock, Benjamin *Baby and Child
    Care* 123-4
state, child seen as asset of 117-18
Steiner, George 175
Steiner, Rudolf 121
Stone, Leo 6
Sturrock, John 28-9
subject, ideologies and disappearance
    of 87-8
sublimation 174, 178-9
suffering 89; paradox of 31-4

super-ego 26; alcohol and 144-5;
    archaic 140-3, 145, 148, 151;
    modern family and 129;
    paternal, collapse of 137-43,
    147, 170-1, 182

teachers: as facilitators 169, 171; new
    mothering role 155-8
television 58-61
Thatcher, Margaret 64
Thomas, Dylan 80
Tillich, Paul 20, 21, 24, 38, 39
Toffler, Alvin *Future Shock* 160
transference 3, 4, 5-6, 7-8; erotic 7,
    37
transitional space 42, 152, 155, 175,
    178
truth, elusive, and psychoanalysis
    18-19

unconscious 3, 44, 91
United States: psychoanalysis in 2, 17;
    Vietnam War and 71-3
utopian ideas in 20th century, failure
    of 83-9

Vietnam War 132; image of America
    and 71-3
violence: in media 61-2; narcissism
    and 146-52

Watson, John B. *The Psychological
    Care of Infant and Child*
    118-19, 121
Watts, A. 23
Weiss, J. 14
Welldon, Estela 101
Winnicott, D. 35, 36, 38, 54, 56, 142,
    151, 156, 183; on adolescence
    168; on crime 149; 'The manic
    defence' 55; on rage 37; on
    transitional space 42, 152, 155,
    175, 178
women: degradation of 94; mass
    politicisation of 95-6
women's movement *see* feminism
work ethic, elimination of 159, 164-5

Yeats, W.B. 58
yoga 23

This first edition of
Cultural Collapse
was finished in March 1994

The book was commissioned by Robert M. Young,
edited by Karl Figlio,
copy-edited by Mandy Macdonald,
proofread by Alan Everett
indexed by Linda English
and produced by Ann Scott and Chase Production Services
for Free Association Books